NORTHROP FRYE UNBUTTONED

NORTHROP FRYE UNBUTTONED

Wit and Wisdom from the
Notebooks and Diaries

Selected by
ROBERT D. DENHAM

ANANSI

First published in the United States of America in 2004 by Gnomon Press.

This edition published in Canada	Distributed in Canada by
in 2004 by	Publishers Group Canada
House of Anansi Press Inc.	250A Carlton Street
110 Spadina Avenue, Suite 801	Toronto, ON, M5A 2L1
Toronto, ON, M5V 2K4	Tel. 416-934-9900
Tel. 416-363-4343	Toll free order numbers:
Fax 416-363-1017	Tel. 800-663-5714
www.anansi.ca	Fax 800-565-3770

Published by arrangement with Gnomon Press.

House of Anansi Press is committed to protecting our natural environment.
As part of our efforts, this book is printed on Glatfelter recycled paper: it contains
60% total recovered fibres and 20% post-consumer recycled fibres and is acid-free.

08 07 06 05 04   1 2 3 4 5

National Library of Canada Cataloguing in Publication Data

Frye, Northrop, 1912–1991
Northrop Frye unbuttoned : wit and wisdom from the notebooks and diaries / Robert D. Denham, editor.

ISBN 0-88784-185-6

1. Frye, Northrop, 1912–1991 — Notebooks, sketchbooks, etc. 2. Frye, Northrop, 1912–1991 — Diaries.
I. Denham, Robert D. II. Title.

PN75.F7A3 2004   801'.95'092   C2004-900706-8

Jacket design: Bill Douglas at The Bang

Jacket illustration: Van Howell

*We acknowledge for their financial support of our publishing program
the Canada Council for the Arts, the Ontario Arts Council, and the Government of Canada
through the Book Publishing Industry Development Program (BPIDP).*

For Richard Outram

∾

*In gematria, the numerical value of the Tetragrammaton
(or four-letter word) is 26.*

NOTEBOOK 24.136

*The total simultaneous pattern always extends
from alpha to omega.*

NOTEBOOK 21.190

PREFATORY NOTE

NORTHROP FRYE, one of the most expansive and visionary critical minds of the last century, is known by most for his study of Blake, his books on Shakespeare, Milton, and the Bible, and his influential *Anatomy of Criticism*. Frye's vision of culture was a continuous one, as was the portrait of the person that emerged from his large body of work—more than thirty books and hundreds of essays. He was a shy and quiet personality, one who drew back from critical arguments, devoting all of his energies to his teaching, and writing with dignity, eloquence, and Olympian detachment. But like everyone else, Frye's personality was more complex than its public perception. We are better able to see this complexity from Frye's previously unpublished papers that are now making their way into print—his correspondence, student essays, diaries, and most importantly his notebooks. The seventy-six holograph notebooks that Frye kept over the course of fifty years are the source for practically all of the entries in *Northrop Frye Unbuttoned*. Several come from typescripts that were not published during his lifetime and from his diaries. Frye's notebooks served as the workshop from which he fashioned his books, but there are thousands of entries in which he speculates on a wide range of topics both personal and impersonal that are at best tangential to his writing project at the moment. They, along with the diaries, reveal a portrait of Frye richer and more unrestrained than the one that emerges from his published work.

Frye remarks in Notebook 3 that his particular fixation is the fear that what he writes in his notebooks will not turn out to be definitive, but this is a fear that he is soon able to vanquish. We do not read very far until we get the opposite impression, and sometimes the pace may seem almost frenetic—the drive of a man possessed to record every nuance of the "obstinate questionings" of his active mind. When we stand back from the notebooks as a whole, however, the mood they convey is neither fear nor frenzy. It is rather a process of speculative free play, "of letting things come & not forcing or cramping or repressing them" (NOTEBOOK 3.120). Frye is in no panic to bring things to closure, moving as he does at a leisurely pace, releasing himself from all inhibitions, and not worrying that his schemes "go bust immediately." "Perhaps that's the reason I have them," he muses (NOTEBOOK 21.203).

In one of his notebooks from the 1960s Frye issues these tactical instructions to himself: "in beginning to plan a major work like the third book, *don't eliminate anything. Never* assume that some area of your speculations can't be included & has to be left over for another book. Things may get eliminated in the very last stage…but *never, never,* exclude anything when thinking about the book. It was strenuous having to cut down *Fearful Symmetry* from an encyclopaedia, but…major works are encyclopaedic & anatomic: everything I know must go into them—eye of bat & tongue of dog…. Give me a place to stand, and I will include the world" (NOTEBOOK 19.333).

From Frye's encyclopedic notebooks (more than a million and a half words) I have selected several hundred entries, characteristic of the free play of his imagination, that I have found to be especially aphoristic, insightful, clever, startling, amusing, powerful, salty, irreverent, or otherwise noteworthy.

In the 1980s Frye wrote,

> I've always wanted to write "my own" book of *pensées,* not like Pascal's but more like Anatole France's *Jardin d'Epicure* or (I've just discovered) Connolly's *The Unquiet Grave.* Neither France nor Connolly is a first-rate mind, so these are examples, not models. Do I have a first-rate mind? Perhaps in some respects I do, but I lack education (i.e., my range of interests is exceedingly narrow). And a book of that type depends on a pretty superior mind that wouldn't instantly start to date. (The model is

Nietzsche's *Gaya Scienza,* probably). The disadvantage of this project is that it can't be planned. (NOTEBOOK 50.568).

Frye never got around to writing his book of *pensées,* but the present collection, which is evidence of a fertile and first-rate mind, might be seen as moving in the direction of what Frye wanted to do.

In a few instances I have omitted material in an entry in the interest of economy (marked by an ellipsis), and I have expanded Frye's infrequent abbreviations, italicized a number of titles, and made occasional changes in the interest of clarity. Editorial additions are in square brackets. The source of each entry is also within square brackets: "NB 3.24," for example, means Notebook 3, paragraph 24; "NOTES" following an entry refers to a typescript, rather than a handwritten set of notes. Diaries are cited by "D," followed by the year of the diary and the entry number: D 49.137, for example, indicates entry 137 of Frye's 1949 diary. I have also provided the page number of the entries that have been published in the *Collected Works of Northrop Frye* (University of Toronto Press):

LN = *Northrop Frye's Late Notebooks* (2000),
TBN = *The "Third Book" Notebooks of Northrop Frye* (2002),
RT = *Northrop Frye's Notebooks and Lectures on the Bible and Other Religious Texts* (2003),
D = *The Diaries of Northrop Frye* (2001).

No abbreviation of a book title in the citation means that the notebook has not yet been published.

I have not encumbered the present texts with the extensive annotations that readers will find in the books just listed, but I have included a glossary at the end that identifies some of the less familiar people, terms, and foreign phrases in these selections.

Frye's notebooks are housed in the archives of the Victoria University Library at the University of Toronto. The selections here are reproduced with the permission of the Estate of Northrop Frye. The caricature of Frye was drawn for me by Van Howell in 1985.

ROBERT D. DENHAM / *Emory, Virginia*

A

Absence. Why did man, or God, or whoever it was, bother to write the Bible anyway? We get the answer at the very end, in Revelation: the real Bible is a sealed book, an apocryphon, a book not to be opened (mentally) until its time has come. Readers of Orwell's *1984* will remember the pathos of the opening, where Winston Smith finds a real notebook and hides it away in the one corner of his room that the telescreen can't reach, to start a diary: his one move out of the hell of the all-seeing eye. The Bible is largely a book of catastrophes, of the disasters caused by the determination of God to interfere in the pattern of human life. It is also a book of refuge and exile, a book of absence, and to that extent a book of comfort. Those poor bastards of Jews and Christians who insist on taking up its burden of the presence of God are denied this comfort. The worst thing we can say of God is that he knows all. The best thing we can say of him is that, on the whole, he tends to keep his knowledge to himself.
[NOTES 52.736; LN, 2:568]

Absentmindedness. Professors *are* absent-minded, & it isn't the fun for them that it is for professional jokers. Like poets, they have to carry their work around with them & can never go about without their mental hands full, so to speak. Absent-mindedness with me is as real a disease as anything can be: great nauseating dizzy feelings sweep over me in waves, I can't seem to lift my brain clear of a directionless & generalized panic, & great forces of resistance make themselves felt as soon as I try to peep out into the Martha-world. I've said that this is all induced by the laziness endemic in academic work, & in fact I find that when the disease is at its

1

worst I'm never concentrating hard on a job—I'm just not thinking of anything at all. It's the state in which I feel so irritated at my stupidities that I get irritated at my irritation, which is a hell of an arse-biting state of mind to be in. [NB 3.58; RT, 25-6]

Abstract Expressionism. I've often wondered why I disliked abstract expressionism so much, and now I think I know: it's pictorial anarchism, the same thing student unrest begins in, the renunciation of the community. I remember some Clyfford Stills I saw in Buffalo: wonderful pictures, but they wouldn't endure anything else in the same room except another Clyfford Still. (I was told later that Still was personally almost a psychotic, and of course I disapprove of putting that fact into a causal relation to the pictures, but the effect of the pictures is unmistakable.) But going through the Uffizi one can see how the pictures of the most towering geniuses still belong in a pictorial community, and hang in a room with other pictures. [NB 12.280; TBN, 199]

Abstraction. Hieratic language abstracts, but evidently there are no original abstractions; they all grow out of earlier concrete images. Abstraction may turn out to be connected with the stage in religion where gods seem to constitute a transcendent order and sit on mountains. [NOTES 54-5.71; RT, 286]

Acceptance. You start life by accepting as desirable an ultimate freeing from all natural bondage which you yet cannot achieve through the will. Then, with this acceptance, or faith, spinning around by itself on top, one goes ahead as before, but now all one's willed acts are provisional, on an "as if" basis, characterized by a kind of tentative pride. At a certain point the will finally is able to relax, the creative spirit surges in from nature & takes charge of it. At this point a Last Judgment takes place, a *Paravritti,* and time is ended. Now of course this passing of will, pride & time into the fullness of time never completely happens in life, but the conviction of acceptance is real enough: tentative pride does succeed to tentative

2

innocence. The "certain point" seems to be reached when something circular (destroying the linear Spectre of Urthona sequence) takes place, when the shape of lost direction becomes manifest. The idea of grasping knowledge seems to me derived from this attempt to reach an end from which one can see one's starting-point, the Bering Strait between extremes of the same world. After that, the idea of knowledge as letting go becomes effective. [NB 3.115; RT, 47-8]

AC/DC. A purely individualized myth is an obsession, sometimes a psychosis. A purely socialized myth is an ideology, which sooner or later also becomes obsessive or psychotic. A myth that has either the direct current of transcendence or the alternating current of imagination rises clear of this grisly antithesis. I suppose the Hitlers & Stalins are the people in whom the antithetical obsessions coincide. [NB 11H.26; LN, 2:716]

Active Evil. Blake's "Active Evil is better than Passive Good" is not sadism …. Blake simply has an ironic hell & a real one, & only the former can be active. Blake comes out for civilization. But the full sadistic content of the phrase needs to be explored. Blake rejected institutional Christianity in order to recreate the New Jerusalem in the soul; a writer like Norman Mailer rejects fascism for a cult of individual violence which is really the same violence. It may be horseshit, & pernicious horseshit, but can evil itself be redemptive? [NB 19.38; TBN, 11]

Active Perversity. You can't get along without the conception of active perversity, the personal devil, even if evil is fundamentally nothingness. What it works out to is something like this. I've said before…that the statement A is never also not-A is true, as it asserts the eternity of form; but the statement A is never also non-A is bullshit. I learned that from the *Lankavatara Sutra*, produced by the same Indian genius that said: it is absurd & inept to imagine that no-number could also be a number. O.K. Let's see what happens when it does. The result was the discovery of zero, and all mathematics turns on similar postulates: a line, a thing of length

3

without breadth, neither exists nor does not exist. That's the doctrine of *Maya,* the attempt to get off the Beulah mattress of a substantial or objective world. The Christian conception of evil as the product of original sin & a fallen world is really exactly the same: the same combination of something that exists & yet cannot exist. We've never looked this in the face: partly, I think, because we've never got beyond a heaven—a Beulah presided over by a father & mother where man is eternal creature—into a conception of real *Kaivalya,* & of course hell is the complement of heaven. The Ptolemaic universe retarded Christianity by postulating a sublunary sphere of fire. I'll figure out what I mean by that later on.
[NB 3.105; RT, 43-4]

Adolescence. The rush of adolescent memories continues: I'm just at the "change of life" period in Jung's psychology, I suppose. They now take the form of wishing I'd spent my youth practising writing fiction: it's silly, of course, but it's part of a general recognition of the damage I did my future life in my earlier years. A certain amount of daydreaming is normal, I suppose, but I daydreamed to excess, and hesitated to start any real work on fulfilling my ambitions because I was so afraid my first efforts wouldn't show true genius. I worried a lot about genius. I think too that my present excess of embarrassment over various failures to achieve perfect life rhythm in social behavior is largely due to an exaggerated picture of myself built up in reverie during adolescence. I suppose that repentance or *metanoia* consists first of all in determining the conditions under which your life must henceforth operate. The irrelevant emotion of regret thereby built up is remorse. [D 50.469; DNF, 401]

Adventure of the Mind. Whatever one thinks of the Tertullian paradox ("I believe *because* it is impossible"), the opposite of it is that trying to reduce belief to the credible is a waste of time and desolation of spirit. One doesn't bother to believe the credible: the credible is believed already, by definition. There's no adventure of the mind there.
[NB 50.290; LN, 1:313]

Adverbs. It's interesting to read persons struggling with residual belief, & watch their adverbs. The word "certainly" almost always betrays the uncertainty of concern. [NB 11F.191; RT, 118]

Advertising. Nobody seriously thinks of television as a viewer's mode of perception; he thinks of it as *his* way (if he's a producer or advertiser) of reaching a viewer. We were astonished when blacks started to smash & loot: we hadn't thought of television as *their* way of seeing an affluent white society gorging itself on luxury goods & privileges. No matter how much he wants people to look at his product, the advertiser doesn't realize that television is their way of looking at him, & not his way of reaching them. [NB 11F.111; RT, 95-6]

Aesthetic Sacrament. When I got nothing out of the [Japanese] tea ceremony I assumed that the limitations of my Christian background made it impossible for me to take in the notion of an aesthetic sacrament. And yet there ought to be a place for an aesthetic sacrament; as part of…religion. [NB 11B.9; RT, 350]

After-Life. One doesn't know anything about an after-life, but one can always invent. We read (experience) a text linearly, forgetting most of it while we read; then we study it as a simultaneous unit. While we live we learn fast but not enough, like a bull in a ring. Meanwhile our dreams store up commentary which we sometimes remember but don't understand. At death we enter into & become the total dream-world we've constructed. We understand it then. The slave, the captive, the exploited, become the compensation-worlds of release & freedom they dream of. Others help & teach us to read. Not so much an inner world as a world of which one is the circumference, seeing it all simultaneously, as we're said to do before death. A world where youth knows and age can. [NB 11E.34; RT, 325]

The Aging Chorus. When I first began to think about a book on the literary context of the Bible, the literary critics specifically interested in the

Bible were few and apologetic; today they are many and confident. The number coming the other way, from Biblical scholarship to an interest in literary criticism, has increased proportionately. I am now, therefore, not a speaker of a prologue, but a member of an aging chorus. Of course every scholar of senior years living in the nineteen eighties has lived through forty or fifty such revolutions even in the fields that directly concern him. This particular revolution may confirm the accuracy of my instincts thirty years ago, but does little for me now. [NB 44.338; LN, 1:175]

Air. We can't live a day without being concerned about food: we can't live a minute without being concerned about air. That's a good reason for the centrality of all the "spirit" metaphors. If we had to eat as much as a shrew we could do nothing but eat: perhaps the incessant breathing, however automatic, is what keeps us from entering into the real "Spirit."
[NB 44.145; LN, 1:132]

Akasa. I say only one soul: the occult tradition, which for some curious reason has got itself stuck to the name of Plato, says only one spirit. The soul-world to them is, first, the total magnet or *anima mundi* which accounts for mesmerism, telepathy, clairvoyance, second sight & magical healing cures; second, Bardo, the world of dead "souls" who in some systems are reborn & therefore unborn, & who are asserted to communicate with spiritualistic media; third, elementals & other non-human forms of more or less conscious existence. I wish I had a consistent idea about this soul-world, which I may call *Akasa.* The Catholic purgatory belongs to it. I rather wish I could throw out this world: I don't like its rumor basis of quasi-fact, its vague Beulah fluidity (it's not a real Beulah, though artists draw on it, as Shakespeare drew on the "elementals" Puck & Ariel, the ghosts (that's different, though, as they aren't in Beulah) & the magical healing of Helena.) I wish I could get a Beulah grasp on this *Akasa* world that would eliminate the subject-object dilemma about it. [NB 3.136; RT, 54]

Alice in Wonderland. I've often said that if I understood the two Alice books I'd have very little left to understand about literature. Actually I think the Alice books, while they carry over, begin rather than sum up— a new twist to fiction that has to do with intellectual paradox & the dis-integrating of the ego. [NB 24.226; TBN, 329]

I suppose the fascination with Alice is not that she's a child in the state of innocence, but that she's a *preternatural* child: what seven-year-old girls would have been like without the Fall. [NB 21.558; RT, 244]

In *Through the Looking Glass* the alchemical marriage is celebrated be-tween the Red King and Alice the White Queen, where it's symbolized by a mutual dream. As Alice is the second white queen, in something like a filial relationship to the bumbling and scatterbrained earlier queen who turns into a sheep, her reaching the Eighth Square is also an anabasis of Kore. The Alice books are inexhaustibly suggestive, one with cards & one with chess, one ending with a trial and the other with a banquet, and the riddle in the second: Why are all the poems about fish? They're a source of the kind of mad and unprintable intuitions that supply most of the real power in this myth game: too bad people are so stupid I have to keep them secret. [NB 50.192; LN, 1:293]

Allegory. The word "allegory" has its uses in criticism, certainly; but when-ever it assumes an either-or category of thinking it becomes junk. Thus scholarship on the *Song of Songs* tends to maintain that it is either a purely physical song of sexual and erotic passion or that it is an allegory of some-thing fuckless: the love of Christ for his Church or what not. I'm saying that both views are conceivable, on condition that neither is wholly rejected. The great Biblical principle that there is no metaphorical contrast between the individual and the social, the male and the female, the physical and the ideal, holds here as everywhere. [NOTES 52.152; LN, 2:452]

Alphabet. I keep wondering why there's such extraordinary magic attached, in Kabbalism and elsewhere, to the Hebrew "alphabet," which is really just a consonantal syllabary. It seems to go with the veneration of *écriture*, and not just because only the consonants are written down. There seems to be an unexpressed feeling that the *silent* word, of moving lips and tongue and the like, is the real communication: the actual sounds produced are variable (e.g., Jehovah for Yahweh, Moloch for *melek*). [NB 27.458; LN, 1:83-4]

Alphabet of Forms. In Christianity truth is the revelation of the person of Christ, where the understanding of a book enables the Spirit to perform again the resurrection of the Word. The only literary form possible for this kind of revelation is that of a discontinuous sequence of epiphanies. The feeling that this "sequence" ought to suggest the cycle of totality produces the conception of the Logos as an alphabet of forms. The *I Ching*, the Tarot pack, & the like, are the Alpha-Omega aspect of the Word. These schemes are used for divination, as is natural, because they're conceived as above time, but they are expressions of the schematic ("all imagination") shape of mythical apprehension of reality. Yeats' circle of the moon and Poe's *Eureka* cloud of unknowing. [NB 6.22-3; TBN, 110-11]

Altar of Introverted Acceptance. If Jesus were sinless he must have kept out of moral dilemmas with extraordinary agility, & if this agility were not purely the result of omniscience and/or omnipotence, which would take away the credit of his incarnation, it must have come from a continuous ability to make the most of every situation he was in from childhood up. Hence he would never have fallen into that state which paradoxically is both fate and chance, & which affects all of us. Things happen unpredictably & involuntarily to us which involve us in moral dilemmas, & more or less sin enters into, not getting out of them, but simply through them. Perhaps the origin of such unpredictable events is always some deficiency in our previous handling of a previous situation. Believers in reincarnation say "man is born into the world he has made"—we believe that only of Christ. Of course for anyone to dodge sin in early childhood not only the family training but the heredity must have been carefully taken care of, which is why so much hullabaloo is made about the Virgin & her immaculate conception, in spite of Jesus' irony on the subject. All this is most irreverent, & I mean to make something of irreverence, to carry the attitude of, say, Shaw into the citadel of faith itself. If I keep my nerve I may encourage & put heart in all those queasy intellectuals who can't resist cutting the throats of their critical reason on the altar of an introverted acceptance of tradition. [D 49.363; DNF, 202-3]

Alternative Career. Every normal man has an alternative career he sometimes dreams about.... I have music. Corresponding to this is the holding of an opposite mental state up as a reflector to the one one has. I'm a Blakean, a visionary disciple: hence the complement is scientific materialism & skepticism of the crudest kind. It used to tempt, or rather tease, but it's losing its appeal, which is perhaps unfortunate. But I'm always torn between feeling that the cock crows because he has a vision of the dawn, or because he feels stimulated by standing on top of a pile of horseshit. [D 42.24; DNF, 12-13]

American Scholarship. To get a grip on the bibliography of the period I'm shockingly ignorant of, I dug out Bernbaum's *Guide through the Romantic Movement*. A primer, with all the critical statements that aren't utterly commonplace either demonstrably false or meaningless. And even I can see that the bibliographies are very bad. What dreadful charlatans there are in American scholarship, some with formidable reputations! It started me wondering again about the possibility of making some money out of a *Blake Handbook* after *Fearful Symmetry* stops selling. Waste of time, though. [D 51.6; DNF, 455]

Amoral Nature. I suppose every new development of romance is really a new development of polytheism, and a new set of heroes or quasi-god figures developed from the tedious amorality of nature. The Bible did point a way and a direction out of all that: why are allegedly creative people so stupid? [NOTES 52.986; LN, 2:608]

9

Analogia Entis. Wonder if the Catholic search for a philosophical infrastructure, the *analogia entis* [analogy of being], doesn't accompany a neo-imperialism, as Stoicism reinforced the *pax Romana.*
[NOTES 54-1.79; LN, 2:680]

Analogies of Existence. My notion of merely human existence as a phantasmagoria, and of education as the encounter with reality: Education is a set of analogies to a genuinely human existence, of which the arts are the model. Merely human life is of course a demonic analogy or parody of genuinely human life. That is, Ulro is pure projection, Eden full recovery; in between come two degrees of recovery, Beulah being that of recovered belief where no dispute can come. Ulro is the projection of tyranny; Generation of constituted authority; Beulah of democracy; Eden of the kingdom of ends, the pure fraternity of individuals.[NB 21.49; RT, 149]

Analogy. People think they're being iconoclastic & realistic when they ask me if there aren't differences as well as similarities in the patterns I put together. Of course there are, but that again is confusing imaginative & conceptual processes. In imaginative thought there is no real knowledge of anything but similarities (ultimately identities): knowledge of differences is merely a transition to a new knowledge of similarities. In conceptual thought analogy is tricky & misleading beyond the heuristic stage: in imaginative thought it's the *telos* of knowledge. The great ocean into which all analogy empties is the *via negativa* approach to God, which the Incarnation reverses into spring rain, the identity of God & Man.
[NB 21.401; RT, 215]

Ancestor Worship. Ancestor-worship is, I think, a projection of a much deeper impulse telling us that the dead have to be redeemed by the creative & charitable acts of the living. Christian doctrines are projections of the go-away-and-don't-bother-us feeling. The dead can do all sorts of things for us...but they're not superior beings, or are in only one aspect. Another aspect lives on in time inside descendants (or others: the feeling that one *must* leave descendants is nonsense) and is beatified by them if they're lucky. Reincarnation may occasionally be a form of this. [NB 11C.13; RT, 345]

Angels. I should do a bit of thinking about the conception of angels. After all, it's damn important in the Thomist set up. Lycidas joins the "solemn troops & sweet societies" of the city of God & gives it his full attention while being at the same time "Genius of the shore," a guardian or watcher of human fortunes. I suppose angels are personal archetypes, & belong on the third level with gods & myths as parts of the whole, the whole being the divine-human society. As substantial existences, therefore, they're covering cherubs, part of the chain of being, Atlases who hold up the sky-god on top of man. That's what the prohibition about worshipping them really amounts to (in the New Testament). Thus far I'm just repeating the ideas I have now: what's new is the ambiguity of the collective "intelligence" that watches human society from outside & simultaneously acts within a divine society. In Dante that's linked with the dreadful pervasive vulgarity which identifies God, not with suffering humanity, but with ruling humanity, & so continually cuts God down to human size, using him just to rubber stamp the standards arrived at by Popes & Emperors down here. Milton has a lot less of that, mainly because his political ideas are in better shape: his heaven is a place of *spiritual* authority, not a series of astral barracks labelled "for officers only." I only wish Milton had done his poem on the Passion. [D 50.126; DNF, 264]

Anima. I am now facing my anima, in a spectre-emanation relationship, trying to separate the anima from mother, wife, ex-girl friend, & fantasy figures. She's a statue I'd like to make come to life. The Great Work is not, after all, the begetting of a child from this, but the recognition that the child already exists: our Perdita is found. A female statue comes to life, a dead female comes to life also, & the two cycles synchronize. No. Perdita is not the dying & reviving female: that's Hermione. Perdita is the child who refuses to die. She isn't born; she's *found*. End of the Magi's journey: all the Magi begot Jesus, & yet none of them did. [NB 11E.98; RT, 338-9]

Annual Elections. The kingship metaphor as an attractive icon. But of course there are many other contexts where the kingship metaphor is a very dangerous idol, and it is because of the dangers in it that democracy has replaced the ritual humiliation of the king with the annual election in which, according to the theory, if you get enough individual imbecilities added together, you get a collective wisdom.
["SYMBOLISM IN THE BIBLE," LECTURE 10; RT, 493]

Anti-intellectual Cosiness. Marxism owed its immense popularity in Western democracies during the thirties to its being a primary or naive social vision, filling people with the great hope of pulling them down to a collective level where they wouldn't have to think any more. Those who couldn't buy that bought Thomism; those who simply hated the whole operation of thought went fascist. The United States never got sold on Marxism apart from the intellectuals, because they had their mattress to sleep on, the American way of life, with all its anti-intellectual cosiness.
[NOTES 53.155; LN, 2:642]

Antiochus Epiphanes. I'm beginning to feel that one of the key figures of history was that repulsive idiot Antiochus Epiphanes: without him neither Judaism nor Christianity would ever have come into focus.
[NB 11F.181; RT, 115]

Anxieties. Words are the only language of consciousness, and the art of words is the only art directly subject to the conflicts of consciousness. Anxieties can only express themselves verbally. They express themselves in two ways: formally, in clichés, and materially, in assaults on the structure. In paranoid writing, where an author is continually digressing to attack the Jews or his mother-in-law, we can see what we see in a different way in doggerel: that every structural achievement in writing is an ethical victory. The average sermon is full of digressions, because parsons are occupationally anxious, anxieties being what the will substitutes for the grace of belief. [NB 19.261; TBN, 59-60]

Anxiety of Influence. Bloom's *Anxiety of Influence:* an embarrassing book to me, because it's about him & not its subject, & I'm one of the influences he's anxious about. I think the fear of death, which the existentialists say is *the* anxiety, is really just the center of a much larger anxiety of metamorphosis. The question *ubi sunt* may turn up in snow or flowers long before it's realized to be death. The anxiety of continuity is salvaged from this, just as the knowledge of good is salvaged from the knowledge of evil. Continuity actualizes itself in the Old Testament forms of wisdom (*hokmah*) & law, & thence develops towards a neo-metamorphosis ("we shall all be changed," says Paul). The Jews, & the Pharisaic survivals in Christianity, knock themselves out keeping their identity continuous (e.g. apostolic succession). [NB 24.248; TBN, 334]

How and why the twenty-first century, if we survive that long, may become the first age in history when primary concern is really primary. Every poem in the meantime an expression of ideology or secondary concern, and this is I think the real "anxiety of influence," not Bloom's psychological Freudian kind, which I think is a by-product of the law of copyright. [NOTES 52.406; LN, 2:505]

The Aphorism. The orator's style is continuous, but the crux is the high-style sententia, which speaks with the authority of concerned prose. An aphorism is not a cliché: it penetrates & bites. It has wit, and consequently an affinity with satire. It appeals to the instinct in us to say "I don't care if a man's right or wrong; all I care about is whether his mind is alive or dead." Naturally this will not do as a guide to thought, but it's normal & healthy as an occasional reaction. Christ speaks in aphorisms, not because they are alive, but because he is. [NB 11F.154; RT, 108]

What is the literary effect of continuity? It isn't really dictatorial: rather it's democratic: one man button-holing you. One can express *aloofness* only in some form of aphorism. Also, continuous prose suggests complete identification with the representing, observing, immersing-in-object self.

13

Aphorisms suggest a richer & varied personality made up more of internal conflicts and decisions. An *epiphanic* sequence suggests the highest mystery of personality. [NB 33.47]

Apocalypse. If everything in the apocalypse is (spatially) identical with everything else, then every moment of time is identical with every other moment of time. And as in the apocalypse unity is particular & universal but not general, & the opposite of uniformity is likeness, it follows that the Parmenidean universe, where every moment is just like another, is demonic. [NB 11F.96; RT, 91]

Archetype Spotting. Many years ago young Woodbury, when a student of mine, spoke of the triviality of "archetype-spotting," and I've always tried to recognize that. I'm beginning to recognize more clearly the identity of what it doesn't consider—I mean my repetition approach. Within the last century or more, and starting with the *symbolisme* movement, poetry began to get increasingly self-conscious about the centripetal this-poem approach. [NOTES 52.723; LN, 2:564-5]

The Archimedes Principle. I've always been a little doubtful about Jung's introversion & extroversion principle: it's really a difference between the contemplative & the active approaches. If, for example, I were younger, could hold an erection, & were interested in the pursuit of women, I wouldn't pursue them: I'd pretend to be interested in something else until they came up to me, virgins to a unicorn. It's the same instinct that makes me a critic, withdrawing from experience until it becomes oracular. It goes back to my lack of physical confidence, or, more accurately, to my realization that that lack of confidence has a very sound basis. I am not one of those who attack & conquer events & surroundings: I turn away until they settle down. I'm an Archimedes who could move the earth if he were standing in a different place, but when he is, he can do his work only in the absence of the murderous louts of Rome.
[NB 11F.199; RT, 120]

Argument. Nothing is more remarkable in the Bible than the absence of argument. There are pseudo-arguments in Paul, but they're not really arguments: they're disguised proclamation & exhortation, at best shadow inferences from premises already held by the reader. Argument is internal continuity. So is logical sequence in narrative: in the Bible the connectives are just "and." [NB 21.317; RT, 200]

Aristocrats and Proletariats. Aristocrats get everything in this life: consequently they're fatalists & accept a shadow Hades-world. Cults of immortality are proletariat. [NB 46.11; LN, 2:692]

Art. One of the major activities of art consists in sharpening the edge of platitudes to make them enter the soul as realities. [NB 3.12; RT, 7]

Art is not simply an identity of illusion and reality, but a counter-illusion: its world is a material world, but the material of an intelligible spiritual world. [NB 27.399; LN, 1:73]

I don't want the reduction of religion to aesthetics, but the abolition of aesthetics & the incorporating of art with the Word of God.
[NB 3.13; RT, 7]

A community's art is its spiritual vision. [NB 21.352; RT, 206]

Art of Words. My professional career has been concerned with the study and criticism of literature, and so I have been aware, from the beginning, of two contexts of the word literature. Literature is an art of words, hence one context emphasizes the "art," the other the "words."
[NOTES 52.384; LN, 2:500]

Astrology. It is not conceivable that stars billions of miles away can "influence" us, but it is theoretically conceivable that stars & their positions could be used as a computer to determine one's character, for what reason we don't know. But not even astrologers can believe in *causal* astrology; as Jung says, synchronicity has to be acausal. Silent *écriture* again. Even at that I'm suspicious of astrology: it's too close to the view that creation was made for man, a notion not only wrong but ultimately sick. But still the possibility remains that as long as it's acausal, in the same way that putting a thermometer outside the window doesn't cause but only records a change in temperature, not only astrology but any number of "mancies" or forms of divination might be alternative ways of recording the phenomena of human (or any other) life; part, as I say, of the silent *écriture* of a newly intelligible nature. [NB 11E.38; RT, 326]

Atlantis. There's a lot of semi-occult fascination with Atlantis in the last two centuries: one very fine book (despite its obvious weaknesses and lapses) is Merezhkovsky's *Atlantis/Europe,* which tries to go all out for the historicity of Atlantis and doesn't mention Thera, but is really based on an ascending-ladder diagram in which we go on to the future, unless we get caught in the same cycle again, while Atlantis is our buried or forgotten past. He links the *Timaeus* and the Book of Enoch in some curious ways, coming close to a lot of the von Daniken mythology, but he's better than that: an example of how yesterday's kook book becomes tomorrow's standard text. [NOTES 52.358; LN, 2:495]

The myth of Atlantis, as I've known from the beginning, is another version of the myth of the fall, except that those who deal with it usually try to place it in history, whereas it doesn't really belong in history necessarily. [NOTES 53.41; LN, 2:620]

Attachment. Montaigne says that one should not love a wife too much, for that is attachment: she might die and then where would you be? The doctrine of non-attachment is mine; the application is not: I feel that in such a passage as that wisdom has outfoxed itself. One should withdraw attachment from possessions & machines, but you remain attached to your right arm, & life without it is a mutilated life. With wives as with arms, one is attached, & simply has to take the chance. The metaphor of "one flesh" is not an idle one. [D 49.139; DNF, 107]

Authentic Knowledge. Authentic knowledge is *ut pictura poesis* knowledge. [NB 11D.23; RT, 269]

B

Bach. I think Bach is the great Protestant poet of the Pathos: not only two *Passions,* but even the B minor centers on the Kyrie and the Crucifixion. Milton and Bunyan are the Protestant poets of the Agon [conflict]: Blake of the Anagnorisis [recognition]. I wonder, if the Mass were analyzed from this point of view, what would happen. [NB5.22]

Though a very Protestant mass, with the weight thrown on the Kyrie & the Credo, the [B Minor Mass] is pure revelation, & that's why it's so brilliant & buoyant. It's such a contrast to the Beethoven mass, where the predominant feeling is mystery, & the big climax is the Messianic Benedictus, which is dependent on a violin solo. Bach takes mystery in his stride: the key word of the mass, for him, is "gloria," & he gives you pure mandala vision. He's also given the real meaning of sacrament, which is commedia, recognition, anagnorisis, epiphany. It's the exact opposite of sacrifice: in sacrifice, which is tragedy, something is killed: in sacrament something is brought to life. That something is the real presence of a single mind which contains both the Mass & the participating audience. No external God can be adored with music He did not compose. [D 50.283; DNF, 324-5]

In the twenty years that I've been listening to the *Passion* I've changed my mind about it. I used to feel that the narration was something to sit through, & one waited for the arias & choruses. Now I feel that the work is primarily narration, as the arias & choruses, with greater familiarity, fall into the background as commentaries. This, of course, brings out its real tragic structure, as it's like Greek tragedy, not only in its use of a chorus,

18

but in its *reporting* of the events. Even Christ, though he does his own singing, is contained within the narration. [D 50.285; DNF, 325]

Bardo Novel. How the hell would one write a *good* Bardo novel? It would have to be short, or get laborious. I don't know how one could introduce incident or dialogue. It wouldn't do at all unless it could acquire a powerfully convincing logic: I'd want something as concrete as Dante and yet carrying its punch within its own argument, and not depending on the traditional Church fables. To do that I think I should have to assume that you get to a certain spiritual abode when you get there, i.e., that one's environment is appropriate to one's character, as the doctrine of karma or original sin establishes for this existence. The trick is to make a logical sequence of experiences without preaching, and yet implying a complete theory of Bardo. [NB 2.13]

Beatrice. I wish [Dante's] Beatrice didn't blither so: she's the most tedious & drivelling spinster in literature. [NB 45.110; RT, 408]

Beauty. I have never understood why the question of "beauty" should have a peculiarly close relationship to the arts. Beauty may be predicated on many things that are not works of art. Works of art seem to me to be concerned with a certain kind of structure, or process, found in them but not in other things. Structure if, with the Classical critics, we assert the priority of the hen; process if, with the Romantics, we assert the priority of the egg. [NB 18.97]

Beginning. We are always in the place of beginning; there is no advance in infinity. [NB 50.129; LN, 1:281]

Being and Nothingness. Let's take a familiar example of the confronting of being with nothingness: I am standing in London on what the guidebook assures me was the very spot where something happened in 1150. The gap between my being & its nothingness is, essentially, time: the connection between them is essentially space. It's Newtonian space, which is why Newton called space the sensorium of deity, following the Christian instinct to call Christ a real presence (space) rather than a real present (time). [NB 19.262; TBN, 60]

Belacqua Fantasy. Every so often I find myself, as now, at the bottom of the mountain, with everything I've done numbered zero. I'm in what Beckett calls the Belacqua fantasy, in no damn hurry to climb. Prolonged, this state would be the paranoia I'm familiar with.... I notice that in this state I tend to think about time, and more particularly the notion that time as we know it is a false or projected form of real time. [NB 19.106; TBN, 24]

Belief. Belief is a highly integrated & concentrated state of mind. William James speaks of a will to believe which is mostly phony. In Christian terms, belief is a matter of grace rather than will. Clergymen are naturally prone to believe that they ought to believe. Many of them can't manage belief, & have to settle for anxieties. One can hardly discern the beliefs of Protestantism through the thick cloud of anxiety-mongering about the "liquor traffic," or the beliefs of Catholicism through anxieties about contraceptives & meat on Fridays. Well, would you let them get into pulpits with nothing to say? As a matter of fact Jesus recommends precisely that, & guarantees their inspiration, given a highly disciplined state of mind in which one has, like Mary as against Martha, got rid of importunate anxieties. As for the man who said "Help thou my unbelief," what he was expressing was doubt about the validity of his doubts: a state of mind that might be called virtuous hypocrisy. [NB 18.145]

Problems of belief are still with me: for all practical purposes "I don't believe in God" and "I believe in no God" are interchangeable. They seem to me to be very different statements, and the agnostic-atheist distinction doesn't exhaust the difference. [NB 27.35; LN, 1:8]

At a class a girl asked me if I "believed" in Jung's collective unconscious.

I don't believe in anything that is to be believed: that is, I don't trust anything that remains in the dark as an object of belief.
[NB 11F.162; RT, 110]

My principle that what we believe is what our actions show that we believe is only a definition of *functional* belief. It's the first step in getting rid of ideology, and ideology is, I suppose, most of what Jesus meant by hypocrisy. But it doesn't even define the sincere belief, for a functional belief may be deliberately chosen for the worst possible reasons.
[NB 21.16; RT, 142]

Another form of silly & irresponsible escapist belief is… muttering darkly about the horrid (unspecified) disasters that would have followed if Europe had succumbed to Arianism or Manicheanism. *Nothing* could have been worse than the beliefs Christianity did adopt (e.g. hell), except a religion more difficult to wriggle out of. Such people are playing with serious ideas, playing not as poets do, but frivolously. [NB 21.19; RT, 143]

Belief has nothing to do with knowledge, & *credo ut intelligam* [I believe in order that I might understand] is horseshit. It was a possible hypothesis as long as the deductive synthesis seemed possible, but not now. The fact that all knowledge is based on accepted axioms is a quite different principle: it has nothing to do with making religious belief a source of knowledge. [NB 21.368; RT, 209]

I should ask myself squarely: do you intend to make this book [*The Great Code*], in one aspect, a Christian apologetic for our times? If you do, why do you? And would such an intention make the book dishonest? The best answer I can give now is to say that if I can show that Christianity is imaginatively possible today, I can show that any other belief is a choice distinct from that, there being no state without belief, & no one belief inevitable for everybody, much less a necessary alternative belief to Christianity. It's that last I should hold on to. I'm a Christian partly *faute de mieux:* I see no better faith, & certainly couldn't invent one of my own except out of Christian assumptions. But some of my other principles are: a) the less we believe the better b) nothing should be believed that has to be believed in. [NB 21.499; RT, 232]

Belief as tactical adoption: to say "my life is in the hands of God" is a tactical way of coming to terms with such data as (a) I can't prolong my life, so far as I know, by an act of will (b) I feel it wouldn't solve anything to kill myself even if I otherwise was led to (c) it may be true that people do shorten their lives unconsciously, but what I'm unconscious of I by definition don't know & therefore can't control. Not everybody finds the above formula satisfactory or necessary; others are simply stuck with it, & believe that any other formulation would be wrong, despite the obviously metaphorical form ("hands"). "The length of my life is not, barring suicide, my responsibility" is what the metaphor means. [NB11E.93]

The state of mind that we call belief is neither ancient nor universal. It's one of those unconscious assumptions we seldom examine that everyone believes. The attitude of the ancient Greek was, obviously, not: "I believe in Zeus the father Almighty…and in Dionysos his Son our Lord." It was rather: "Some say that Dionysos was born from the thigh of Zeus; others that he was nursed by Amalthea," etc. And today Christianity would go bankrupt overnight if it were supported only by the people who believe. People accept it, realize it's there, respect it, even turn to it for help, but don't necessarily believe or disbelieve it. [NB 13.64]

A belief is a course of action inspired by a shaping vision. This shaping vision is the opposite of idolatry. In both cases you become what you behold. One is the total "I am" building up inside you; the other is the *tabula rasa* approach to the objective. [NB 24.196; TBN, 322]

Benediction. I've just done another benediction job: I said knowledge was the food of the spirit: it had to be shared, & if hoarded would spoil.

There is a metaphorical identity link between food & knowledge: the spoiled hoard has its type in manna and its antitype in the parable of talents…. The benediction itself said: "May the presence of God consecrate our studies and transmute their elements. May what we offer in ignorance be accepted in providence. May the reverence for God's creation, which all the arts and sciences express, grow in us and unite there with his will to create all things new." I transcribe this because I asked for help with it and feel I got it. It links with a lot of *Words with Power* themes, or what ought to be themes. [NB 50.562, 565; LN, 1:371-2]

The Bible. Without losing its specific historical orientation through Judaism and Christianity, the Bible is an archetypal model of a perennial philosophy or everlasting gospel. At least, that's what I'd call it if I were writing a book on religion. We really do move from creation to recreation. [NB 27.151; LN, 1:28]

This book [*The Great Code*] does not say that the Bible is literature: it says that it is literary, that it has literary qualities. It will be said (that the Bible is not just a work of literature, &) that it is ridiculous to put Moses & Jesus into the same category as Odysseus or Oedipus. Of course it is; but the Bible is not "just" a work of history or doctrine or factual statement either, & there are (also difficulties, perhaps) equal difficulties, in putting them, Moses & Jesus into the same category as Lycurgus or St. Francis or Charles V or Loyola (Alfred the Great or St. Augustine). [NB 11F.60; RT, 83]

Approaching the Bible as myth or imaginative construct is the first step in a genuine reformation of Christianity. The next step is the razor principle: the less you believe the better. The third step is: belief is the derivation of action from vision: no belief that isn't a visible axiom of action is a real belief. (There may be possible beliefs or hunches that are cherished but not acted on, but you aren't justified by those). [NB 21.229; RT, 182-3]

23

I am not interested in the relation of religion and literature, where there may be any number of "either-or" contrasts and dilemmas—aporias, we knowledgeable people call them—but in the relation of the Bible & Western literature. That is, I'm interested in the Bible specifically, because it's written in the language of literature, the language of myth, metaphor, figured speech, rhetoric, symbol & analogy. I want to make a few suggestions about what that feature in the Bible has helped to shape in our imaginative culture—I can't do without "imagination" as my central building block. [NB 44.267-8; LN, 1:160-1]

The function of the Bible is to give us knowledge of myth (and metaphor). Not experience: that the reader's response. The Bible guides and girds the experience: unorganized mythical experience is hysteria or insanity. [NB 11B.22; RT, 352]

The Bible never calls itself the Bible nor does the phrase Word of God ever mean the Bible. Hence one of the things the Bible is is a Bible of misreadings. The misreading paradox turns on a constant recreation, & we can't trace the Bible back to a time when it wasn't being recreated. [NB11E.79-80; RT, 336]

Blake. People in Blake's day couldn't understand why man was born free & was everywhere in chains, or why the oppressed put up with oppression when "Ye are many, they are few." Blake saw that if your myth-created ideology was hierarchical, you couldn't function outside that hierarchy. As for his lack of influence in his time, the only commentary needed on that is the line: "Wisdom is sold in the desolate market where none come to buy." And, of course, it was Blake who saw that the real Bible was a revolutionary structure, founded on the Exodus type and the resurrection antitype. [NB 50.327; LN, 1:321]

Blasphemy. We must cling to a God who approves of blasphemy because he hates Jehovah & Nobodaddy & Zeus & Isvara & all the other kings of terrors & tyrants of the soul. To a God who appreciates obscenity because he looks not into the secrets of our hearts but into the hearts of our secrets, & knows that our bloodfilled genitals & cocking guts are the real battle-fields. [NB 3.39; RT, 19]

Bloody-Mindedness. The question of play, of it's not really happening, is inseparable from all cultural development. In an Aztec ritual a man is flayed alive & the priest puts on his skin. Spring festival, you see: put off the old man & put on the new, reviving what's dead in a new form. O.K., but if you were to watch such a rite being performed, the beauty & appro-priateness of the symbolism is not what would strike you most forcibly. Here as everywhere the literal-minded is the bloody-minded. The only thing we can take literally in the gospels is the Crucifixion.
[NB 44.123; LN, 1:127]

Bodily Revelation. Iconoclasm, the turning to the ear away from the eye, geometrizes the visual arts & so abstracts them. So what? In Moslem art I notice that the effect of a great mosque is overall, in contrast to the cathedral where you move from point to point. Yeats has two suggestive koans: that the Word is number in movement & that Pythagoras the mathematician planned the erotic beauty of Greek art. A lot of notions which in themselves are just clichés (e.g. why is the sense of shame about the body, especially the female body, rationalized as decency or propriety in sky-father religions?) are sloshing around in my noddle, but I hope they'll take a pattern that isn't cliché. Most of it as usual comes out of Blake, but Blake calls the *Greeks* prudes & the Biblical tradition a bodily revelation, which will take some showing.
[NB 21.340; RT, 204]

Body. All the clean-minded authorities, from Patanjali to Castiglione, insist on an absolute identity of mind & body. All religions including the Protestant (alcohol) made taboos and fetishes in diet, for instance, & that's the legalistic analogy of the fact that one does find oneself being

25

poisoned by certain things (the most obvious instance in my case being an overdose of coffee) and perhaps narcotics & stimulants, perhaps even meat, do gradually fade out of the diet. I find myself unusually sensitive to alcohol: I feel perceptibly more stupid after a single drink. Breathing, too: I find it advisable to change the "lean" of my breath, as I often catch myself breathing in for a long time, which I think is a symptom of laziness and timidity. We're told that the heartbeat comes under control in later stages, perhaps the adjustment of heart & lungs rhythms is the basis. Ascetic practices are said to be useful in breaking up habit: I should think it more essential to build up habits, & get rid rather of physical fears & phobias. I haven't got this clear: Suso seemed to know what he was about. [NB 3.6; RT, 5]

Body and Soul. The thing that gets me down about the Hellenistic philosophies, including early Christianity, is the incessant war of the soul against the body, where the soul is always right and the body always wrong. This heads-I-win-tails-you-lose situation is applied to God and man by Kierkegaard. There's a close parallel with the Indian conceptions of gunas, where we have a Rajas Guna, all will and aggression, and a Tamas Guna, all passivity and resistance. There's also a Sattva Guna that transcends them, not by reconciling them, but by breaking clear of their antitheses. Christianity has this third principle in Paul's doctrine of the Spirit, but for the life of me I can't see where Christians made any effective use of it. There's a parallel with Freud's picture of an ego-centered consciousness sitting on top of a repressed one. Faith, in this setup, is the soul insisting on the truth of what the body knows ain't so, and telling the body to shut up. The "body" doesn't know anything either, of course, except that the soul is wrong. Not that I know what "body" means in this context. [NOTES 53.51; LN, 2:622]

Body as Metaphor. My much suppressed & censored hunch that the symbolic universe must have the form of a conventionalized human body is still there. The Logos vision of order is the spherical head. The romance section is the trunk, with the point of epiphany at the brain stem. I've always thought of this as square, but it may be more naturally an upward-pointing triangle. The ironic section is certainly a down-pointing triangle, with the point of demonic epiphany at the prick, the "instrument of production" from which all revolution starts. Below this is the cloven fiction of feet & legs, or the advance through contraries, depending on how they're used (often with a cyclical vision attached, like Molloy's bicycle in Beckett). The end of the Theseus quest is of course the arsehole, which is why there's so much anal demonic symbolism. In the center the axis of *nomos* [law] & *nous* [mind], is the systole-diastole movement of heart & more especially the lungs, with its alternation of inspiration & expiration. [NB 12.184; TBN, 175-6]

Body of the House. The metaphor follows a quest like the second half of the *Odyssey*—the least-likely-to-succeed old beggar turns out to be not only the master of the whole house but the body of the house. That is, metaphor, the bridge between consciousness and nature, is the microcosm of language. [NOTES 52.590; LN, 2:540]

Body Parts. Many illuminating thinkers come to grief on practical politics, & the profoundest wisdom often sounds merely silly when working on the newspaper. One major blunder is taking the men-in-one-man symbol the wrong way, & making the social human being a *fallen* body. This was Plato's blunder, and Paul's, & all arguments about heads & bellies & members & the natural supremacy of honorable to dishonorable parts of the body are founded on the fallen body, never on the risen one. Hence the analogy symbols of Shakespearean drama (*King John* & *Julius Caesar* particularly) are ready-made: cf. the frontispiece to *Leviathan*. The brain doesn't rule; it thinks. The heart doesn't obey; it pumps. Plato was right in regarding a flexible caste system as the basis of freedom; grotesquely wrong in mixing it up with ruling & being ruled. [NB 32.34]

Boehme. I have very few religious books, & those I have stress the mystics.

27

I have great difficulty, nonetheless, in reading, say, Boehme, because mystics (less true of Boehme than of others) seem so masochistic: isn't this stuff just wonderful that we have to say we believe anyway? But now Boehme is making more sense as I move closer to light and signature symbolism. Once more, it's not that I "believe" him but that this is the kind of link between the Bible and the creative imagination that I'm looking for. [NB 27.197; LN, 1:35]

The Book. Derrida on the book between two covers as a solid object enclosing an authority is, as Derrida must know, complete bullshit: nobody believes that a book is an object: it's a focus of verbal energy. What he should be attacking is the dogmatic formulation that eliminates its own opposite: that's the symbol or metaphor that can kill a man, and has killed thousands. It's always self-enclosed and opaque; no kerygma ever gets through it. [NOTES 53.176; LN, 2:647]

Books. I'm at the age to reread books I've forgotten: when an undergraduate F. H. Anderson told us to read Havelock Ellis' *Dance of Life*, & I read it with interest, but picking up a second-hand copy in a bookstore, I found I'd totally forgotten it, yet its spattery encyclopaedic style has certainly influenced my idiom, & it begins by saying that the fundamental arts are dancing & building (my freedom & shelter concerns). A footnote includes the sexual concern (mating dances of birds). (Unfortunately the stinker who sold the shop the book has razored out five pages, so I'll have to find another copy. I won't keep a mutilated book on my shelves). [NB 44.81; LN, 1:117]

For some time now I've been scolding myself for not reading a lot of the "good books" on my shelves, or opening them and not having the guts to finish them. Then I take book after book from my shelves and find that I've read it carefully all through, with marginal comments that prove I have. What gives? Is senility just the flipside of human existence? [NB 50.535; LN, 1:365]

Brains. Once in Pakistan it began to rain: a man from Belfast walking with me had an umbrella & spread it over me, saying he was glad to help preserve "a better brain than my own." There are many obvious reasons why I should find such a remark irritating: the most important, perhaps, is that I feel that within the very wide area of normal intelligence I think all brains are pretty well alike. I have always loved music better than words, but I think I'd have been a second-rate musician, a commonplace church organist. In other areas, like business, I'd be a dunce. We all start from scratch: the immense differences in where we arrive are largely a matter of luck, plus conditioning of various kinds. That's one reason why one *has* to believe in a God who knows what people are and pays little attention to what they do. [NB 50.212; LN, 1:297-8]

Breathing. Perhaps if from early youth I had practised regularizing my breathing—just regularizing it, not trying any fancy yoga tricks—instead of spending my entire life in short pants, I'd have developed an inner authority despite my physical weakness and outgrown the masochistic self-betrayals that have tripped me up at intervals all my life. God, the things the bull learns the first and only time he is in the ring. [NB 44.451; LN, 1:200-1]

Brutality. The writers of the Gospels say that crucifying Christ was wrong: it did not occur to them that crucifixion was wrong in itself, and worse than anything the criminal did (cf. Luke 23:41). So Christianity had no defences against its own brutality when it came to power. But burning heretics is wrong whatever the motivation, and this eventually draws out the discovery that the good motivation (zeal, charity, etc.) was phony. [NB 21.9; RT, 141]

Buddha and Beer. I think now I have finally grown to distrust yoga & Buddhist insistence on diet, not that I ever had the least intention of observing a vegetarian or teetotaller diet. Bernard Shaw made the initial impression on me. It's a kind of empiricism I think one can do without.

If beer makes me feel stupid & sleepy, I have to put more energy into remaining awake, that's all. Of course there are limits. One should not say, with Lawrence (T. E.): "the only rule is to have no rules" because that's self-conscious, & still negatively preoccupied with the rule. Gandhi, perhaps even Hitler, is a more difficult case than Shaw. Such things with them may be indispensable symbols of concentration. Being an introvert, I tend to attach oracular significance to outward events, & the latter are at present partly alcoholic. [NB 3.156; RT, 62]

Buddhism. Buddhism is superior to Christianity in the way it gets past the aural-visual time-space antithesis: Revelation gets to the panoramic apocalypse, invites us, like Rabelais, to have a drink, and that's it. Buddhism understands that the next step, or participating apocalypse, is interpenetration, which destroys the antithesis of the inclusive and exclusive. Hence being a Christian is one way of being a Buddhist. Christianity has the spiritual crusade, the effort to consolidate the death-principle & hell-principle, and get rid of them by clarifying their nature.
[NB 50.34; LN, 1:262-3]

Building Temples. I'm told that the structure of the *Anatomy* is impressive but futile, because it would make every other critic a Gauleiter of Frye. People don't realize that I'm building temples to—well, "the gods" will do. There's an outer court for casual tourists, an inner court for those who want to stay for communion (incidentally, the rewards of doing so are very considerable). But I've left a space where neither they nor I belong. It's not a tower of Babel: that tries to reach something above itself: I want to contain what, with a shift of perspective, contains it. Why am I so respected and yet so isolated? Is it only because I take criticism more seriously than any other living critic? [NB 44.93; LN, 1:120]

Business of Life and Death. The business of life is to make a path for the incarnation: the business of death is to make a path for the resurrection.
[NB 11B.31; RT, 354]

C

Canada. I was disappointed, years ago, when the Supreme Court of Canada was established in place of the British one. The myth involved was the analogical one: a colony is a child, a sovereign nation an adult: puberty comes with taking one's own powers. I wish Canada had junked this dismal cliché and been the first nation to vest supreme legislative powers in another nation: the kind of super-national conception that the Commonwealth of Nations permits. [NB 18.146]

I've been reading Yeats' letters & wondering why Canada, apart from the lack of a historical tradition, hasn't anything corresponding to what he found in Ireland. Ireland was the last stronghold of the old world—the world that lasted from the New Stone Age to 1940: Canada is a symbol of the new world that floats in space & has no center, the world of cars & motels & shopping centers, & high rise apartments that's replacing the sense of a fixed center "downtown" or, earlier, in a market square.
[NB 3.180; RT, 70]

Canadian Will. I have a limited faith in a historical process myself: I cannot believe that the Canadian nation will blunder and bungle its way out of history into oblivion, raising with its name only ridicule or at best a sympathetic smile from the rest of the free world. I do not remember any other time in history when a nation disintegrated merely through a lack of will to survive, nor do I think ours will. [NOTES 53.262; LN, 2:662]

Capital City. I think there is a real meaning in the conception of a "capital" city, not in the technical sense (i.e., New York is the real capital of the U.S.A., of North America, perhaps of the world). The city is the community become conscious: it is to the country what man is to animals. Animals live; man knows that he lives; people live in the country & often live very well, but in the city some additional consciousness comes to life. I've said before that only the bourgeois is creative man: in some respects I think culture is impossible except in a capital city. There are more people in Cincinnati than in Shakespeare's London; but Cincinnati *cannot* produce genius. It isn't the capital of anything: no organization of state or nation or anything else with a body comes to a head in it. [D 49.120; DNF, 99]

Caricatures and Character Types. So many people show a curious tendency to live up to their own caricatures: one would swear of many middle-class Canadian families that they had taken pains to make every remark typical of the Canadian middle-class. Not only caricatures either, but simply types: a man sells a story & buys a pipe & a dog; a man gets to be a professor & lets his hair grow & his pants go out of press, like me. When one meets such a person, one is forced to see with overwhelming clarity what he is; one therefore both likes him & feels superior to him. [NB 34.20]

Casting out Devils. Jesus' fundamental act is to cast out devils, to locate the pharmakos in man & by driving it out achieve his catharsis. To identify the devil-state with an individual, to make him a scapegoat or a pure devil is the ultimate act of evil, & can come only from one who has made himself into a pure accuser, & so by a ghastly paradox becomes the Satan he attempts to project on another. [D 49.262; DNF, 155]

Cat and Mouse. A man sitting reading a book in a library while a mouse ran past him unobserved would not be in a more subjective state than a cat, but he would appear so to the cat. A desire for a contest with reality is psychologically quite different from a desire to escape it. [NB 3.144; RT, 57]

Censorship. A work of literature can be ideologically wrong, or thought of as such by the general attitude of concern: Kipling's *Kim* and Lawrence's *Plumed Serpent* would be examples. But no one sympathizes with assaults on them. On the other hand I read a trashy thriller on a train once that suggested that all Chinese in American cities were involved in kidnapping white women and selling opium. It would be against the law in Ontario now to write such stuff: I thoroughly approve of the law. But when we get a "moral majority" organized, it always tends to regard genuine literature as its enemy, instead of as the thing it ought to be defending. [NOTES 52.212; LN, 2:468]

Center and Circumference. I think there are two degrees of hierarchy. Underneath the Freud-Marx one is another that Freud didn't see & Marx didn't care about, the hierarchy of man on top of woman. The true symbolic relation, male as central and female as circumferential, then comes to light. The woman poet's business is circumference, as Emily Dickinson said. There are two perversions of this: one is Blake's Female Will, which keeps man an embryo, the other is the male will, which tries to expand into and dominate the circumference. Berkeley says too that "all speech concerning the soul…is metaphorical." [NB 44.118; LN, 1:125]

The sacred is the symbolic, the holy marked off *temenos*. What's it symbolic of? Ultimately, the profane is the symbol of it: the sacred represents an eternal world where there are no symbols. As with the Temple symbolism of the Bible, what begins as a center ends as a circumference. [NB 12.262; TBN, 195]

Century of Meditations. It would be nice if God willed that I should write a Century of Meditations. But I wouldn't want to plan such a book as a dumping ground for things I can't work in elsewhere or as a set of echoes of what I've said elsewhere. Such a book would feature (a) completely uninhibited writing, like my notes on the romance book (b) completely uninhibited metaphor-building, as in some of my undisplaced plot-reconstructions. Ideally it's a book to be put away in a drawer and have published after my death…. It would be wonderful to write a whole book in the discontinuous aphoristic form in which things actually come to me: I'd still have the sequence problem, but not the crippling angel of continuity to wrestle with. The hell with it, at least for now.

[NB 44.667-8, 671; LN, 1:238]

Certainty. Some critics seem to talk as though, because we can't have absolute certainty in criticism, nothing is left for us but absolute uncertainty. And we're past the bicentenary of the *Critique of Pure Reason*!

[NB 27.361; LN, 1:64]

C'est à Moi. I *hate* making a whole chapter out of second-hand information. *Other* people, for Christ's sake. Maybe some day I'll get to a point of sanctity where the difference between my ideas & other peoples' ideas will cease to exist, but I'm sure as hell not at that stage now, & every *word* of the Frye Encyclopedia is going to be mine, do you hear? mine! mine!! *mine*!!!

[NB 21.250; RT, 186]

Chance. *Toute pensée émet un coup de dés,* says Mallarmé. Cf. Heraclitus' axiom about the child moving pieces in a board game. Wyatt's sonnet, "My galley, chargèd with forgetfulness" is based on the same analogical metaphor, a shipwreck enclosed by the dialectic of will and chance.

[NB 27.255; LN, 1:45]

Charity. It's curious how insistently one tends to make cheap & flippant epigrams about things of which one is ignorant, & how much progress in wisdom is concerned with discovering the positive values of more & more things, or writers, & interpreting even their errors sympathetically. I still feel that in criticism everything positive stands, everything negative dates. As writing gets wiser it drops the tone of polemic, & I think it's as literally true as so figurative a statement can be that without charity one is a sounding brass.

[NB 3.43; RT, 20]

Charm and Riddle. Tales are told: the oral tradition is behind them, a listening audience: they're paced in incident, following the beat of time, and they charm, they beat being hypnotic and punctuated with archetypes. Stories (=histories) are read: they're epiphanic, and have symbolic emblems. Thus what we read is a riddle; we guess the meaning of the emblematic object, or we gain an insight (epiphany) into a certain human situation. [NOTES 55:4.65]

Chastity. "Make me chaste, Lord, but not yet" is an exceeding sensible & pious prayer. Let me enjoy the lasciviousness you planted in me while I can: then, in due time, deliver me from its inconveniences. The attitude to death is the same: receive my soul & deliver me from the sorrows & cares of the world—but not yet. [NB 23.36; RT, 372]

Childhood Impressions. I have a feeling—probably it's just one of those would-be profound feelings that it's comfortable to have—that I cannot really get at the center of a problem unless something in it goes back to childhood impressions. Thus my New Comedy ideas, the core of everything I did after Blake, probably go back to my Alger reading, and now I think the clue to this labyrinth is the sentimental romance of the 19th century, the roots of which are in Scott. While I lived on Bathurst St. [early 1940s] I was constantly reading ghost stories with similar patterns in mind, & Poe & Hawthorne have always been favorites. Underground caves; the Phantom of the Opera, & the like, are all part of the Urthona *penseroso* pattern. [NB 12.49; TBN, 141-2]

Children. The sound of children playing is a cliché of innocent happiness. I have listened to it, and what I hear is mainly aggressiveness and hysteria. Living with children is recognized to be purgatorial, differing from hell only in having some sort of end. This is assumed to be an inscrutable but unbreakable law of nature, but I wonder if it is. I think children are aggressive & hysterical because they're in an aggressive & hysterical society, & would be serene and dignified if society was. Compare the song of birds, which also is sexually aggressive & which we interpret as innocence, tweet rhyming with sweet. Both are aspects of *homo ludens,* an aggressiveness with a shift of perspective seeing it as exuberance or free play. It's like vanity in man—or woman—which has an oddly disarming & innocent quality to it even though it's an aspect of pride. [NB 18.148-9]

Children do lots of silly things, but they also do a lot of things they should keep on doing. Thus a child who tries to see how far he can go without opening his eyes is beginning an imaginative exercise, designed not to forgo the advantages of eyesight, but to increase the sensitiveness & confidence of the other senses. But because he finds nothing in his environment to encourage himself to explore the neglected regions of touch & kinesthetic rhythms, such games fade as quickly as the rest of his imaginative flowering. [NB 3.77; RT, 32]

I feel that children go into a spiritual vacuum if they're over-indulged. A child in a tantrum is working up toward an orgasm, a union of his libidinous will with a censor, & if he doesn't get slapped or bawled out or in some way "brought off" he feels gypped and frustrated. There's nothing to give him the nervous shock and squall that's the erotic end of his tantrum. And just as there may be a real connection between unloved children & supporters of power politics (being unloved is the only sure way to acquire the essential proletarian archetype of exclusion from society), so there may be a real connection between indulged children and their predestined victims. It seems to me that coddling is likely to breed masochism, partly by consolidating the child in his protected & privileged bourgeois environment, & so making him unable to resist any challenge to it, in fact making him hanker for the stern denials he's been denied. On the other hand, the whacking that 19th-century children got enabled them to keep their feet firmly on lower-class necks & build empires at the same time. The battle of Peterloo was won on the flogging-blocks of Eton. [NB 3.169; RT, 67]

For all their tedious cuteness, Lewis Carroll's Sylvie and Bruno are closer to being actual children than Alice is. Alice is a *preternatural* child, and an astonishing achievement: I know of nothing in all literature remotely like her. But she belongs to another world than the world of our seven-year-olds, though she is utterly real in her own terms.

[NB 27.265; LN, 1:47]

Children's Fiction. The first book of *Paradise Lost* shows the devils discovering the two infallible formulas of children's fiction (boys anyway: I don't know about girls): the golden treasure hidden underneath the world and the conspiratorial society about to overthrow the world. I suppose even such genuinely evil things as the Nazi myth of a conspiracy of Jews sitting on a treasure of the world's gold belong to it. Gold and shit, of course.

[NB 50.331; LN, 1:322]

China. The current of world history is now [1942] going through Asia & ...Europe has ceased to be of any organic historical significance. China will probably have the next century pretty well to itself as far as culture, & perhaps even civilization, are concerned. Western historical dialectic gives me a pain anyway. God thought of us. He started us back in Nile slime & Euphrates mud, then the Greeks added reason, the Hebrews God, the Romans law and the British fair play, until here we are. Asia is irrelevant: it has no real history because it didn't contribute anything to our great Western omelette. Phooey. In Sept. 1939 the *New Yorker* wrote a stentorious leader about a world of peace being plunged into war. Two hundred million people, if that, go to war in Western Europe and that's a world at war. Half a billion people have been fighting for years in Asia and that's peace. I expected something better from the *New Yorker*.

[D 42.63-4; DNF, 27-8]

Choosing Moods. The existential philosophers, Nietzsche, Heidegger, Sartre, build up structures containing moods or emotional reactions like absurdity, anxiety, nausea, & the like. But that's because they *choose* these moods. What they've really chosen, as the key to reality, is the tragic structure. Comedy includes the victory of dialectic, hence the essential philosophers, from Plato on, are choosing the comic form. [NB 9.336]

Christ. The crisis for my questionings at the moment is: is Jesus a Bodhisattva, or rather, that being obvious enough, does one reject the essence of Christianity by rejecting the uniqueness of Christ? I know the alleged "Catholic Church" is an analogy or physical perversion of something, & maybe the real Catholicity that permits one to feel that Christ is universal & not unique, & therefore Buddha & Krishna as well—or rather what Buddhists mean by Buddha, which is a far bigger thing than Gautama. The lunar madness of the Occident seems to me connected with this centrifugal expansion of an analogical crusading religion from a central point in time & space: Christianity, Mohammedanism, Communism, all have it. All these things are unique & exclusive, therefore analogical. Empirical science has something of the same movement. Is a literal understanding of "no man cometh unto the Father save by me" something that turns Christ into a Peter or a Covering Cherub, a unique doorkeeper? Does this, if accepted, make some "Catholic Church" inevitably accepted too, in place of the Everlasting Gospel? The craze for uniqueness in Christians would take, if visualized, the form of a pyramid, narrowing to the single point of Christ. But, if we see in Christ *a* God-Man rather than *the* God-Man, are we forced into reincarnation thereby? Anyway, I'm trying to work out this idea of centrifugal expansion as the analogy of catholicity from Morris, in a different way. Spiritually there's only one Christ, of course; but must he be attached to only one historical analogy of himself? Is there only one Bible? Is it possible not only to preach Christ to the heathen, but to find Christ there? [NB 3.125; RT, 51]

It may be only a Christian prejudice, but I think if I were a Jew I'd be strongly tempted to accept Christ as at least a plausible working model of what a Messiah would be like. Which means that on the basis of imaginative literalism there's no real difference. [NOTES 54-1.49; LN, 2:675]

Christian Position. My Christian position is that of Blake reinforced by Emily Dickinson. At what point did Christianity throw away Paul's spiritual-natural antithesis and pick up his dismal shit about a soul-body combination that separates at death, leaving us with a discarnate soul until God gives the order for the resurrection of the body? This evil notion was concocted to keep man under the priest-king hierarchy. I suspect the Filioque clause was added to subordinate the Spirit to the Son and reduce the former to continuing the priest-king authority in time. Not that the Eastern Churches did any better with it. Even if you do this, as Joachim of Floris realized, you turn history revolutionary and go through a "reformation." [NB 11H.13; LN, 2:714]

Christianity. To see Christianity in imaginative terms is to see its pure form: that's the vision of the Spirit. To begin with belief is to follow Antichrist & sin against the Spirit even if Christ does appear to be urging that in the Gospels. I wouldn't say that the outward ceremony is Antichrist. The outward ceremony belongs to the redeemed, not the elect. People who resent my imaginative portrayals of Christianity do so because they're afraid that the hook of belief is buried under the bait of imaginative vision. I sympathize with that, up to a point, if they don't snap at Zen or Marxist or other baits on the assumption that the same hook isn't there. [NB 21.227; RT, 182]

Christmas. The Christmas festival is really a New Year festival, its main figures being the Infant of the New Year and the old man (Santa Claus) of the old. A new year is normally a time for trying once more to align life with myth, & such periods, according to Eliade, are preceded by periods of chaos. Christmas season then is a deliberately induced period of chaos & hysteria designed to assume stability after the New Year. In contrast to Easter, which is carefully synchronized with the Passover, the Gospels don't seem to care when Christ was born: the infancy stories are late anyway, & they seemed content to let the half-apocryphal notion of the *birth* of Christ be taken over by the old winter-solstice festival. The result is that

39

Christmas, as the Puritans kept insisting, never was primarily Christian. Its Germanic Romantic framework expressed a pastoral myth centripetal in shape, the large family installed in a big home eating huge amounts of food, which seems oddly in contrast with this very centrifugal civilization. Hence although the New Year resolutions don't amount to much, there is a curious stock-taking at Christmas, an attempt to face one's childhood perspective. [NB 3.182; RT, 71]

Our society lacks festivals: our Christmas is an introverted German Romantic affair, & its Dickensian propaganda assumes a retreat into the cavernous depths of the middle-class family. [NB 11F.185; RT, 116]

Christmas note: the city-jewel world and the pastoral world are grouped around the infant Christ, the former with the wise men and their gold-shrouded gifts, the latter with the shepherds & the ox & ass in the manger. Gozzoli & Gentile da Fabriano are particularly good on the jewelled-world setting of the wise men. In the calendar the pastoral reclamation comes on Christmas Eve, at the moment of birth: the renewed city at the very end, at epiphany, with the new year in between: millennium, end of the seventh cycle, & apocalypse. Note in Milton's *Nativity Ode* how the entry of the wise men is designed to follow the poem, the *claritas* succeeding the Incarnation itself (*integritas*) and the telos of time (*consonantia*). Gold and green are the colors of new beginning. [NB 19.160; TBN, 36]

Church. The purely spiritual gospel preached by Jesus is also known to what Augustine called the *anima naturaliter Christiana,* to Buddhists and Stoics and what not. What isn't known to them is the specific historical development known as the Christian Church, which is useful to have around as long as it doesn't make absurd and blasphemous pretensions. It's one of many ways in which the Holy Spirit operates: one can renounce the church without sinning against that Spirit: in fact one may well be working for it. Otherwise, why do contemporary writers on religion keep quoting Nietzsche, Heidegger, Marx, Freud? Fold my ass. There is no such thing as a Holy Catholic Church, but a church that knows it isn't catholic and is sincerely trying to become so is certainly worthy of respect. [NOTES 53.93; LN, 2:630]

Church Going. All theology is designed to persuade people to go to church, but I'm rather obstinate about not going to church, even when I do nothing better—and it's very easy for me to do better. As I don't believe in a substantial real presence, I don't believe anything *happens* at a church service. I don't understand the "this do in remembrance of me" aspect of Christianity: it seems silly, & I must think about it. Religion is still where medicine was in, say, 1750: its practitioners are sincere, but it can't really cure. [D 50.26; DNF, 223]

Churchill. Watching the funeral of Winston Churchill, one felt that a whole conception of human personality was being buried with him: that his heroic personality had something archaic about it, the last of its race. Kennedy, at least an equally admirable person, had nothing of it, but was already in a different world. [NB 13.106]

Church Man and Scripture Man. The church man has a structure of ideas derived from the institution he's attached to, and he translates everything into conformity with the structure. The scripture man tries to keep the "dialogue" open: he respects an oracular residue that pulls him beyond the structure. The closed & the open way are perhaps better, though they imply comparison of value. I'm returning here to the remark in the *Anatomy* about criticism being part of a general activity of keeping verbal structures intact while transforming their meaning. The "church" man in politics is a supporter of *de jure,* a legitimist: the "scripture" man has a greater respect for the *de facto.* Conservative & radical distinction at bottom, I suppose. For one, the informing principle is also conforming, or sacramental; for the other, it's a liberating one.
[NB 18.117, 119]

Circumferential Terms. Meditation on Hegel: some terms, like God or mind or soul, have practically no meaning as point-terms (denotative meaning). They are circumferential terms. Zoology is the study of animals, but it's of no value to zoology just to think of "all animals." One spends one's life filling in a tiny part of the area covered by this circumferential term. But then *all* conceptions are circumferential: when we point at them we see at most only their shells or seeds. Again, I just record this: I don't know what I'm talking about, but am revolving the notion of interpenetration again. [NB 19.387; TBN, 87-8]

The Circus. The circus was the most spectacular entertainment ever designed, & much of its appeal had to do with the circus coming to town, with people in Podunk seeing elephants & zebras. Today the circus is as dead as the great auk, because nothing can come to anywhere anymore: it's already there. [NB 11F.120; RT, 99]

Cittamatra. *Cittamatra,* the doctrine of Mind-only, has otherwise no Western counterpart. Its rival of the Yogacara school, *Vijñtaptivatra,* sounds very like Platonic idealism. And when we read that all things exist only insofar as they are seen of Mind itself, that suggests pantheism to a Western mind. Such pantheism corresponds to the hazy impression the Westerner has of all "Eastern" philosophy: that it is an attempt to forget that one is an ego & try to hypnotize oneself into feeling that one is a part of the great All. But it is clear, first, that the Lankavatara is based on a conception of a divine man; second, that it does not teach a doctrine but inculcates a mental attitude. Buddha is represented as saying that he discourses to the ignorant & helps the wise attain self-realization. And as here he is addressing a highly sophisticated audience of Bodhisattvas who can be trusted not to make the obvious mistakes, it follows that this Sutra [the *Lankavatara*] is not really a discourse. [NB 3.111; RT, 46]

Clunkheaded Teutons. The demons of the four quarters are Jung (N), Spengler (W), Heidegger (S) and Husserl (E): four clunkheaded Teutons. [NB 12.80; TBN, 150]

Colin Still. Something *else* is involved in the Bible of hell that begins with Blake. So far I've thought of it as a straight Heraclitean reversal: the un-differentiated alienating Absolute at the top, under it the two estrangements of ascendant object & ascendant subject, & under that the identity. The book that started me on all this was Colin Still's book on *The Tempest*, which I found by "accident" in the Public Library (Toronto) in 1930. Its influence is earlier than Blake's. Eventually I picked up both it & its successor, *The Timeless Theme*, & put them on my shelves, where they sat for years uncracked. Now I'm reading the second book for the first time & it's a bit disappointing to see how much of it is already part of my make-up. *And* my diagram. [NB 24.99-100; TBN, 296]

Collective Unconscious. I suppose the collective unconscious is originally the hallucinating voice of wisdom, urging caution & prudence and obeying social conditioning. It chatters and jibbers incessantly inside me whenever I'm writing, and is a bigger hazard than the steaks frying in my ears. That's why I can't read hostile critiques of me: most of them come from people who have nothing but a collective mind, so all they do is externalize all the monkey chatter I keep hearing anyway. Whether this collective mind is in Jung or not, it's certainly in Samuel Butler as well as in me. [NB 50.481; LN, 1:353]

The soul-consciousness is aggressive and asserts: the spirit renounces. It's the creative element in man, which creates by renouncing expression and accepting conventions of speech…. Jung's collective unconscious has to be expanded into a collective consciousness, and so it does. But that doesn't mean a collective soul-consciousness: nothing could come of that except listen to me, to me, to me. The collective spiritual consciousness is, as I keep saying, the conventions and genres of a cultural tradition. [NOTES 53.119; LN, 2:635]

Color Mnemonics. The six-day perspective, which as Browne says is a chaos, sees man as merely the child of & successor to the animals. Consciousness,

or man in the image of God comes next. The first light was a violet light; the firmament is blue; the forests of the third day green; the second light yellow or gold; the creatures of water & air orange, the creatures of land, including man, were formed of red earth. The return unites man as total spectrum or microcosm, the second He, with the white first He, the God-Man or Son, the black Father, & the indigo Spirit (the seventh essence hidden in the spectrum that produced life from the firmament). I think these associative fantasies may help to give at least a mnemonic structure to my material, as long as I don't let them take me over. I can't associate my sevens with the keys of music, because they run into the arbitrary color scheme imposed by the wooden blocks of my childhood. Thus E is always green, B blue, A violet, F black, D orange, C red in music but not verbally, G red verbally but colorless in music.
[NB 21.200-1; RT, 176]

Communication. Communication is the force holding together a community; at the center of community is communion—the icon or concept symbolizing unity. In a medieval town the market place was a community focus; & this in turn was around the church, where communion in a single body was going on. The Queen draws crowds for the same reason. The Protestant sense of a *Word* being revealed in church was theoretically even better than Catholic real presence; but both became spectacular dramas, & so ultimately boring. Why don't people go to church today? Because the kind of communion it stands for no longer holds the community together: if the faith in community goes, nothing will get them back.
[NB 11F.109; RT, 95]

Communication is an expression of community, a two-way street, a shared myth. The one-way street always means a sales pitch, whether it's a comedian selling toothpaste, an educator selling integral calculus, or a clergyman selling Christianity. And a sales pitch meets resistance, even if one buys the toothpaste, learns calculus, or accepts the religion. It pretends to be sharing a myth, but it's really interested in something else. Resistance is

44

an unbreakable datum—theories of education, for instance, ought to be based, not on a student's alleged willingness to learn, but on a teacher's willingness to share. Communication simply *must* outgrow the whole baited-trap or product-selling aspect, including the government-propaganda type. [NB 11F.118; RT, 98]

Communism. We've reached several ideological deadlocks in history. Communism in my youth (the Depression period) was widely assumed to be both more efficient and morally superior compared to capitalism. But capitalism didn't evolve into communism: the two systems settled down into an adversary relation in which they could improve themselves only by borrowing features from each other. The Reformation produced a similar deadlock. [NB 44.10; LN, 1:103]

Communities. It appears that communities are on four levels: an Ulro or subjective community of involuntary participation through birth, mainly of the family & symbolized by father & mother; a Generation objective community of voluntary participation through choice, mainly of the party & symbolized by the comrade; a Beulah symposium community of affinity, mainly of the university & symbolized by the fellow, & an Eden community of super-voluntary incorporation of one divine & human body & symbolized by the (communion of) saints. [D 49.352; DNF, 198]

Community of Love. If we pursue either liberty or equality we lose both. The *tertium quid* of one thing needful is fraternity, or interpersonal relation, the kingdom of ends, the community of love, relaxing into tolerance and good will at a distance. [NOTES 58-8.71]

Comparative Mythology. There are many books on comparative mythology, but mythology cut away from the mythology that inherits, disseminates, and ramifies it becomes a sterile and readily exhausted subject. Literary criticism cut off from its roots in mythology becomes also a sterile & quickly exhausted glass bead game. [NB 11H.27; LN, 2:716]

Computers. Curious about the computer mystics: they talk of an "alien intelligence," meaning that they're searching for a personal Other, a machine God. It's the Babel story over again. What they leave out is the fact that human beings are not just conscious but conscious wills: they keep a continuum of identity going from infancy to old age. Machines have no will to do what they do: they have to be plugged in or turned on, so they're not really alive. In the Old Testament it's the continuous will of God that's invariably stressed: "I will be what I will be." His consciousness is not obviously better than ours, in spite of being so often said to be so. [NOTES 54-1.51; LN, 2:675]

I've been reading a book about computers, full of very muddled arguments about whether a machine can be said to think or have intelligence. The difference between a mechanism and an organism is not one of intelligence but of will. An automobile can run faster than a human being can, but in itself it has no will to do so: it will sit rusting in a garage indefinitely without the slightest sign of impatience. There's no reason why man should not develop machines that can reproduce every activity of the human brain on a vastly higher level of speed and efficiency. But nobody has yet come up with a computer that wanted to do these things on its own: as will, so far, every machine is an expression of the will of its makers. In the Clarke-Kubrick movie *2001,* the computer Hal suddenly develops an autonomous will, a power of using its intelligence for its own ends. That makes Hal a nightmare, of course, but it also makes him a fellow-creature: he's now a *he* and not an *it,* and the depiction of his gradual destruction had a genuine pathos. [NOTES 54-2.2; LN, 2:682]

Concealed Thirteenth. Linked to [the theme of twins] is the concealed extra number, the most familiar one being thirteen. There are thirteen tribes of Israel, because of the division of the Joseph tribe into two, but what is interesting is the number of lists, ranging literally from Genesis to Revelation, that give twelve and leave out one. There are always plausible reasons for the omission—Dan is the tribe of Antichrist, hence left out of Revelation; Levi got cities and is hence left out of the Canaan map; Simeon was absorbed by Judah, so is left out of one list, and I think Gad is omitted in another. The reasons don't matter: what matters is that thirteen visible presences is unlucky: we have to have twelve with a concealed thirteenth who's the essence of all of them. Thirteen presences in the Gospels, as at the Last Supper, mean martyrdom. The concealed presence is the Resurrection one mentioned in the fifth part of Eliot's *Waste Land*. I have to work out some more of these: the fourth concealed in threes, such as the Trinity; the eighth concealed in sevens; the concealed number you get by adding all the numbers before the one you're interested in: that is, the sum of the numbers up to seven is twenty-eight and up to twelve seventy-eight, both of which have important overtones in various places. [NOTES 52.170-1; LN, 2:456-7]

Concentration. I'm proud of my ability to swivel easily from work to distraction, to find ideas crystallizing on streetcars or restaurants, to be relatively undisturbed by yelling children, & the like. I think this ability really is valuable, & should be developed, but concentration when alone should be developed too, as long as no resentment at being interrupted affects me. If I can't always get the sort of thing I used to get with coffee & solitude at 2 a.m., I should get as near it as possible, as often as possible. I find too that concentration & a sense of efficiency in work increase the general competence & assurance of all the rest of my activity: I'm never so confused in behavior as when I think I am thinking & ain't. [NB 3.84; RT, 35-6]

Conditioning. Discoveries of the extent to which psychopaths & criminals are socially & parentally conditioned to be what they are have, it is said, made moral standards too relativistic, in fact have eroded such standards. But knowledge of conditioning has also opened new avenues of freedom in showing how some (perhaps everyone: I'd say the great majority) can escape from these prisons. [NB 46.63; LN, 2:699]

Consciousness Raising. The paradox of nothing. One can only get out of the prison of Narcissus by raising the level of consciousness: maybe religion today has to pass through the Oriental meditation techniques. But then I've always insisted that works of art are also objects of meditation no less than mandalas. [NOTES 52.515; LN, 2:526]

As I've said so often, living things are animated by a continuous will, and the continuity of the will accounts for the sense of identity between infancy and old age of the "same" person. Human beings have conscious wills, but human beings in bondage, slaves and the more brutally exploited, get little chance to do anything except survive. Among the leisured and privileged glimpses of genuine consciousness may emerge, even to the point of glimpses of what consciousness could be.
[NOTES 54-1.72; LN, 2:679]

Consubstantiality. The authoritarian universe goes with the desperate effort to preserve a definitive interpretation of sacred scripture. The modern universe follows another rhythm entirely. Montaigne said his book was consubstantial with himself, a speaking or written double of himself. The dream of all one's work forming a single structure of this kind—Burton, Wordsworth's cathedral, Valéry—goes very deep. It's linked with the sense of the apocryphon not so much as a hidden book as a hidden aspect of an inexhaustible book. Kabbalism says the Torah contains all possible books; similar things are said about the Koran somewhere in Islamic traditions; in Christianity there's the last verse of John. I suppose it's a metaphor derived from the alphabet, the potential source of all utterance (God as Alpha and Omega). [NOTES 52.684; LN, 2:555]

Correspondence. My ideas do hold together, God help me: the myths of contract & telos correspond not only to creation & apocalypse in religious myth, but to the first two essays of *Anatomy of Criticism*: the historical & the ethical contexts of a work of literature. [NB 19.80; TBN, 19]

Cosmetics. I suppose the motivation for the overuse of cosmetics by women

is to be sought for in the economics of competition. When the only competitive trade for females was either whoring or courting (in the sense of hanging around a court), only whores & duchesses painted; now that all women are walking the streets and now that the middle class has captured all the aristocratic phenomena, all women paint.
[NB 34.19]

Cosmology. Cosmology is the process of assimilating science into a mythology. It's always temporary, because it's always wrong—that is, it's full of fictions. The use of mythical analogies to scientific principles (evolution, relativity, entropy, indeterminacy) is cosmological. See what comes out of Teilhard de Chardin. [NB 19.313; TBN, 71]

Note that contemporary poets can still deal with the phases of the moon, the four elements, even the word "universe"—in short, with out-of-date cosmologies—because cosmology, like mythology, comes eventually to speak the language of imagination. [NOTES 52.931; LN, 2:598-9]

The objective cosmos usually tends to think in terms of a development from chaos to creation and order, from the simple to the complex, from fortuitous collocations of atoms to like attracting like. The imaginative cosmos, on the other hand, thinks in terms of a past Golden Age or a lost Paradise, because it naturally starts with an ideal or model in the mind, of which the present situation obviously is a degenerate form. *Timaeus,* etc.
[NOTES 53.79; LN, 2:627]

Counting. When Paul Tillich was asked whether he supported the Protestant theory of two sacraments or the Catholic view that there are seven, he answered that he didn't think there was any future in counting the sacraments. I wonder if there's any future in counting the Persons of the Godhead. There may be three; there may be four and a half; there may be three hundred and sixty-five billion. If it's bad luck to number Israel, it may be even worse luck to number the names of God. Nowadays we have a stronger feeling about the reality of polytheism, or what Emily Dickinson calls refunding our confiscated gods. [NB 6.33; TBN, 113]

Courage. Even if I have only a shrivelled last rose of summer to lay on the altar, I won't blame it altogether on the lateness & sophistication of the age. Granted that a late age of culture breeds a self-consciousness which tends to inhibit the creative powers of the soul by a premature knowledge of their processes, this knowledge is not itself untrue, & yet it has undermined the old forms. Take the question of tolerance. The Spanish mystics in their monasteries were trying to live in the garden of Eden after the Fall, surrounded, like Brynhild, with a wall of fire, a hideously cruel & foolish Covering Cherub fed by the burning bodies of heretics. I do not deny Loyola's kind of courage, but I am more impressed by the heretics' kind, & hope it will prove more acceptable to God. [NB 3.38; RT, 18-19]

The Courtier. Joseph, in Genesis, has always totally baffled me: he bulks so large and so crucially in the Bible's greatest book, but what to make of that I don't see. I've encountered several times the assertion that he's a type of Christ; but what's really Christlike about him? I've investigated Mann, but without result. The one thing that interests me is that he descends to Egypt and becomes, not the Pharaoh or temporal ruler, but his adviser, a Castiglione courtier. Castiglione's book has always fascinated me, although it would be easy to call it a futile and silly book, because it grasps what for me are the central myths of education: the guardian angel teacher, the attendant spirit who doesn't interfere with the ruler's will but whose advice directs and shapes that will. That would make him a type of the Spirit rather than the Word. [NB 50.404; LN, 1:337]

Cranks. History of ideas deals only with ideology: history of mythology, or real literary tradition, takes a crank or a nut like Frazer or Graves or me. Also mythological history develops a curious optical illusion of complete myths in the past. Actually myths complete themselves as they go on, because the area of communication is the conscious mind, not deep calling to deep. But whole subject still in the "here be dragons" stage of map-making. [NOTES 52.972; LN, 2:605]

Creation. Creation includes fraud: it has to if the original model was better than what we have now: efforts to shuffle off the fraud on the devil don't work. The goddess of Metis is a trickster; so is the divine wisdom. [NB 10.58]

The chief *motives* for creation, or rather motivations, are eros & logos, creation by desire & creation by the Word. [NB 11B.78; RT, 359]

Our bodies are so conditioned that what we see (perceive with any sense) *can only be* the subhuman, or at most the merely human. What we see is inexorable law, Newtonian or Darwinian, struggles to survive & the like. What we create participates in our creation & comes as far alive as the limits of imagination permit. [NB 19.10; TBN, 6]

"Creation" is not only a metaphor: it expresses the fact that both life & art achieve an identity out of an analogy. *Integritas* is identity; *consonantia* is interpenetration; *claritas* is I+ (i.e. the recognition of identity, *satori* in the individual or the beatific vision in the analogical context, but usually erotic or sexual). [NB 19.143; TBN, 32]

To unite the dream world with the waking world is to create. [NB 10.38]

Creative and Critical. Everyone knows with half his brain that the language of religion is myth and metaphor; with the other half we continue to use rhetorical adaptations of conceptual and dialectical language.... We need both languages, for one is "creative" and the other "critical" i.e., one presents and the other explains. Kerygma uses the language of presentation, but it isn't self-sufficient: the critical & explanatory ideological reserves have to be brought into action too. They are even in the Gospels (e.g. the parable of the sower & its silly commentary). [NB 50.603-4; LN, 1:379]

Creative Process. I've been thinking of Smart's *Jubilate Agno* as a very good example of how the creative process starts, in paronomasia & free association. Wherever we have "madness" we have glimpses of the creative process in action: Lear is a good example. *Finnegans Wake* may be something else again…. *Jubilate Agno* also has a passage on rhyme words & the orchestral sounds of words that shows how the original paronomasia process articulates itself into a metrical structure. The counterpart to this is the elaboration of diagrams in thought. [D 50.72; DNF, 242-3]

Creative Sin. Early Christianity discovered that Christianity would be much more saleable if you perverted its good news into bad news, and in particular if you put at the center of your teaching the doctrine that after death, unless you did what you were told at this moment, you would suffer tortures for eternity, meaning endlessly in time. Every system of organized priestcraft has had a doctrine of that kind, and the only thing to be said in favor of it is that it makes sin creative: that is, we owe a great deal more to the people who went on sinning in spite of it than we do to the people who tried to restrain sin by threatening it. ["SYMBOLISM IN THE BIBLE," LECTURE 13; RT, 515]

Creative Superstition. I am intensely superstitious; but there are two kinds of superstition, related as self-destructive melancholy is to *penseroso* melancholy. There is the superstition based on fear of the future: this is based also on my character as a coward & weakling, & is of course to be avoided. There is another kind which consists of removing all censors & inhibitions on speculation: it's almost exactly what Coleridge calls fancy. It may eventually be superseded by imagination: but if there's no fancy to start with there won't be any imagination to finish with. Let's call it creative superstition. It works with analogies disregarding all differences & attending only to similarities. Here nothing is coincidence in the sense of unusable design; or, using the word more correctly, everything is potential coincidence — what Jung calls synchronistic. [NB 12.327; TBN, 211]

Creative Trickster. God's power works only with wisdom & love, not with

52

folly & hatred. As 99.9% of human life is folly & hatred, we don't see much of God's power. He must work deviously, a creative trickster, what Buddhists call the working of skilful means. [NB 44.510; LN, 1:212]

Critical Constructs. The opening sentence of *Anatomy of Criticism* said I attached no particular importance to the construct *qua* construct. I think I've got past that now, and that it's only by means of such dizzily complex constructs that one can ever get anything substantial out of criticism. Those who appear not to have such a construct, like Johnson, are attached to an ideology: those who do often don't get it worked out, like Coleridge. [NB 44.99; LN, 1:121]

Critical Language. I am old and on the shelf now, and much that is going on I no longer understand. I'm reading Samuel Delany, a science fiction writer interested in semiotics, and he begins with a sentence from Julia Kristeva I can no more understand than I could eat a lobster with its shell on. I wouldn't discourage anyone from masticating and ruminating such sentences, but I'd like to think (or perhaps only my ego would) that my greater simplicity came from a deeper level than the labyrinth of the brain. [NB 27.347; LN, 1:61-2]

Critical Method. If there is such a thing as a key to my critical method, it is that I look at the image as revealing or illustrating the essential shape of the author's thought. I never think of it as purely decorative, & this means, of course, that I find any author who does deficient in his sense of reality. The corollary of this is that I look directly at the form and subject-matter of the completed work: I do not try to peep through it and make critical generalizations about some substratum of its substance. Quality to me means whatness, essence, substance, not attributes, as it generally means in critical writing. I know that I am on solid ground here: if I were a creative writer, say a novelist, I should adopt the same principle to a technique of studying character. Character is revealed in the images we choose; in the concreteness of our thinking, never in the generalities we pack around them like excelsior. Everyone has a private cosmogony, complete with diagrams: no novelist has worked out the full implications of this, though there are those who have specialized in various aspects of it. [NB 34.1]

Critical Principles. Any critical principle that will not work for the Bible in an unprivileged position is unlikely to be of much relevance to it in a privileged one. [NB 11C.24; RT, 347]

The Critical Y. I may be nearing the end, although my powers seem to be as lucid as ever. After finishing Blake I faced the critical Y. Either spread into general theories and make endless mistakes in detail, or dig into one period and do it thoroughly. I chose the former: many of the mistakes I have made have been pure laziness, and could have been avoided. But I think perhaps no one else could have done what I have done, and I think perhaps what I have done has been worth doing. [NB 44.452; LN, 1:201]

The Critic as Bard. No human language can constitute a revelation. Something must arise from contemplating the infinite variety of literature, of the sort indicated in the epilogue to *The Tempest*. Of course this makes the literary critic a prophet, or at least gives him a prophetic function, but I can't help that. Hear the voice of the Bard. Whatever the Bard has heard himself, he's making too much noise to hear himself, or, more accurately, what most bards have heard is a damn garbled version of the Holy Word. [NB 21.73; RT, 153]

Criticism. I am still bewildered by the betrayal of criticism that turns all literature into an alphabet soup in which one can never find the crucial letters Alpha & Omega. That's why I've turned to the Bible, which simultaneously constructs & deconstructs (a) metaphor (b) holistic form. My main reason for thinking this a betrayal is my conception of primary concern. [NB 27.424; LN, 1:79]

Criticism approaches a literary work which is a metaphor-cluster made explicit. Why do we need the critic? Because there's so much implicit in the metaphor-cluster that he didn't make explicit. Mainly, of course, the relation of context, to other cultures of words. "Deconstruction" is such a dreary negative word for all this. [NB 44.44; LN, 1:109]

Criticism is the primary act of human awareness: it expresses detachment without separation. First, the natural sciences criticize the natural environment, then the social sciences criticize the human environment, treating man himself as an object. Then imagination moves from actualities to possibilities, involving primary concern, and the criticism of that leads to spiritual vision. [NOTES 53.242; LN, 2:658]

Critics. A critic realizes he agrees with other critics, as a rule, when he renounces his ego. I can't of course say quite that, but I have to keep it in mind, because it's true. Second-raters who can't think but just think they think have to adopt some pre-fabricated position, feminist or Marxist or whatever, to disgorge whenever they're asked about anything. Of course they could do it with Frye criticism too, and some have, but there's something about me that discourages automatic patter. [NOTES 53.148; LN, 2:641]

Crucifixion. The Crucifixion is the story of how man tried to kill God and failed. But as that God was man as well, it follows that wars and massacres and holocausts, apart from all their evil and horror, are simply *futile*. I don't want to make that a smug statement, but I think it's part of the picture. [NB 44.205; LN, 1:145]

Fire burns, but fire-walkers are a tourist attraction: in other words there is apocalyptic fire in which man can live. I know of no experience showing that a man can lie at the bottom of a lake without drowning; but apocalyptic water of life must be equally "possible." That's why I think Jesus was required, or felt himself required, to give up all such powers & privileges in the Passion, and enter the world of those with no faith. This world being hell, the Crucifixion was a descent into hell. [NB 11E.72; RT, 334]

Cultural Poverty. The charitable attitude to undeveloped countries is another aspect of the one-way street. How can we help Pakistan to become nearly as good as we are? I saw poverty & disease in Pakistan, certainly: I also saw, in the midst of it, many beautiful & utterly serene people. What impresses me, by contrast, is the poverty & disease of my own country. Cultural poverty in the appalling ugliness & meanness of our streets; disease in our noise pollution & the subtler polluting of the eye from the millions of glinting hard metal surfaces & the like. The ribbon development of used car lots & hot dog stands is *filth*. [NB 11F.123; RT, 99]

Culture. In our society genuine culture is a counter-culture, not a sub-culture, as the latter either doesn't exist or gets quickly absorbed into the establishment culture. It is set up to fight the ascendancy of advertising, in our society, or propaganda, in socialist societies. Its ultimate aim is the creating of a counter-environment, the opposite…of the one being built by the architects of desolation, the anti-creators of a uniform world. [NOTES 52.680; LN, 2:554]

Cup. I've read a lot of crappy books on the Grail, yet there remains a fascination with it. Christ breaks bread, says "this is my body," & the bread disappears into the disciples' guts, including Judas' (John 13). Then he takes the cup, but after the wine is drunk the cup *must* be left behind, like the mantle of Elijah. So it's a central symbol for what persists in this world as a communion with Christ. [NB 27.274; LN, 1:48]

Cutting Losses. Even the biggest book is fragmentary: to finish anything, you have to cut your losses. Nobody ever writes his dream book, like Coleridge's treatise on the Logos. That's why we make scholars finish a thesis first, that is, a book which, almost by definition, nobody wants to write or to read, to show how closely the reproductive & excretory systems are connected. [NB 33.54]

D

Dale Carnegie. I've been reading Dale Carnegie, whose book [*How to Win Friends and Influence People*] is exactly what I thought it would be. It's not really naive, but it meets a remarkably naive audience (it seems to me) on its own level. I imagine that its success is partly due to its complete integrity: Carnegie is no fool; he has a sharp insight into human nature as he knows it; & he begins with the human nature of his reader, who is the friend he wants to win & influence, so that his book must give an impression of continually practising what he preaches. His book is however only for extroverts, salesmen & executives, who have energy but lack imagination. Introverts like me, who are almost morbidly aware of the other fellow's point of view (though not less egocentric on that account) need a companion volume on How to Stiffen Your Backbone even at the Cost of Losing your Influence Occasionally…. Thousands of Americans, including the author, regard Carnegie's book as of far more value than all the Latin & Greek that were ever jabbered, the book itself containing testimonials to that effect; and it is very difficult to answer that assertion except by postulating a relativity of culture, the postulate on which the conception of the classic is founded. His book might have real value if he had mentioned the importance of applying his techniques to the chorus of egos inside oneself. [NB 3.106; RT, 44-5)

Dance Music. The radio is going: why is so much dance music thin, wailing, dismally melancholy and wistful, like a train going through a forest at night? Is it intended to reproduce the complaining of the libido? Certainly it's aimed at below the waist, & suited to a dimly lit dance hall with adolescents shuffling up & down the floor rhythmically rubbing their genitals together. [D 42.92; DNF, 36]

Dancer and Dance. If we find it difficult to tell the dancer from the dance, why should we destroy our vision of the gospel by trying to separate the word from the speaker of the word? All those words are coming from inside ourselves. That is, the existential metaphor is evoked by the verbal one, and we join in the play, or dance. [NB 44.313; LN, 1:170]

Dandyism. It is curious how closely the cult of the unfeminine male is connected with a protest against matriarchy. Actually, heroism & dandyism are apt to go together…. The only men who patronize beauty parlours & get permanent waves are professional hockey players: it's people like me who are most careless of their bodies & least vain of their personal appearance, my hair being an accident. Again, it's sedentary & soft males who have the longest penises & the most appetite for the sex act: the athlete is much more easily celibate, & to the average sailor the tart he fucks is merely a different kind of public urinal. *His* body has no affinity with percale sheets. I am merely concerned to show here that the "tough guy" is not nearly so virile a type as a dandy who wept copiously on all occasions, used women very rarely, & was capable of great abstemiousness, might well be. [NB 34.3]

Death. Death is the *basanos* [touchstone] of life, the ultimate test or touchstone of detachment. It's also a torture to those who have misunderstood the ordeal. [NB 27.346; LN, 1:61]

Death is a process, not a condition. A stone is not dead: when did it ever die? Death is not the opposite of life: it is the opposite of birth. Hence the world that for Christianity is undying is for Buddhism unborn. One says you get born but don't die; the other says you die but haven't been born. [NB 21.11; RT, 141]

One of the things that literature is all about is the relation of ordinary life, a current moving toward death, with whatever it is that begins with death. I know how violent the prejudices are on this subject, pro & con, but what the imagination, as distinct from rationalized commentary on traditional myth, says on the subject must be looked into. One lead is Yeats's remark that dreams are the current of the dead moving through us, the opposite way. And my "point of ritual death" is really a point where the hero gets renewed strength from contact with the world of death. Well, it looks as though I hadn't yet thought enough about this to formulate anything new: I thought the context would help, but it doesn't. The point of introversion is perhaps always the world of the dead, disguised traditionally as gods, ghosts or what have you. Being is a life-death complex: I don't mean that the dead are still alive: I mean that to have been is a part of being. That which is to be is not part of being, but that which was is. It's the other half, like the world of anti-matter in physics, where entropy goes into reverse. God is dead; therefore God exists.

[NB 19.342; TBN, 78]

I said in *Fools of Time* that death was what defined life: perhaps it's also what permits the variety of life which is the other aspect of its unity. If there were no death, life would be uniform, as in the monotonous vision of heaven. This connects with one of my favorite superstitions: that in order to rationalize the utterly pointless & hideous tortures men have inflicted on each other, one has to think, not of reincarnation, but of one man getting the total variety of all possible experiences, of hell as well as of heaven. In the Last Judgment everything that has done this becomes part of the body of death & disappears: everything that has suffered it is part of the redeemed body of Albion or Adam Kadmon. One comes to a focus in Barabbas & the other in Jesus: the former is the "scapegoat" sent out to Azazel, the Gadarene swine driven over a cliff (the word Azazel means cliff) out into the deep of annihilation. The scapegoats or Gadarene swine are the temporary kings, i.e., Blake's "Elect," the rulers of the time-establish-ment. Not as people, but as phenomena: the sinister goat-world that's abolished. [NB 24.90; TBN, 292-3]

Death's Alternatives. We must be free or die, says Wordsworth. We must love one another or die, says Auden. We must grow older or die, says Northrop Frye at the age of seventy-eight. [NOTES 55:1.6; LN, 2:721]

Decentralization. I have often said that our age is one of contrasting movements: a movement from nationalism to imperialism, huge federated states forming a world-wide Holy Alliance, gigantic cartels and internationalized business in banks, trusts & merged industries is what we are in for politically and economically as the world begins to establish a digestive system. But for expert craftsmanship in wines, glass, linen and all the creative arts, we need a corresponding decentralization. To give our unqualified support to one movement in everything is foolish & disastrous, either hazily international (all metropolises are exactly alive & equally sterile) or defiantly provincial, like the men of good will in the Protestant & Catholic churches respectively. Previously the great movements of art have combined an extreme localism (which means the imaginative recreation of the immediate environment) with an idealized catholicity. The Greeks had the fact of tiny Attica and the idea of Hellenism; medievals had the fact of Provence and the idea of a Christian empire; Elizabethan England had London and their curiously effective idea of the catholicity of the Church of England. Now [1944], the British, American, and Soviet federations seem to be working out a possible solution. There is a great deal to be said for the British Commonwealth, but everything connected with the British Empire, from the Indian question to the defense of Singapore & Hong Kong, is entirely vicious. The capture of Calais & the American Revolution in the past, and lots and lots of hell with India in the future, manifest the same thing. [NB 42.5]

Decision-Making. I suppose the most difficult decisions for an inspired man to make are those that don't matter a damn. For the swift & automatic certitude of inspiration is always consciousness and reason in slow motion, & for a man in the position of a donkey equidistant between a thistle & a carrot—say between two turnstiles—there is no underlying reason, at most only some compulsion which a perfectly disciplined man shouldn't have. I suppose he'd wait for several minutes, & then slowly turn anti-clockwise north of the equator & clockwise south of it, or whichever it is. [NB 3.22; RT, 11]

The Decline of the West. Malraux says Spengler's book started out as a meditation on the destiny of art-forms, then expanded. What it expanded into, I think, was a vision of history as interpenetration, every historical phenomenon being a symbol of the totality of historical phenomena contemporary with it. That's what fascinated me, though of course I didn't know it for many years. [NB 44.709; LN, 1:245]

Deconstruction. I've said that what Pound, Yeats, Joyce & Eliot do with staircase & spiral symbolism forms a series of deconstructions of the old chain of being. Deconstruction, however, is a birdshot technique: it aims at the horizon and bags what it accidentally hits. I'd prefer to pick out a real target and aim at that. [NB 27.390; LN, 1:70-1]

I suppose the vogue for deconstruction has to do with its Romanticism: it takes off from the Romantic conception of creation as something opposed to *the* creation. [NB 44.142; LN, 1:131]

I don't see how deconstruction techniques fit the Bible at all: you have to start with a *lisible* text by an author you can "supplement," and such a text doesn't exist. "The Word made flesh" certainly sounds like the supreme logocentric claim, but there isn't any "transcendental signified" except the Father, who disappears into the Word. So I think there must be what Derrida doesn't allow: a polysemous structure that directs all the "deconstruction." [NB 44.224; LN, 1:150]

Surely, if "deconstruction" starts with a construal text, that text prescribes a *direction* for deconstruction, otherwise you wander forever in a wilderness of words. Such a direction involves one at once in polysemy, whatever the particular steps in the verbal ladder may be. Surely too the conception of "supplement" indicates this. I suppose the traditional fears about how "dangerous" a speculation may be if it doesn't stay on the track provoked this reaction. [NB 44.229-30; LN, 1:151-2]

I wish my mind were clearer about Derrida: it's silly to make him into a sort of critical Antichrist trying to abolish incarnational texts. To me all texts are incarnational, and the climax of the entire Christian Bible, "the Word was made flesh, and dwelt among us," is the most logocentric sentence ever written. My only hunch is the one I've recorded: that if you start with one text rather than another, that text prescribes a certain *direction* of comment & deconstruction & what not, and the direction reduces to a polysemous pilgrimage. You can't just wander in the wilderness of words forever. A lot of post-structural stuff seems to me just irresponsible and undirected polysemy. [NB 44.241; LN, 1:154]

The old idea that all kinds of mysteries of knowledge can be extracted from myth is, in modern terms, the fact that discursive prose is verbal work, while myths, like literature, are verbal play, & consequently can be "deconstructed" endlessly. Except that in practice you have to set up a straight polysemous path from your construal starting point. This conception of play integrates the kookiest notion of criticism into the center of contemporary theory. [NB 44.281; LN, 1:163-4]

It's curious the vogue for deconstruction in America today: there's something hysterical about it, something out of focus. My own view that it makes it possible for anybody to become a critic, or at any rate to produce critical articles, may be part of the point. It's curiously antithetical to the Zen Buddhist vogue at the other end of the intellectual society. Koans, parables, & the like, are designed to stop you talking all around the subject & looking for additional meanings. They don't, of course: they just add one more convention to literature and keep yacking about it. Still, it's interesting that a Zen master confronted with the logic of supplement would reach for his stick. Perhaps at the back of the deconstructive critical mind is some hazy analogy with atom-smashing: eventually we'll break down my gross accumulations of rhetoric into protons, hadrons, quarks. I think that's a false analogy. [NB 50.542; LN, 1:367]

Deep Hermes. Every so often I get an itch to get a grip on what I think of as the Egyptian tradition in thought, the one that runs through Plato's *Timaeus,* Plutarch, the Alexandrian neo-Platonists, the Hermetic literature, and so on. The Egyptians kept the descent to the mother open. The hieroglyphic is one of the cipher-images in deep Hermes.
[NB 24.11; TBN, 274]

Deifiers of the Void. The deifiers of the void do get me down & they start with a conception so wonnerful there ain't no words to describe it, & then they weasel & slither their way down through as many intermediate stages as possible before they approach with a shudder of distaste what's at the bottom, which is our old friend Mother Nature, Cabbalists, Neo-platonics, Gnostics, the lot. [NB 10.114]

Democracy. Today few writers in U.S. or Europe feel any particular loyalty to "capitalism," or are even continuously conscious of living under it; but many of them do feel a loyalty to "democracy." And by democracy they mean something that includes a respect for the authority of their art. Some of them of course project their dissatisfactions with their own society on some imaginary Communist system, identified with some pastoral-myth conception of Russia or China: this is a central part of the *trahison des clercs.* But it is no wonder if a large number of writers are politically fools: literature has no obvious standards to appeal to: it represents a second twist on concern itself, and I see no way of demonstrating that it is a second twist. [NOTES 52.202; LN, 2:465]

Demonic Parody. Curious the number of times people have sold out to some silly cause because they couldn't distinguish the demonic parody from the real thing. Heidegger has some remark in an essay about National Socialism being essentially the struggle against technology: he wanted so much to have peasants woo-wooing around the soil that he didn't see that the Nazis were interested solely in demonic technology. Similarly with all the jerks who went in for Stalinism, and disregarded all the evidence that Stalinism was the demonic opposite of Marx's goal. [NOTES 54-5.154; RT, 304]

Demythologizing. I seem to be shocking the local religious community with my notion that "demythologizing" is a doctrine of Antichrist—well, anyway, of W.H. Auden's Herod. Essentially it means "up with ideology," which is why Barth is so tolerant about Bultmann. But of course it's supposed to mean "up with fact & down with fantasy." I have a lot of thinking to do about the paradox that in religion there's no such thing as a fact. The fact is annihilated by the myth. It's Theseus' two worlds of apprehension & comprehension again: fact as fact is incorporated in historical & parallel syntheses: fact that's really experience disappears & is reborn as experience. Fact is the grain of wheat that is buried and "dies"—incidentally, what a violation of fact the word "die" is! [NB 27.453; LN, 1:82-3]

I'm glad I'm not concerned with belief, but only with trying to understand a language. I simply can't believe (there's that word again) that the people talking about demythologizing are really as stupid as they sound. *How* can they be so damn cocksure about what the modern man can and can't believe? I've never tried drugs, but it's obvious that with enough pot you can believe anything, and with enough LSD you can visualize anything. We can't believe all the stories about casting devils out of people because we can't believe devils cause diseases. How the hell can there be any other cause of disease, for God's sake? We can't accept everything Jesus says about the end of the world because it didn't end as soon as he thought it would. Didn't end for whom? For fools and cowards like ourselves, perhaps; but we're the ones who are wrong. [NOTES 54-5.151; RT, 303]

Derrida. Derrida says structuralism is wrong because you can't get outside a structure to examine it. That's a misleading metaphor: you enter a structure from the "inside" & it becomes a part of you. Only it doesn't stop at the individual, but creates a spiritual substance: it's one's infinite extension. [NB 44.559; LN, 1:220]

I don't know what the Derrida people are talking about, and am too lazy & cowardly to find out. I *don't* know why "God is dead" should become (so ironically) a dogma; I don't know what's wrong with being "logocentric." My first tentative guess is that deconstruction is a Lenten criticism, where the Word wanders in the desert, most vulnerable to temptation, as Eliot says, never making contact with the Spirit. The contact with Spirit is like two gases that will burn combining to form the liquid water that won't. [NB 50.574; LN, 1:373]

de Sade. de Sade is just as right about "nature" as Wordsworth is: he simply points to its predatory & parasitic side. But no animal acts with the *malice* that man does: that's a product of consciousness. [NB 27.311; LN, 1:56]

Detachment. In Jungian terms, I'm a thinking type, with feeling undifferentiated & likely to break over me in waves. As a thinker, I'm committed to detachment: my feeling works as tempter trying to make me attach myself. If I could turn Roman Catholic, for instance (which would appeal to me more than my inherited evangelism because of its legal completeness of ideal phrasing), that would be the tempter's supreme triumph, the achievement of giddiness designed to make me throw myself off the pinnacle & trust to angels to get buoyed up. Jung would call it *sacrificium intellectus.* [D 50.90; DNF, 250]

Detachment without Withdrawal. We are at a period of history when we recognize the all-pervasiveness of ideology but are disillusioned with all existing forms of it. The "conversion" to religion or Marxism so common up to a half-century ago now seems utterly futile; yet withdrawal from all ideologies merely confirms the power of the one there. The next step is detachment without withdrawal, the study of the mythology of concern. [NB 11H.37; LN, 2:718]

Detective Stories. Why am I obsessed with detective stories?... I've completely forgotten the Freudian explanation I came across recently. In my own terms (which wouldn't of course exclude Freud) a really top-flight detective story has two levels of meaning throughout. Every sentence, every fact given, may be potentially a "clue": it has its surface meaning in the narrative, and its teleological meaning as a part of what you "see" in the final *cognitio.* Also, of course, the descent of the police as a Last Judgment symbol, searching for the guilt that's in everyone, and the scapegoat as the primal anxiety symbol. [NB 27.493; LN, 1:90]

The detective story is written backwards, & belongs to creative & dream time, not to the ordinary beginning-to-end, cause-to-effect time. It's written in the way one composes a dream after having the alarm go off. This event-to-cause order is the mythical as distinct from the historical order.... I think my *dream* life demands these stories. [NB 21.309; RT, 197]

There are obvious Freudian reasons (except that I've forgotten what they are) for the appeal of detective stories: Freudianism itself owes much of its popularity to the same kind of appeal, Freudian therapy of a neurosis being essentially a search for who done it in childhood. Or what done it. [NB 44.517; LN, 1:212]

I have often wondered why I'm so hooked on detective stories.... One thing that occurs to me is double meaning: a casual remark or incidental episode suddenly becomes *relevant* in that second world where the murderer is identified. Miniature apocalypse with Satan cast out and all the other details moving together in identity. [NB 50.255; LN, 1:306]

I don't think that I have either a highbrow or a lowbrow pose about

66

detective stories, but I don't really quite understand why I like reading them. I read them partly for the sake of the overtones. I'm not a connoisseur of them: I can never guess what the hell's up when the detective suddenly pulls out a watch and shouts: "My God, we may yet be in time!," shoves the narrator and half the country's police force into a taxi, dashes madly across town and finds the girl I'd placidly thought was the heroine all equipped with a blunt instrument & an animal snarl. I'm always led by the nose up the garden path in search of a false clue, and I never notice inconsistencies. And I always get let down when I find out who dun it. As I say, I like the overtones. A good style, some traces of wit & characterization, a sense of atmosphere, and a lot of the professional intricacies of the game can go to hell. Yet I want a novel in that particular convention & no other. The answer is, I think, that I'm naturally a slow & reflective reader, & make copious marginalia. In the detective story I live for a moment in the pure present: I'm passively pulled along from stimulus to stimulus, and, ignorant & idle as that doubtless is, I'm fascinated by it. Yet I seldom finish without disappointment. [D 42.32; DNF, 15]

The whole conception of a holiday or break in routine derives from the sacrificial festival, & the cuddliness or cosiness of the detective story is connected with the holiday atmosphere inspired by a murder. All the details of life that are so boring ordinarily: the layout of rooms in a house & of furniture in a room, the trivial movements of one's personal habits, all become irradiated by a sudden novelty of significance. A trace of a Last Judgment in this, perhaps, worked out in a human context: somebody dies & there is a general summoning to account for one's actions. The whole appeal of Sherlock Holmes was connected with his ability to notice ordinary details. Here again is the dialectic between the all-seeing eye of God & of the spy of the state with his "telescreen." [NB 33.43]

"De-" Words. Bultmann decided to talk about demythologizing the Bible, which is like removing the skin and bones from the body. I don't understand the twentieth-century attraction for these antiseptic sounding words beginning with "de." I don't know why Bultmann speaks of demythologizing the Bible when he means remythologizing it. And I don't understand in literary criticism why Derrida speaks of deconstruction when what he means is reconstruction. But that's just original sin. ["SYMBOLISM IN THE BIBLE," LECTURE 24; RT, 606]

Diagrammatic Interpretation. Poetry, says Aristotle, is more philosophical than history. As there is no obvious sense in which Sappho, say, is more philosophical than Thucydides, this remark must be interpreted diagrammatically, as Sidney & others did interpret it. [NB 18.78]

Diary Writing. I have occasionally wondered why I couldn't keep diaries. The answer is that I'm too busy with other writing—the only times I succeeded in keeping a diary more than a week or two were in doldrum periods of writing. Now I'm so full of commissions & deadlines I can't even keep notebooks. [NB 18.105]

Dictatorships. The reason why "Christ is in me" is not the same statement as "I am Christ" but its exact opposite is that practically all of "me" is a stupid and rebellious mob, forever setting up its own muddled leaders. Hence all the metaphors, from at least Plato's *Republic* downwards, about the wise commonwealth as an allegory of the wise man's mind, and of the latter as a dictatorship. The Christ in me can never be a dictator: all dictators turn out to be Antichrist sooner or later. [NOTES 52.167; LN, 2:456]

Dilemma. In the gospels note the pericope of dilemma. Jesus is asked a two-way question; either way gets him into a difficulty, & trying to avoid the dilemma would get him into an unseemly (for a prophet) wriggle. What he does is to break through the dilemma formulation. [NB 12.440; TBN, 239]

Discipline. One of the major efforts of all discipline is to unbury the consciousness of the moment that Satan can't find, as Blake calls it. [NB 3.15; RT, 8]

Discovery. It's common knowledge that Kekule's discovery of the circular atomic structure of the benzine molecule is linked to a dream of the ouroboros, and that the DNA molecule is linked to the double helix. Nothing is discovered out there that isn't in some sense already here.
[NB 50, 154; LN, 1:285-6]

Dog in the Library. William James' figure of the dog in the library has always fascinated me: what are the areas of meaning around us of which we're unconscious? I'm not suggesting that one can answer such questions, only that there should be a literary convention to deal with them: something in the romance and anatomy traditions that can be given a new shape.
[NB 20.14]

Don Quixote. Our lurking assumption—myths are by hypothesis unrecognized. Don Quixote is a very subtle example of a man who has developed a mythology in order to reveal an infinitely deeper destructive impulse. He's the first of a line of lunatics who try to destroy the present under pretext of destroying the past. [NB 4.87]

Doubletalk. Movements that consider themselves revolutionary, like feminism and Marxism, go in for a kind of conscientious dishonesty in their pseudo-arguments. Here's a feminist saying that most of the poets I refer to are male. That's exactly the doubletalk I used to get from Communists: (a) it isn't true that nearly all great poets, for whatever reasons, happen to be men (b) of course it's true, but you must be a mean old chauvinist to assume that it's true. Nothing can be done about this except to wait for it to stop. The instinct to lie deliberately to support an ideological cause is in Christianity, of course, God knows how deeply. If there's anything in that book about a censored gospel of Mark and Clement it's pretty deep, and one suspects it even in the gospels. Orwell's principle of who controls the past controls the present is involved here. It's a more or less degenerate offshoot of the fact that myth inevitably lies about history.
[NOTES 53.160; LN, 2:643-4]

Doublethink. Orwell's doublethink is not correctly defined by him as the holding of two contradictory opinions simultaneously. The real demonic parody of the double vision is the feeling that those who utter what everyone acknowledges to be the truth should be treated as criminals. This in turn reflects the inner doublethink of the natural man: of course the God of the Old Testament is a shit, but you're an infidel, etc., if you say so. [NOTES 53.175; LN, 2:647]

Downsizing. Well, here I am in the Alonso stage, pursuing a will-o-the wisp through forthrights & meanders. One day I'm sure it's two volumes I'm contemplating; next day I'm not sure. Experience has already presented me with a number of books the size of *Grove's Dictionary* that folded up into two or three hundred pages.
[NB 23.60; RT, 375]

Dragon Killing. The two dragons I want to kill are Bultmann's "demythologize" and Derrida's "logocentric." The Bible is myth from Genesis to Revelation, & to demythologize it is to obliterate it. The climax of the (Christian) Bible is "The Word became flesh, and dwelt among us," which is the most logocentric sentence ever written. But I must be careful to make sure I understand them & am not just saying that my views of mythos & logos are different. [NB 44.253; LN, 1:157]

Dream-Memories. I have archetypal dream-memories which I can trace to childhood, or rather to one or two of the experiences of childhood that helped build it up. One involves gray city streets, a late afternoon, a rain, and sombre dark red houses with little gnome-like lights in them. The vision eludes me, though it points to Sherbrooke, & I think my year in England helped to nourish it. In any case it conditions my reactions to city streets, late afternoons, rainy days, & T. S. Eliot's early poetry. A much more recent dream concerns a maroon-colored book which mentions St. Augustine & explains everything; an archetype that started with Spengler in Edmonton & grew through the spring of 1940 when I was holding

Lovejoy's *Chain of Being* in my hand and trying to find out about Neoplatonism. In my dream I don't write the book myself; when I wake up I know I have to. The difficulty with dreams is that they bring with them an emotional supercharge of significance which makes every approach to realizing them an anticlimax, a descent from Beulah into Generation. No, I don't want to be psychologized: I know what sort of thing would come out, & psychoanalysis is just medieval medicine all over again: it's guided by a mythical theory of the "temperament," and all it knows is purging & bleeding, along with an allopathic "occupational therapy" drug cabinet. Freud's id & ego & libido or "censor" (how Austrian that word is!) explain a lot, but so did the medieval theory of humors. The psychoanalyst's couch is Promethean, & perhaps Procrustean. [NB 3.75; RT, 31]

Dreams. Dreams can be read &, even if they can't, are continually translating themselves into action & further thought. Dreams are the digestive process of the mind. They rearrange the data (food) of experience into the libidinous form of either a comic resolution or an "anxiety" tragic one. [NB 3.138; RT, 55]

The dreams we don't remember are likely to be the important ones. Normally some experience will remind me, like the echo of a plucked string, of something I dreamt the night before & cannot otherwise remember. Freud says nothing about the therapeutic value of sleep & why we spend a third of our life unconscious. The facile "rest" theory is nonsense. Nothing vital rests, not even the brain—least of all the brain. Animals sleep lightly because they never really wake up. No, I think sleep is the key to memory, the continuity of consciousness. If I can't sleep, thoughts race through my head in a stream or else circle around one point—often an anxiety point. Sleep digests the stream of impressions & transforms them into a mental circulation of ideas: the myths of dreams are the chyle of sense experience. Even Freud says that the content of a dream is that on which the mind has not yet slept, & everyone knows how problems are solved by a night's sleep. Old people sleep lightly & lose

71

their memories. Sleepiness comes when we have wakened to repletion, & need to digest the sense-stream. [NB 3.141; RT, 56]

On my mission field 14 years ago I was awakened suddenly at 5:30 a.m., & surprised my mind churning up some kind of pattern in which [Francis] Quarles & John Wesley formed links in a continuous evangelical tradition. Doubtless there were sexual wish-fulfillment allusions here, but the primary point is that dreaming is a kind of thinking that is necessary to consciousness yet cannot be done by consciousness. Last night all I can remember of my dream is an attempt to realize that Bernard Shaw is not of the tradition of Mill, as I say in lectures, but of Carlyle—this links with the "frustrated royalist" idea of Shaw I have always had. If I had not remembered that dream it would have affected my thinking about drama anyway. [NB 3.143; RT, 57]

The therapeutic role of dreams must ultimately be that of enlarging vision, & dreams should be interpreted on the same principles as works of art: observe faithfully (literal), note all references to external events (allegorical), place in relation to your own libidinous urges (moral) & then aim for anagogic completeness. [NB 3.148; RT, 60]

Yeats says dreams are really dreamed by the dead, & create worlds we enter at sleep. Has anyone explained why we need all that sleep? Hours & hours of it. It can't be to "rest the brain"—the brain doesn't work all that hard. And what, if any, is the biological function of dreams? What use are they if nobody can understand them, least of all the dreamer? It's the same question that gets asked about the arts. However, I think I have ideas about dreams & art. The private Freudian wish-fulfilment dream is part of the egocentric subject, & partakes of the same unreality. There's an individual that isn't an ego, & there must be a dreaming individual that isn't just preoccupied with a wish to screw his mother. In waking life the storm clouds of the ego keep blinding us to reality, but every so often they clear & we see clearly & objectively. Something similar happens with dreams—everybody feels that some dreams are more oracular than others. But this doesn't tell me anything about the analogy between the dream world & death. [NB 19.6-7; TBN, 5-6]

Everyone admits that the dream comments on the previous day, & everyone knows that the problems of that day are sometimes solved by sleep alone. Does not this imply that the dreaming consciousness rearranges material from waking consciousness in a wish-fulfilment form, & that this material, now dramatized, is assimilated to the archetypes below it, from whence it reemerges to consciousness? This would explain how dreams hook themselves onto the key experiences of childhood, as I'm convinced that impressions taken in the first few years of life recreate for the individual all the primary archetypes. Thus the dream assimilates the haphazard and involuntary experiences of waking life, the becoming world, into the archetypal world of being where everything is a wish-fulfilment comedy. Each dream is a personal episode of a universal comedy of the human collective unconscious, a drama broken off from the one great epic. If the individual is not progressing, then his dreams will be Freudian sex-dreams or Adlerian power-dreams, concerned solely with an antithesis between reality & desire. These fall into the childhood archetypes & reemerge autonomously in life: the whole process is involuntary, sterile, & regressive—or rather, it follows the organic curve of life, & becomes regressive from 35 on, ending in the dismal poverty of ideas one sees in age. If he is progressing, his individuality, Jung's self, takes form at the center of the wheel, instead of being one of the foci of an ellipse, the other being a point in the dark. [D 49.30; DNF, 61]

Drunken Monkey. I suppose the basis of the apophatic, contemplative, "hid divinity" tradition is the implication in Paul that "we are known," that God already has total knowledge of us. What you do, then, is turn off the chatter in your mind, which is making more noise than a punk rock band ("drunken monkey," the Hindus call it) and relax into the divine knowledge of us which is one of the things meant by a cloud of unknowing.

Not as easy to do as it sounds: I've never known an instant of *real* quiet in my mind. [NB 44.270; LN, 1:161]

For *The Great Code* I tried a different experiment: typing notes. They started off in the regular way, but before long I realized that I was just draining the "drunken monkey" babble of the so-called conscious mind off my skull. It didn't really work: I want to destroy those notes. [NB 44.326; LN, 1:173]

I know from experience, and I've read the statement often enough, that if one could turn off the incessant chatter in one's psyche one would be well on the way to freedom. In all my life I've never known an instant of real silence. That, of course, is because I've never gone through the years of discipline and practice in meditation. To come to it cold (as I've said in another notebook) would be like rolling back the waves of the Red Sea and walking across the bottom. [NB 44.448; LN, 1:200]

The Orientals say you should get outside the rush of thought through the mind, & realize that it isn't you thinking—in other words all such gabble is at best ideologically conditioned, at worst just ego-shit. Stream-of-consciousness means something that's never really conscious. The verbal sewer is an infiltration of "historicity" into the individual: it's nonsense to say we can never get clear of it. [NB 44.573; LN, 1:222]

Why do I set up such a deafening clatter of inner talk in my mind? Probably for the same reason that villagers gossip and urban people intrigue: to keep myself reassured about the reality of the ordinary world. If I'd shut up and listen I might be able to hear other things. It corresponds to the senses' filtering out and giving us the reality we can take.... How to distinguish the clatter & chatter from my central work with words? No real boundary; but I know well enough when it's nothing *but* chatter. I can't turn it all off, but I could, perhaps, get more control of it. And perhaps after a couple of years of trying to shut off babble I might

get a second or two when I'd realize what genuine quiet would be. Even before that, a quieter mind might increase the intensity of experience. The aim would be the receptivity of the infant Samuel.
[NB 50. 52, 54; LN, 1:267]

Dualism. I've been called a (Platonic) dualist, but I'm not one, and neither was Plato. There is only one form of dualism, the Cartesian cloven fiction of subject & object, a formidable barrier to thought because our language is Cartesian. But it isn't dualism to say that an embryo and a baby live in different environmental worlds, nor to say that before and after death are also different worlds. I said that, dammit. [NB 44.347; LN, 1:177]

Dussek. In playing through an edition of Dussek's sonatas, I had a curious sense of the ambiguity of the word "invention." The greatest composers, we think, are those who make up the best music out of their own heads. This is part of the subjectifying of creation that we've come to take for granted. It's the ghost of the old idea that God is the only objective creator. Gurdjieff has a remark about "objective" art that impressed me, although in his context it was probably all balls. But I wonder about "invention"—I get a strong feeling that Mozart and Beethoven found things that were really there, in the ground Dussek surveyed. (Of course Dussek found things too, especially in the fine F minor sonata). Maybe the "greatest" artists are also the greatest realists: they discover, like the scientists, patterns & constructs actually latent in nature. This would explain the sense in, e.g., Eliot, that the poet is a fisher king trying to hook and land one thing, his poem, which is his only because he happened to catch it.
[NB 12.467; TBN, 245]

$\mathcal{E}$

The East. What people like Whitehead mean when they say that the Greeks began a tradition of *reason* which makes 50 years of Europe significant in a way that a cycle of Cathay isn't I don't know, & I don't know either how anyone could bring himself to write down such obvious horseshit. If there is any spot in the world where reason had a clear field it's India; & the whole set-up in China is—or rather was—an enlightened liberal Deism which makes our 18th century look like what it was—cheap *chinoiserie*…. The one unique thing about the West is its inability to perceive its lack of uniqueness, its dogma of peculiarity, its belief that God planned a high road for the West, with the Greeks contributing reason, Hebrews moral virtue, Romans law, English liberty, & Americans atomic bombs & sanitary napkins, & left the East to rotate helplessly around its own navel until rescued by the West. The fact that the bloody world is round is one of the first things we learn & one of the last we ever believe. [NB 3.48; RT, 22]

The goal of Eastern training appears to be a world in which the imaginative, the imagined, the imaged & the imaginary are all the same, a world which is not nothingness because nothing is a dogmatic antithesis to something. It would be better described as anything, a world of total potentiality. Now according to the East, the difference between the imaginative & the imaged, the conscious & unconscious perception, is accounted for by a *habitus* built up over a series of previous existences, which is all right with me if we give the previous "habit" a Samuel Butler interpretation. But in the East's revolutionary conception of break with habit there is, having entered the world of anything, no reason for doing one thing rather than

76

another. One has left *the* creation for creation; one is now God at the opening of Genesis; but one has got there by losing the desire to create. Blake's doctrine of creation is more consecutive: there is evolution, & that means there is a next thing to do, a development on the consolidation of habit to make. This is connected with the fact that the West has what the East has not—care, a very different thing from the Buddhist's compassion. This care, or *caritas,* or *charis,* is the cause of all our intolerance & persecution, but it is also the reason why Western imaginative developments assume a social & educational ("democratic") form. [NB 34.46]

Easy Satisfaction. It isn't that Freudians are stupid, but that they're so easily satisfied with what they (think they) know. Similarly with Marxists and Christian fundamentalists. Discovery, for them, is not interesting. [NB 44.402; LN, 1:190]

Economic Creed. I have always believed that to have several competing firms scrambling for my business on all lines was Utopia. A delight in this and a horror of any monopoly that could get along without me is my one real economic feeling. It has a censor in the fact that all my intellectually respectable friends are socialists & therefore it must be all wrong (no doubt because delightful: the feeling of jealousy of the gods leaks through every open pore of my imagination), but it persists. [D 42.8; DNF, 6]

Education. Education is, or has something to do with, a process of transforming the continuum of identity from the ego and the memory to the individual and the imagination. In the process memory becomes practice memory or habit. [NB 19.124; TBN, 28]

Education in Criticism. The only features in human life that are genuinely human are creation and criticism. They intertwine of course: the thing is right now that all education is education in criticism, and that criticism and education are synonymous. [NOTES 53.225; LN, 2:655]

Educational Dagwoodism. The old notion of four years of gentlemanly training in preparation for life during the mating season is on its way out. There's no longer that kind of race against time—the Spencer kind, I mean: how much can be squeezed into preparatory years? What's essential & what belongs to the fill-up-the-cracks stage? These questions are obsolescent. Herbert Spencer said: why learn the archaic superstitions of Greece & Rome when you could learn contemporary facts & ideas that would be useful? We say: why learn contemporary facts that will be archaic superstitions in ten years? Why try to "adjust" to a society that won't be there when you've adjusted to it? Educational Dagwoodism, trying to jump on a bus that's just vanished around the corner. [NB 19.271; TBN, 62]

The Ego. As soon as one makes the original act of self-knowledge, the feeling that "Je est un autre," the ego, the instant it's *recognized,* begins to bite and scratch—on one's own flesh. It gibbers and lampoons & mocks: it drags all one's associations over toward some embarrassing or foolish thing one did—that is, *it* did—in the past, & generally it behaves like the accusing Satan or betraying Judas it is. Once thoroughly roused, it'll never go back to sleep, hence one has to be all the more careful of not taking one's eye off it. The ego is a perennial adolescent, with the adolescent's ready combination of personal resentment & acceptance of external (i.e. outside the family) authority. (Or rather, any authority that's of the gang, or aggregate of egos, as against anything that's a *telos* or community.) It keeps the mind as an adolescent keeps his room—fully lighted & with a noisy record of music playing. The fact that I'm an introvert doesn't make me love solitude unless I'm really working, because otherwise I'm just alone with my ego, who will always waste my time.
[NB 3.170; RT, 67-8]

"I am a wise and good man" is grammatically impossible, because such predicates cannot be attached to anything beginning with "I am." Even Jesus resented being called good. The ego doesn't co-exist with wisdom & goodness. [NB 27.20; LN, 1:6]

It's doubtless my own ego that wonders why critics didn't feel more called to order by the piece I did for the PMLA centenary ["Literary and Linguistic Scholarship in a Postliterate World"] [NB 44.26; LN, 1:106].

Ego-abstraction and Spiritual Body. The natural abstraction of the ego or body has nothing to do with the soul or spirit, the first act of which is to reach beyond the body into other relations. A man's social life, for instance, is clearly a part of himself, & it's impossible to think of life after death as a mere survival of the ego-abstraction. Everything I have loved—my emanation, Blake would call it—is as much a part of me as anything else in my character, & must survive if anything else in my character does. Helen [Frye's wife] is eternally part of my life as I am of hers, & so we are all members of one body & yet not married, for the Helen in my life is mine, & not the ego-abstraction people refer to when they name her. I attach my love to that abstraction, but love it only approximately. Your spiritual body is the invisible house you build of which the ego-abstraction is the doorkeeper or covering cherub. The person is the incarnation or visible mask of the real Self or Atman. [D 49.282; DNF, 164]

Either / Or. The best known of all Oriental stories is the one about Chuang Tse dreaming he was a butterfly, and, waking, not knowing which was dreaming which. But this must be badly translated: it can't be an either-or question. The real question was asked by the butterfly in Chuang Tse, and was: "Isn't that big lout of a larva awake yet?"
[NB 44.424; LN, 1:195]

It's always been a feeling of mine that my conception of myth was the resolution of all "either-or" dilemmas, not only Kierkegaard's, where it's fairly obvious that "either" is just as mythical as "or," but the far more impressive Marxist one, where it's either revolutionary action on the right line or some eroding ideology. Different versions of either-or dilemmas are constantly turning up: the martyr for a cause we sympathize with always raises guilt feelings. [NB 12.56; TBN, 143]

79

Elemental Spirits. Spirit I've connected with agape & dialectic, & soul with eros & cycle. But this leaves out the central area of elemental spirits, the things created or commanded by the Magus. I've never really understood this complex, though I've revolved around it all my life. [NB11E.71; RT, 334]

A theme I've never got clear is the role of elemental spirits, who are so often sulky, unwilling & dangerous—demonic, in short, & quite often devils. But, as in *Comus,* they can include guardian angels. Goethe's *Faust,* in spite of my growing disillusionment with Goethe, has a lot to do with this: Erdgeist, Homunculus, the lot. [NB 50.311; LN, 1:318]

The elemental spirit is the spark in nature touched by human consciousness: things like Annie Dillard's teaching a stone to talk and some book on my shelves about how a spirit in a stone can be evoked. Such a spirit is to a natural object as a dog is to a fox or wolf. There are two such spirits in this room: the Chinese lady, who's a guardian spirit, and the African reliquary. Helen [Frye's wife] loved them both, so they're not just objects, but have something of what they were designed to be. There are undoubtedly evil spirits too, but not here. [NB 50.460; LN, 1:349]

Elusiveness. I give the impression of elusiveness sometimes, and rightly, because I really do have an inner chamber in my temple I'm not mature enough to open. [NOTES 53.26; LN, 2:618]

Emancipating Spirits. Marx and Freud are the great emancipating spirits of the 20th century because they attacked the natural-man hierarchical setup in society and the individual: it's nothing against them that more is needed in both areas. [NOTES 53.105; LN, 2:632]

Emigrés in Time. I've said that American youth coming to Canada as draft-dodgers suffer from an emigré mentality: they're not coming to Canada, but only leaving the States, & they live in a social limbo awaiting an amnesty or similar change. However, they may get their amnesty: they're not as badly off as the *emigrés in time* of the younger generation, who expect some gigantic revolution which will not come, or if it does will be in a form more disillusioning than the status quo. I don't see much future for them except psychoneurosis. It's all very well for Blake to say that fear & hope are vision, but when both fear & hope are concentrated on what are not & cannot be there, the vision becomes fantasy, of a drugging and will o' the wisp kind. [NB 11F.174; RT, 113]

Energy. The omnipresence of spirit and its independence of simple location: angels are spirits, and the number that can stand on the point of a pin is either none or an infinite number, depending on whether they occupy space or not. I think I can risk speculating on the fact that the spiritual body consists of energy rather than matter, but I hate to think of some form of Whitman's "body electric." Not that anyone knows what electricity is. [NOTES 53.137; LN, 2:637]

Engineering Metaphors. Engineering metaphors or thought models start of course with fire and the wheel. One gives metaphors of spark, scintilla, energy & the like: most of our organism metaphors take off from it. The wheel is of course the source of all cyclical conceptions of fate, fortune & nature. The pendulum is involved in all Yin & Yang theories like those in Plato's *Politics;* it's also part of Hegel. But in Hegel, as still more in Marx, we begin to get all the "feedback," "governor" & other self-regulating metaphors that run through 19th-century thought from Burke to Butler. Internal combustion is in *anima mundi* & all vitalist metaphors; ball bearings, in myths of individuality; gears in metaphors of compulsion & interaction & so on. *Organism* metaphors, as in Spengler, may be reducible to mechanisms. [NB 18.10-11]

English Literature. As soon as one begins the serious study of English literature one makes two paradoxical discoveries about it. One is that there is no such thing as English literature, and the other is that there is no such

thing as literature. The former is because the two obvious criteria, "literature written in English" and "literature written in England" don't coincide,
and because, for instance, Virgil is a vastly greater name in English literature than the *Beowulf* poet. The latter is obvious. Yet, just as a written
orthography exercises a constant check on pronunciation, so a language
exercises a constant check on a literature, even before 1600. Again, some
kind of normalizing principle, perhaps the metre of poetry, exercises a
constant check on literary form. [NB 42.7]

Englishness. Henry James' pansy mannerisms and distilled snobbery don't
put me off as much as Butler's inverted snobbery about the upper class:
the latter, however disguised as parody, is the real pain in the ass. Because
that's the Englishness I had to put up with when I was principal.
[NB 44.112; LN, 1:124]

Epiphany. Epiphany is not a new experience: it is the knowledge that one
has the experience: it's recognition or *anagnorisis*. The wise men did not
need to journey to it: it was their own wisdom in the only form wisdom
can take, the divine infancy or fresh beginning. Epiphany is the containing of change, or the other, by bringing it into line with identity: in short,
it's the awareness of growth, when the line pointing from the object
reverses its direction. [NB 19.152; TBN, 34-5]

The end of art is epiphany, perceiving the particular as universal, the grain
of sand as the world. The end of non-literary verbal disciplines, and I think
of mathematics, is the intuition of a network of relations or laws.
[NB 19.159; TBN, 36]

Eros. Eros is primarily a reversal in time, a movement toward reversal
of youth (*Faust*) or childhood (*Purgatorio*). Hence the first movement is
toward the mother, or more accurately the virgin or inaccessible mother. It
goes back through earlier stages of history & culture, often idealizing them
(both the Bible & Renaissance-Classic & Romantic-medieval idealizings

show this; also Virgil, even Homer's bronze age), its ultimate goal a lost Paradise. Here possession & being possessed are the same thing ("know as I am known"). So primarily there's the ascent to the virgin mother, the *hortus conclusus* who's also Paradise, sometimes represented by the moon at which a phallic mountain points. Beatrice first appears as a scolding mamma: Matilda is the image of pre-sexual innocence.
[NB 50.437; LN, 1:344-5]

Eros Symbols. The six arts produced give us culture; the six arts applied give us civilization. Architecture: wonder why there always has to be a prick and a cunt: I wondered this when sitting in the Skydome with the CN tower beside me. Islam had a mosque and a minaret; Christianity a basilica and a bell-tower; even the New York fair had a trylon and a perisphere. Something points to the sky and something contains on earth. Wright wanted to put up a building a mile high and Fuller wanted to build geodesic domes. These are Eros symbols, and just as kerygma is verbal imagination coming the other way, so Agape is Eros coming the other way. After all, God creates us by the power of Eros. I'm just circling: I haven't caught my mouse yet.... Of the prick-and-cunt pairs in architecture...I should have added the menhirs and stone circles of Neolithic times. I suppose in another area this pairing becomes the one-and-zero binary form that's the basis of number. Erik Erikson: leave children alone to play and the boys will build towers and the girls paddocks.
[NOTES 54-1.41, 44; LN, 2:673, 674]

Escaping from Time. Christians & Buddhists have the same sense of escape from time, but the Westerner says we never die because he thinks of immortality as continuity of energy, & the Easterner says we have never been born because he thinks of immortality as release from karma or causation. But both are equally true, or untrue, whichever you like. When the Westerner tries to absorb the idea of unbornness, he tumbles into the "predestination" pitfall; when the Easterner tries to get clear about deathlessness, he gets into the "reincarnation" one. [NB 3.119; RT, 49]

ESP. I've noticed a curious form of e.s.p. in me: whenever I dream of writing something in fiction somebody else who really does write gets the idea instead. This has happened to me so often that it was no surprise to me after thinking about a historical novel situated at Trebizond, to find that Rose Macaulay had the same idea. (In my childhood I dreamed of becoming a great astronomer & discovering a new planet beyond Neptune that I was going to call Pluto). [NB 3.172; RT, 68]

Esse est Percipi. Esse est percipi; but we know the world keeps on existing whether we see it or not: hence, for Berkeley, we trust that God keeps on watching it, the world being a perceived idea in God's mind. It's a good thing that, as the Psalmist says, God neither slumbers nor sleeps. [NOTES 53.208; LN, 2:652]

Eternal Existence. I come back to the feeling that one's eternal existence is to be connected, not with where one is going after death, but with where one is at death. I suppose that senile people who have lost their memories are in effect dead in this sense. [NB 21.30; RT, 145]

Evocations of Forces. I want to avoid phrases that sound as though I were a Jungian trying to psychologize everything: it's not just human creation but human response to something other that I'm interested in. Jupiter and Venus were never real until the human element in their creation became obvious; but they aren't *just* human creations: they're evocations of forces common to man and his environment. [NOTES 52.40; LN, 2:428]

Exclusive and Inclusive Approaches. Sidney's theory of poetry implies that one course is right & two wrong, the two wrong being the exclusive & inclusive approaches to the integrity of the art. Exclusive gives Poe's theory of poetry, Cézanne's of painting, & a lot of music, concentrating on the accidents…. Inclusiveness leads to the black mass, Wagner & Scriabine, to literary painting & pictorial music. The right way is to use other subjects in, e.g. painting, but not make a pictorial synthesis of them.

Also the difference we feel in saying Spenser is allegorical & Shakespeare isn't means that Spenser is explicitly a teacher of allegorical language. Note that the inclusive *social* theory of response is sentimental (Tolstoy) & won't work; the exclusive one is snobbish (ivory tower) & won't work either. If Shakespeare is greater than Spenser, it's not because of his greater range of appeal; if Auden is greater than Edgar Guest, it's not because his audience is more restricted. [NB 7.25]

Excremental Vision. Swift's notorious poem on a woman's dressing room is usually cited as simply Swift himself being obsessed by the fact that women shit: "insanity," says Lawrence; "excremental vision," says Norman Brown. Well, it's that, all right: if you haven't got an excremental vision you have no business setting up as a major satirist. But "Celia shits" isn't *Swift* screaming: it's Celia's lover Strephon, whose love for Celia is of the insipidly idealistic kind that hasn't taken in the fact that women, *mutatis mutandis,* have the same physical basis to their lives that men have. Besides, if, like the hero of *Berkeley Square,* one of us were to wake up in the middle of eighteenth-century London, assailed by all those unfamiliar stinks, wouldn't we be just as nauseated? *That's* the mark of the great writer: who sees his own time, but with a detachment that makes him communicable to other ages. [NOTES 52.786; LN, 2:578-9]

Eye of Bat and Tongue of Dog. Tactical directive: in beginning to plan a major work like the third book, *don't eliminate anything. Never* assume that some area of your speculations can't be included & has to be left over for another book. Things may get eliminated in the very last stage of preparing a book for publication, as an alleged "epic" chapter did from *Anatomy of Criticism,* but *never, never,* exclude anything when thinking about the book. It was strenuous having to cut down *Fearful Symmetry* from an encyclopaedia, but if the encyclopaedia hadn't been there *Fearful Symmetry* would never have existed. That of course doesn't apply to single essays or short books made out of them, or public lectures on a definite theme; but major works are encyclopaedic & anatomic: everything I know must go into them—eye of bat & tongue of dog. It follows I suppose that all my major books are the same book with different centers of gravity: interpenetrating universes. Give me a place to stand, and I will include the world. In *Fearful Symmetry* I was standing in Blake's *Milton;* in *Anatomy of Criticism* I was standing in *The Tempest;* the only other place that I can stand that I know of is *Paradise Regained.*

[NB 19.333; TBN, 74-5]

Ezekiel. Ezekiel's valley of dry bones does mean resurrection, whatever the historical scholars say. That doesn't mean it prophesies Christianity, which would be an even more future event than the return from Babylon. But what burst out of Ezekiel without his conscious knowledge was the vision of an expanded present, a spiritual world existing here and now, where past and future are gathered, in Eliot's phrase.

[NOTES 53.234; LN, 2:657]

F

Fairies. Fairies are the detritus of the oldest mythology in the world, the beings in nature that are close at hand, form the earliest stratum or the "supernatural," are present in rivers and trees and stones (they later become nymphs and satyrs and the like), and are closely related to the dream world. They belong to what the theosophists call the astral world, the closest to this one, where auras and similar phenomena that can be allegedly seen by certain people belong. They do seem to have predominantly Celtic affinities, and they do seem to have some connection with Arthur.... The demonizing of the fairies was tried by the godly but didn't really take. They're linked to mirrors and mirror-worlds.... John Crowley's *Little, Big,* a book the author handed to me when I was lecturing at Smith College, seems to move in and out of this world with considerable expertise. [NOTES 55-3.8-10]

Faith. Faith is the recurring sense of revelation, i.e., an existential reality beyond the hypothetical. This revelation is the vision of a "new" creation —new to us, that is. Such a faith, if attained, redeems and justifies all literature. [NB 27.70; LN, 1:14]

Faith is based on what is *not* "there," & has to be realized by action. It may be "there," but to say "I believe that it is there" is off the track. I'm presenting this here as my own views, not as literary criticism of the Bible, but I imagine I can show the views follow from looking at the Bible as a book. The principle of the less belief the better goes here too, even its consequences for belief in an "after"-life. [NB 21.332; RT, 202]

Faith: as I've said so often, it's the negation of faith, or indifference, that's the real opposite. The contrary, doubt, is a fertilizing influence on faith. Out of their interaction a new antithesis forms: the negation of faith-doubt becomes faith as uncritical acceptance, a retreat from reason & evidence—what's ordinarily meant by faith. Similarly, I suppose, hatred, in the sense of what I call abhorrence, is the contrary of love which produces the new negation of gregariousness. The contrary of hope, not exactly despair but Hardy's full look at the worst, forms the new negation of the donkey's carrot of progress & the like. [NB 21.494; RT, 231]

Curious how the faith-doubt dialectic blocks so many people off: if they don't believe or lose their faith, they just back down the ladder. [NB 11C.5; RT, 344]

I wonder how far I could get with the conception of faith as negative imagination—faith in the sense of asserting the existence of a construct and then making one's life a sacramental analogy of that. The weak spot in imagination is that it has no subjective counterpart, which is why people are always asserting that art is no substitute for religion. [NB 19.109; TBN, 24-5]

Faith, Hope, and Charity. Hope is the virtue of the past, the eternal sense that maybe next time we'll do better. The projection of this into the future is faith, the substance of things hoped for. Love belongs to the present, & is the only force able to cast out fear. If a thing loves it is infinite, Blake said, & the act of love is itself a vision of a timeless world. Oh, God, how well I talk. *Deteriora sequor.* Or do I just say that because of an obscure feeling that such statements are somehow approved of by some atavistic God in my infantile shadow world? [NB 3.146; RT, 59]

The terms word and spirit—the dividing and uniting aspects of human awareness—move in the direction of obliterating all the nonsense of either-or and God plus man. Is there *a* God or not? Can we get along with just man or do we have to have God too? Is God dead or alive? (Any God of whom that question can be asked is certainly dead; but the place of asking it may be his tomb & the time may be the last Sabbath. At that time & place resurrections are unpredictable.) My guess is that all this stupid nonsense comes from the conception of faith as simulated knowledge. Such faith *limits* hope instead of providing its *hypostasis* [substance]: it limits because it tries to define. Meanwhile, both word & spirit can be used either with or without any sense of the "supernatural." Without infinity of hope, we have only the accuser's record: human history is the record of the only animal in nature more repulsive than nature. We can hope for nothing in either man or nature: there has to be an apocalypse within man. I personally don't see why humanity still exists without some power that cares more about it than it does about itself, as history records nothing persistent or continuous except the impulse to self-destruction. But that's not an argument: the principle is that everything charitable makes for the elimination of the sacred-secular antithesis in Word & Spirit. Spirit (*esprit, Geist*) can be freely used with no suggestion of the "supernatural," but it doesn't eliminate such suggestions either. [NB 50.545-6; LN, 1:368]

The criticism of faith says "I believe there were certain historically true events, or logically valid propositions, of which the words we find in the Bible are the servomechanisms." That's balls. The criticism of hope says "I don't know what the hell happened, and probably never will know, but I sure hope it was worth all the to-do that followed." That's balls too. The criticism of charity says the text is the presence. The response to the above rendering of the first verse of Genesis ["to begin with, everything is a (divine) creation"] is *not* "Yes, I believe everything is a divine creation," but "I assume that what I am still about to read is roughly consistent with this." [NOTES 52.27; LN, 2:425]

False Analogies. One hardly knows which are the more absurd & dangerous: the false analogies to business at one end of the university, or the false analogies to democracy at the other. [NB 21.137; RT, 164]

False Symmetry. False symmetry is my worst enemy, because, founded as it is on arbitrary association, it is perpetually elaborating a total form too restricted to contain the pullulating swarm of ideas I get. The general clarifying process is one of pulling apart. [NB 32.21]

Family. The real curse imposed on Adam & Eve was the family: not just a patriarchal family, even though that may be the worst form of it, but simply the family, in which children are brought up in a hierarchical structure with the design of losing their childhood when they become adults. The genetic child (the child*like*, not the child*ish*) is prehistoric: post-historic man is the creator or recreated (not the adulterated) child. Hence Jesus on preserving the child in us; hence the way that fundamentalist devil-worshippers go in for periodic orgies of child-spanking, preferably, of course, girls. (At least the fundamentalist journals I get sent occasionally seem to have regular cycles of such articles.) The family is a cyclical principle. [NB 50.322; LN, 1:319-20]

Fantasies of Greatness. I had the usual childish fantasies, when very young, of wanting to be a "great man"—fantasies that in our day only Churchill has realized. But Churchill's greatness was archaic: his funeral really buried that whole conception of greatness as a goal of ambition. Then I had fantasies of wanting to be a great composer & a great novelist —both obsolete conceptions today. The novel is breaking up into other forms & is no longer central as it was in the 19th century: the great composers ended with Bartok, and Boulez & Varese & Cage are not "great composers;" they're something else. When I settled into my real line I naturally wanted to be "great" there too: but maybe the great mind is obsolete. In the 19th century one wants to read Hegel & Marx & Kierkegaard & Nietzsche; are there really any 20th-century equivalents of that kind of "great thinker" Sartre? perhaps. But something about greatness *ended* around 1940. We're doing different things now. Marshall McLuhan is a typical example: a reputation as a great thinker based on the fact that he doesn't think at all. [NB 12.66; TBN, 146]

Fear of Spirits. While…the whole "secular scripture" has to do with the wanderings of the soul, the overtones of "spirit" seem to be fixed. In English, spirit seems to be something you can put in a bottle: even Jesus uses the bottle metaphor. The image of fermentation, as a symbol of meta-morphosis of substance, and the fear of enzymes, the feast of unleavened bread & Moslem & much Christian prejudice against liquor, have much to do with the resistance of institutions to spiritual development. Goethe's homunculus & the symbolism of alchemy with its flasks & retorts & alembics hermetically sealed, come back in the picture. Likewise the early theories of metabolism & the transforming of food into spirits. [NB 11E.58; RT, 331]

Feminist Criticism. I can't say what I really think here: I'd kill the book [*Words with Power*] if I did. I think social feminism, genuine social & intellectual equality between men & women, a centrally important issue. Feminist *literary* criticism is mostly heifer-shit. Women frustrated by the lack of outlet for their abilities turn to pedantic nagging, and the nagging pedantry of most feminist writing is a reflection of frustration unaccom-panied by any vision of transcending it. As Newman resignedly said of English literature, it will always have been Protestant. Perhaps female (not feminist) writing has a great future, but that doesn't make its effort to rewrite the past any less futile. [NB 44.580; LN, 1:223]

Fiction Writing. I am not today a great novelist because I have never been actively interested in fiction. Had I been, I should, from the age of eight or so onward, have been reading incessantly any form of contemporary fiction that came to hand, not passively for entertainment, but actively for analysis & imitation. I should have been analyzing plots, to begin with, & imitating the stories in the slicks, rewriting them in different forms, fitting different characters to the same plot or vice versa, & copying out or not-ing every bit of description or information that would supplement my very imperfect knowledge of life. After many years of incessant practice at this, I should have acquired a technical facility in handling formulae and a capacity for divining potential stories in situations that might have begun to pay off surprisingly soon, in spite of my grotesque social immaturity. I grew up imagining that literature was a product of life, and needed direct experience of life to nourish it. It has taken me a long time to realize that literature is an autonomous verbal organization, & that one should not copy life but other books. Not having done this work or anything corresponding to it, I now find myself in a mental block about writing fiction: I've by-passed all the simple stages, & now the themes which it seems worthwhile to handle demand vast technical powers I don't possess. [NB 3.164-5; RT, 65]

I have been struggling for some time to think of a new fiction formula, and all my ideas tend to revolve around Rilke's idea of the poet's perceiving simultaneously the visible & the invisible world. In practice that means a new type of ghost or supernatural story, possibly approached by way of some science-fiction development. The idea is a vision of another life or another world so powerfully plausible as to make conventionally religious & anti-religious people shake in their shoes. I've begun notes on this many times, but threw away my best notebook, written in Seattle, in a London (Ont.) hotel. By "shake in their shoes" I don't mean threats, but the ecstatic frisson or giggle aroused by plausibility. [NB 20.1]

It's good exercise to collect ideas about a work of visionary fiction that would perhaps show a modulation of science fiction (a form that fails to interest me much). Anyway, without committing itself to any given visionary system, it would elucidate how, so to speak, reality may be differently added up. It may not come to anything, but it's a place for relaxing the censor. [NB 20.11]

One idea I had a long time ago was a variant of the Jesus novel. Archeologists dig up a fifth gospel, which sheds a quite different light on the rise of Christianity (more Gnostic, I should think): authenticity unquestionable. The churches can't absorb it, so their struggles are interesting experiences in doubletalk. If I could invent a Gospel that sounded authentic it'd be terrific—a Grand Inquisitor theme. [NB 20.26]

All my life I've had an ambition to write fiction, either as a series of novels, or as one big novel. Some of the motivation is dubious: I want to prove to myself and to others that I can be "creative" in the conventionally creative genres. The idea of a series of novels has gradually faded or has left me with the desire to leave, like Santayana, a single work of fiction behind me. My first efforts were in realistic and representational form which is not only out of fashion (and is most unlikely to come back in fashion in that form) but entirely unsuited to my temperament. I simply don't know enough, haven't observed enough, don't think enough in those terms, for any kind of realism to be possible for me. So that's *out*. Since the popular success of Tolkien and the rise in seriousness of what is called science-fiction, I've been attracted to the notion of the philosophical romance. It would have to be entirely "software," as I don't know anything about hardware, and I notice that most of the hardware is used to transpose the characters to a remote spot in some other galaxy that turns out to be a category of something on earth. So why not stay on earth? The taking off point is the relativity of what the sane waking consciousness sees to other perspectives. These are, chiefly, those of (a) dream (b) madness (c) mythopoeic imagination (d) existence following physical death. If I never write such a book, collecting notes for it could still be a valuable experience in loosening up the imaginative faculties. The idea is to write what I myself would be most interested in reading. And I find great difficulty in finishing most works of fiction: they don't tell me enough. A really great writer could achieve tremendous effect by localizing what science fiction (or some form of it) projects into distant space (or, as in Tolkien, distant time) as different aspects of life here and now. The key phrase is "a separate reality," though I never finished that book [Castaneda's *A Separate Reality*] either. I succumbed to the charm of Tolkien, like everyone else, but one *Lord of the Rings* is enough. I read Fowles' *Magus* with the highest expectations, but finished it thinking he didn't know what the hell he was doing. [NB 28.1-6]

The idiom of what I have written [in my novel, *The Locust-Eaters*] seems to be wrong: I don't seem to be fundamentally interested in writing the way novelists write, collecting the sort of data they collect, or throwing myself into the novelist's attitude with any conviction. What I write, with all its wit, is still pedantic. Like a schoolgirl, in order to stick to what I know I have to duck & dodge away from business, war & all the extroverted pursuits real novelists have to grapple with. Part of the reason for this is that the novel is decidedly not my main interest, & so is hard to integrate to the rest of my activities. Anything that would so integrate would have to be mock-pedantic, intellectual slapstick as I call it. I feel that the *Locust-Eaters,* though clever, is mediocre, fits a too-well-established pattern, & would embarrass my friends. It's crotch-bound: it hasn't the Frye swing & confident brilliance, & represents the sort of careful synthetic wit I should have been producing at twenty & couldn't. As a novelist I suffer from abnormally arrested development. I'd do better in something closer to Waugh than Forster, closer to Surtees, Borrow, Peacock & Lever than to Thackeray or Trollope: something more bookish than Rabelais and less so than Burton: something that strikes a glancing blow at fiction but is fundamentally a reader's synthesis of life.... What I shall be collecting are the notes for an intellectual's *Bouvard & Pecuchet.* I should be listening to professors, including myself; reading half-baked intellectuals on psychology & sociology, hearing university presidents talk about a gray deal of this and a great eel of that; making notes on people like Currelly, & not worrying about plot so much as about fantasy. Universities installing dictaphones to get students' reactions, e.g. to pictures, Voaden's idea of getting music, reading & pictures all into the same piece—that sort of thing. The essential thing is to give the Frye *high spirits* a chance to emerge.
[NB 1.54-5]

Fictions. Fictions exfoliate from the identities of myth, but very profound fictions recapture their ancestry. In the Old Testament the relation of Ruth to Naomi suggests a Persephone-Demeter cult, but in avoiding the structure of a Canaanite myth the author goes back to a simpler convention of no priests, no temples, spirits rather than named gods, and a feeling of sympathy between man and nature. [NB 27.384; LN, 1:69]

Fine and Useful Arts. The turning point between fine & useful arts is architecture, which is fine when conspicuous (cathedral & castle) & useful when essentially a matter of housing. [D 49.137; DNF, 106]

Finishing the Book. The Bible *is* a colossal literary tour de force, whatever "more" it is, and the canonical instinct is so sure, in the large view, as to suggest a direct intervention by God. I don't see this in the Koran, & I don't see how anybody could see it in the Koran. But what does this lead to? Apparently to the reflection that God is exactly like me: in a world howling with tyranny and misery all he cares about is getting his damn book finished. [NB 44.661; LN, 1:237]

Finnegans Wake. Finnegans Wake is a kind of hypnagogic structure, words reverberating on themselves without pointing to objects (but not without *naming,* as in Mallarmé). This may be the hallucinatory verbal world within which God speaks. [NB 50.716; LN, 1:399]

First Law of Philology. Egyptian texts speak of a Habiru or Apiru, who sound very like "Hebrew," which is not the name of a nation but means something like "dispossessed people" or proletariat. This association is, of course, subject to the first law of philology, which is that every association of words that looks in the least interesting has been shown by scholars to be a mere coincidence. [NB 11B.23; RT, 353]

Fishing. The two big things I'm fishing for I may not get. One is a key image or idea for the literary universe itself, something so overpoweringly obvious & convincing that nobody will be able to argue with it. The other is the formula for what kind of genuine knowledge, as distinct from mere desire, mythical or concerned thinking is based on…. And there's a third thing I'm fishing for, more important than either of the others: the way in which informing ideas in history, philosophy & religion are derived from poetic myths. [NB 12.113-14; TBN, 158]

Fixation. I've spoken of my fixation about musical composition in my adolescence. I find the same pointless machinery operating in these notebooks. I have a notebook fixation: afraid to write anything in one for fear of its not being definitive or something afterward. Particularly true, as one would expect, of my "creative" writing fantasies. [NB 3.178; RT, 70]

The Flexible Mind. The contempt of the limited for the flexible mind is one of the ultimate demonic data of life, & it has nothing in it to be noted except its danger. [NB 3.166; RT, 66]

Flogging. I think education needs the moral equivalent of flogging. Flogging itself is not a simple or unnecessary evil: it is, like war, a perversion (largely a sexual perversion, like war too) of a genuine thing in education. For that reason it didn't do the things educators assume it did, like killing the desire to learn, though it was no less an evil for that. It dramatized the awful authority of the subject; it dramatized the sin of laziness; it brought fearful questionings of one's adequacy & sickening apprehensions of ordeals into education. It brought responsibility & reverence, and the thing it perverted would be a good thing. It brought excitement too, and violent emotions into play. No, we've abolished it without releasing what it accompanied, and if the student is no longer apt to hate school, he is in some danger of growing to despise it. The modern high school class, the brilliant students bored to death, cretins capable of grade five work sitting in the back and believing they're in high school, and the teacher driven crazy by the lack of unity and morale in the class, is not an image of democracy: it's a clear satire on it, and a picture of what democracy is trying not to be. [D 52.108; DNF, 505-6]

Flow of Information. The thing is, not to think of communication as a message from A to B, from a mouth at one end to an ear at the other, from an active to a passive center. This is what produces the elitism of "this is good for you," & the subversive "this is what you want" underneath it. So, as explained, the latter becomes not the popular but the commercial, & as more & money gets bound up with the commerce, producers, including the CBC no less than the producers, lose the power of creating or initiating & simply carry on the situation they've inherited. The A to B notion of communication survives in the phrase "flow of information." Anybody in a field like mine—literary criticism—knows that most of the information available to him is actually misinformation, & the trick is to get rid of it, not to absorb it. [NB 11F.117; RT, 97-8]

Fools. Regarding things like silly reviews of me: what is important about free speech in a democracy is not only that everyone has a right to express an opinion, however ill-considered, but that fools should have full liberty to speak so that they can be recognized to be fools. [NB 50.774; LN, 1:410]

Forest and Trees. I've said many times that man is born lost in a forest. If he is obsessed by the thereness of the forest, he stays lost and goes in circles; if he assumes the forest is not there, he keeps bumping into trees. The wise man looks for the invisible line between the "is" and the "is not" which is the way *through*. The street in the city, the highway in the desert, the pathway of the planets through the labyrinth of the stars, are parallel forms. [NB 44.53; LN, 1:111]

The Form of the Fourth. At school I was taught that substances keeping form & volume were solids, those keeping volume but not form liquids, & those keeping neither gas. Even then I could see that there ought to be a fourth class keeping form but not volume. And there is a tradition, though admittedly a very speculative one, which says that there is a fourth class of this kind, & the one that includes all organisms or living beings. Also, that just as solids, liquids & gases have a symbolic connexion with, respectively, earth, water & air, so organisms, especially warm-blooded animals, are units of imprisoned fire. [NB 21.365; RT, 208]

One often sees medieval pictures of the Coronation of the Virgin, and some of them have not just the Son but the Father flanking him and a dove over her head. I've said that one of my major themes is the entry of the human fourth into the Trinity, and of course the human fourth would be symbolically female. This lines me up with the Jungians, but I can't help that: some of their intuitions are sound, despite all the tedious preaching they do. [NOTES 52.712; LN, 2:561]

Forms of Communion. The simplest form of communion is sexual communion, represented by the male singer & the hordes of squealing damsels, or by the strip teaser & the bald-headed row. A more sublimated kind is critical communion, which is the ideal of education, symbolized, though seldom represented, by the seminar, a discussion or similar social event focussed on knowledge. Watching a hockey game is not directly a spectator sport, because anyone interested enough in hockey to watch a game knows how the game is played, & through that knowledge can see much *more* of what is going on, with or without a commentator, than the players. Modern theories of education assimilate it to the bridge table, where *learning,* or acquiring information, corresponds to waiting with bowed head while the hands are being dealt, so that you can pick up your information and start playing. Similarly with the newscast. Newspapers are, or should be, addressed to those who have already heard the newscast, & are prepared for a more participatory role.
[NB 11F.110; RT, 95]

Fraud. Creation includes fraud: it has to if the original model was better than what we have now: efforts to shuffle off the fraud on the devil don't work. The goddess of Metis is a trickster; so is the divine wisdom.
[NB 10.58]

Freedom. Articulateness is the only freedom, and relates only to the individual. All society can do is to arrange for conditions of this freedom.
[NOTES 54-8.61]

French Music. The French have consistently ignored the great forms, the sonata and the fugue, and have stuck to dainty descriptive pieces not to be taken too seriously. It seems to be an outlet for their crotch-bound paralytically caesured poetry. [D 42.3; DNF, 4]

Freud and Geography. Europe is an ego, the East an id, & the barrier between them, which isolated the West & made it into a Thomist-Cartesian frenzy of consciousness, was Islam. Islam thus occupied the place of the superego: it held possession of the married land where the tomb of the Son was. If the Crusades had achieved their objective, the center of the world would have moved back from the Ego (Rome) to the Self (Jerusalem). [NB 3.147; RT, 60]

Freudian Nits. Some years ago I tried to read Marcuse & Norman Brown. They were Freudians, & both referred to Jung in passing as a "reactionary," therefore useless. People who took that way are nits. Marxists are therefore nits. Nobody is inherently reactionary or revolutionary: it's the use made of him that determines what he is. It doesn't matter what opinions he held: Freud had a lot of reactionary "views" too. The belief in the magical inherence of reaction or what not is a squalid humanized version of the Mark Apocalypse, which is about sheep and goats, but could never have been about people, as nobody is good enough for heaven or bad enough for hell. [NB 12.289; TBN, 202]

Fright. Military officers & policeman are apt to be stupid because they're frightened, and frightened of being frightened, so they fall back on prejudice for security, the more perverse the better. The same thing is true of old men facing death: senility usually takes the form of obsession. [NB 11E.45; RT, 327]

Frustrated Centuries. Paul could explain to Romans that Christianity was the fulfilment of the law, & to Corinthians that it was the fulfilment of love. But he was unable to explain to the Athenians that it was the fulfilment of intelligence also. Hence the New Testament lacks an Epistle to the Athenians, & the growth of Classical thought & imagination as an analogy to Christianity took many frustrated centuries. [NB 11B.66; RT, 357-8]

Function of Art. The function of art is to awaken faith by making us aware of the imaginative world concealed within us. [NB 21.572; RT, 246]

Function of the Critic. I've been reading Loomis and A.E. Waite on the Grail. Loomis often seems to me an erudite ass: he keeps applying standards of coherence and consistency to twelfth-century poets that might apply to Anthony Trollope. Waite seems equally erudite and not an ass. But I imagine Grail scholars would find Loomis useful and Waite expendable, because Waite isn't looking for anything that would interest them. It's quite possible that what Waite is looking for particularly doesn't exist —secret traditions, words of power, an esoteric authority higher than that of the Catholic Church—and yet the *kind* of thing he's looking for is so infinitely more important than Loomis' trivial games of descent from Irish sources where things get buggered up because the poets couldn't distinguish *cors* meaning body from *cors* meaning horn. Things like this show me that I have a real function as a critic, pointing out that what Loomis does has been done and is dead, whereas what Waite does, even when mistaken, has hardly begun and is very much alive. Not that this is new. [NOTES 52.184; LN, 2:460]

Fundamentalism. The "fundamentalist" creed in which I was mainly brought up asserts that it sticks by the Gospel: actually it's founded on the Gnostic heresies. One, there is only one Gospel, for the four existing ones are reconcilable at every point. Two, Jesus, or the Holy Spirit, *wrote* the Gospel, the four evangelists being merely dictaphones. Three, it was written in such a way as to guarantee the complete purity of the text & infallibility of translations. These all being clearly nonsense we are brought back to the question, Why didn't Jesus write, or dictate, or, better still, invent the printing press? The answer has something to do with the inspired tact which keeps my adherence: the Biblical counterpart of the tact that Catholics find in the history of the Church & the Papacy, & which I certainly don't find there. [NB 11F.195; RT, 118-19]

The "fundamentalists" did have one sound instinct: their conception of truth was baloney, but they did see that if the Bible's *primary* aim was truth in the sense of descriptive accuracy, whether historical, scientific or doctrinal, a sacred book, to be accepted as such, would have to be *definitively* accurate in those directions. [NB 21.212; RT, 179]

Funeral Prose. Gorgeous brocaded prose belongs to funerals, partly because you want the impersonality of ritual, & gorgeousness in the proper context is impersonal (purple is both penitential & royal), & partly because it presents death as a high adventure of the soul in which the dignity of man is preserved. [D 49.301; DNF, 173]

Fusion. I think the difference between the animal & human is that animal activity is a sum, & specifically human activity a product, of subject & object. Not all, though; if a building is a product so is a wasp's nest. But everything an animal does can be explained in causal terms, because it's part of its natural impulse to preserve the integration of the subject, & persist in that integration. We can explain a good deal of animal ornament: mating etiquette, the peacock's tail, & so on, as adaptation (plus relationship) to environment & expression of natural needs. The human capacity for *variable* ornament is a leap, like the leap in mathematics from the mathematical world of numbers to the algebraic world of X's & Y's. And the source of that is the ability to fuse subject & object into a product, a compound & not a mixture. Every word, symbol, sign, image, concept, or what have you, is a unit of subject-object fusion, a formal atom or minute particular. [NB 32.11]

Future. There are two areas for which the future is the only metaphor: the predictable and the possible. The former is the basis of the vulgar, non-resonant, "foretelling" aspect of prophecy, & is now emancipated as scientific method. The latter is the apocalyptic hope, hope being a virtue greater than faith, but one relating to the future as faith does to the past. As in Bunyan, we can be faithful only unto death, but hope goes through the Red Sea to the other side. [NB 15.2; RT, 312]

G

Gates of Ivory and Horn. All human creativity drifts upward through the ivory gates from libido to ego, bringing a mixture of vision and violence, love and cruelty. A sense of articulate order comes down through the gate of horn. Creativity is a purgatory fuelled by the "blood-begotten spirits," refined into love & wisdom through words. Without words it's only the Babel of power with its confusion of tongues. [NB 44.603; LN, 1:228]

Gay Science. *My* approach to faith turns it into *gaya scienza*, a joyful wisdom: most of the conventional approaches turn it into a burden of guilt feelings. Critics who distrust me because I don't seem too worried about inconsistencies (Murray Krieger, Bill Wimsatt) can't tune into this notion of faith as a dancing ballet of intuitions, affirmations, counter-affirmations, "doubts" or retreats from dogma, & a pervading sense of "anything may be 'true' or 'false,' but whatever it is, the whole pattern has a design and a movement." [NB 44.649; LN, 1:234]

Generic Difference. Looking at a row of books by Carlos Castaneda, I note that the early ones are labelled "non-fiction" & the later ones "fiction," although there is no generic difference between them. Doubtless an interesting story behind that, but not one to illuminate genre criticism. *Zen & the Art of Motorcycle Maintenance* is a confession-anatomy form also labelled "non-fiction," though the author's preface emphasizes its fictional form. People are stupid. [NB 27.436, LN, 1:79]

Genius. I do feel that genius is a power of the soul and that powers of the soul can be developed by everyone. If to be a son of God is greater than to be a genius, the greater should include the less, not exclude it—there's something more than mere word-jingles there. The fact that under the stimulation of a "great age" or certain period of clarity in art a wider diffusion of genius becomes actual suggests to me that it is always potential. [NB 3.14; RT, 8]

By the standards of conventional scholarship, *The Great Code* was a silly and sloppy book. It was also a work of very great genius. The point is that genius is not enough. A book worthy of God and of Helen [Frye's wife] must do better than that. [NB 44.265; LN, 1:160]

Statement for the Day of My Death. The twentieth century saw an amazing development of scholarship and criticism in the humanities, carried out by people who were more intelligent, better trained, had more languages, had a better sense of proportion, and were infinitely more accurate scholars and competent professional men than I. I had genius. No one else in the field known to me had quite that.
[NOTES 91-28-3; LN, 2:725]

Genuine Critics. The final value-judgement to be made is not on the poem but on the critic. Is he a genuine critic or does he only start on the cultural level of a bazaar letter-writer? In these days of tens of thousands of people engaged in scholarship & criticism, not all can be genuine. And even genuine ones like Leavis can set up wrong conceptions of criticism to mislead others. The genuine critic is traditionally a judge, but illiterate judges make for injustice: if they are not servants of the law they are of little use on a bench. The law in this case can only be scholarship or knowledge of literature: criticism from start to finish is knowledge, not a guide to the love of beauty. [NB 18.99]

Geometrical Metaphors. Geometrical metaphors come mainly from the spatial orientation of the body. Ladders, staircases, chains of being & pyramidal hierarchies of shapes are all "up lifting" thoughts: divers & miners suggest profundity, depth, & the resurrection of gold & pearls from the dead. "On the other hand," we have metaphors of parallelism, balance & dual symmetry. Church, army & feudal system are degree-models; metaphors of discontinuity come into the absolute monarch, Providence, & the Cartesian soul. [NB 18.12]

Ghosts. When I am asked if I "believe in" ghosts, I usually reply that ghosts, from all accounts, appear to be matters of experience rather than belief, & that so far I have had no experience of them. Similarly, the question "did it really happen like that," when applied to, say, the feeding of the 5000, is one that cannot be answered either by a believer's "oh, yes" or by a doubter's "I should imagine not." A better way of putting the question is "If I had been there is this what I should have experienced?" It is only in these terms that belief or doubt arises, & what does rise is nearly all doubt. The doubt is of oneself rather than of the event, which, as just said, shows us the categories of doubt & belief.... If I had been on the hills of Bethlehem in the year one, I do not think I should have heard angels singing because I do not hear them now, & there is no reason to suppose that they have stopped. [NB 11F.5; RT, 73-4]

Gift of Life. Dante and the monstrous moral perversions the priestcraft of his day compelled him to accept. Hell is human life as "mere nature," as Blake says: purgatory is the effort of the spirit to emerge from this. I have now a skin cancer and a hiatus hernia, besides other ailments—very petty compared to what other people have. If I say "thank God," it's only because that seems ordinary politeness; my thanks are really for the gift of life and consciousness, and I'm not fool enough to think my ailments are punishments or trials or that the fact that they're relatively minor has anything to do with my virtues or merits. Diseases are the revenge of nature for getting born: a lifetime of the nervous irritability of my lifestyle was bound to produce these particular diseases. If I recover, my spirit is throwing them off in an effort to continue life on this plane; sooner or later something will separate them for good. Even Lazarus, on the narrative level anyway, would have had to die again. So would all those healed of palsy and the like in the Gospels. *All* healing is casting out the devils of nature. *And* the psyche we acquire from nature.

[NB 44.746; LN, 1:253-4]

Global Village. The "flow of information," which is mostly misinformation, is actually a presentation of myths. And people are increasingly rejecting the prescribed myths & developing their own counter-myths. Take another McLuhan phrase, "global village"—one early satellite broadcast was called "town meeting of the world." The myth behind this phrase assumes that every technological development creates new amity & understanding—that a village is a community of friends. But, of course, a village may be a community of cliques & feuds & backbiting & gossip of a ferocity far worse than any metropolis, like those hideous little towns at the divisional points of railways, where the conductor's wife couldn't compromise her dignity by speaking to the brakeman's wife. So when communicators, with a schoolteacher's bright & glassy smile, say: now we're going to be able to create a dialogue with Paraguay & Tanzania, & won't *that* be nice? the reaction is, very often: we don't want all those people in our living room: we want to get together with the people who speak our language & share our beliefs & prejudices, including, if we're lucky, a minority that we can have the fun of kicking around. Separatism, except when it is a genuine effort to escape from tyranny, is in most respects a mean, squalid & neurotic philosophy, but it is the strongest force yet thrown up by the age of total communication.

[NB 11F.116; RT, 97]

Glumpy Germans. Those glumpy damn Germans, Heidegger and Nietzsche, strike poses that forget a lot of things about Being.... Both of them are examples of the tyranny of Greece over Germany, the paranoid obsession that makes them oppose themselves to especially the British tradition, which adopted the Hebrew culture as its main parent—of course it's revolt against the Lutheran German strain, but it's strange that the Greek obsession has so few adherents in England: Shelley's one of the few. [NOTES 54-5.100; RT, 292]

God. The principle of the master being taken over by his slaves, the contemporary fear of being taken over by our machines & the automatisms of a police state, applies to God himself, or at least to the metaphor of "sovereignty," which is drawn from the worst social systems. Theoretically, God has no need of man: in practice, all gods are fed by human offerings & sacrifices, & starve & die when human imagination is withdrawn from them. If God owns us, he gets taken over by man. [NB 21.536; RT, 239-40]

The conception "God," considered purely as a conception, need not & should not be taken seriously. If "God" doesn't mean a living presence who is not experienced as such, the word means nothing. That's what I feel, even if I haven't had the experience, or rather, haven't become aware of having had it. [NB 21.569; RT, 246]

God must be thought of as the inconceivably transcendent: all thoughts of that psychotic ape homo sapiens being divine have to be dismissed. The sheer bumptiousness of Carl Sagan & others who want to communicate with beings in other worlds amazes me. They should be saying: look, there are several billion Yahoos here robbing, murdering, torturing, exploiting, abusing & enslaving each other: they're stupid, malicious, superstitious and obstinate. Would you like to look at the .0001 per cent of them who are roughly presentable? [NB 44.425; LN, 1:195]

A god who isn't just a concept has to be an incarnate god. There are no gods except incarnate ones. If Attis is a god of the trees, he is the trees. The other kind, I suppose, are, when real, transcendent or Other-gods, teloi of human effort. [NB 10.42]

Thoughts about God: (1) the conception of "God" is qualitatively different from that of "gods," even when one supreme god grows out of them. Hence missionaries, working on the fallacy of the *analogia entis* [analogy of being], often begin by saying "What is *your* word for God?" The word may mean something quite different, as I think perhaps it always does. (2) The miserable futility of constructing a theology which at any moment can go back to square one and say "Is there, or is there not, a God?" That the word has no place in scientific thought is generally acknowledged. Whitehead, even Tillich, give me the impression of saying "Here's this damn word God: what are we to do with it?" In such philosophies the meaning of God gradually pulls away from its Biblical context. In scholasticism it does duty as a kind of linguistic model: a perfect person, St. Thomas' God who hates nothing. (3) I think the real conception "God" must start in typological metaphor: God is the existential reality of the "all one body we" metaphor. After that, one can try to work out his connexion with nature, but if we start with that we just get old Nobodaddy. God "exists," then, only as the will to love and unite: or rather, he's called into existence by that will. [NB 11B.6-8; RT, 350]

The doctrine of the uniformity of God, that he is always good, just, merciful, etc., sounds like devotion to God: actually it's devotion to finite human categories of what man is determined his ideals of God should be. Niels Bohr is said to have advised Einstein to stop telling God what to do: the advice would be relevant to a lot of people besides Einstein. That's why, of course, there's so much about a whimsical, irritable unpredictable, tricky and downright mean God in the Old Testament. [NOTES 53.129; LN, 2:636-7)

Literature is always and everywhere polytheistic. Here are gods, says Heraclitus, lighting a fire; Heidegger, speaking to an audience 2500 years later, says the same thing of the water-jug on his desk. [NOTES 52.643; LN, 2:548]

God as Artist and Critic. The problem of *ethics* becomes more complicated with an open mythology. In a closed one it was assumed that conscience was equipped to tell one the right thing to do. Well, it soon became obvious that conscience itself was motivated by compulsions. So everybody jumped to the conclusion that ambiguity & relativism were the answers. But the thing is that one has to think of God, through the conscience or whatever it is, functioning as a literary artist, seeing a possible ironic pattern, a possible heroic pattern, a possible sentimental-romantic pattern (which he doesn't reject out of hand because he's a genuine critic), and so on. Jesus doesn't promise a Comforter to tell us the one right thing to do: his Spirit thinks the way he does, in parables. [NB 19.325; TBN, 73]

God of Progress. There are, of course, genuine and false gods. The god of progress, who demands that we sacrifice everything for a posterity we know nothing about is a Moloch demanding adult sacrifice for (unborn) children. [NB 50.82; LN, 1:273]

Going Deeply. "Going deeply into" a subject is not necessarily to go into it profoundly. Neither is its opposite necessarily being superficial. If one's aim is comprehensiveness, one has to avoid "going deeply into" a subject to keep one's sense of proportion and perspective about the other subjects. If you're building a fence, you don't batter one post into the ground so far that it gets out of alignment with the other posts. [NB 23.79; RT, 378-9]

Golden Bough. It's possible that if you could take a golden bough with you all the way in the original plunge to sleep, Alice's fall down the well, you would never need to sleep again. The Tibetan Bardo has something of this idea of an initial plunge & then a gradual rise back to the same old grind. [D 49.77; DNF, 80]

Gospels. I find the Gospels most unpleasant reading for the most part. The mysterious parables with their lurking & menacing threats, the emphasis placed by Christ on himself & his uniqueness & on a "me or else" attitude, the displaying of miracles as irrefutable stunts, & the pervading sense of delusion about the end of the world—those are things for intellectual ingenuity to explain away, & the fact that they're there recurrently comes to me out of the delicate tissue of rationalization. The Christian Church with all its manias had started to form when the Gospels were written, & one can see it at work smoothing things away & making it possible for Christianity to be kidnapped by a deformed & neurotic society. I wonder how long & how far one can dodge or resist the suggestion that the editorial shaping of Scripture is a fundamentally dishonest process. [D 50.143; DNF, 270]

Grace. I want the grace of Castiglione as well as the grace of Luther, a graceful as well as a gracious God, and I want all men & women to enter the Abbey of Thélème where instead of poverty, chastity and obedience they will find richness, love and *fay ce que vouldras* [do what you will]; for what the Bodhisattva wills to do is good…. I don't know what free & prevenient are supposed to mean; but surely the fact that so few develop spiritual power in life is a natural & not a supernatural fact. The rarity of saints represents, like the rarity of all forms of human greatness, the contraceptive & abortive apparatus of that whorish madam Nature operating on a plane where it has no business to be. The wind bloweth where it listeth because it's wind, & doesn't know any better. The utter rejection of natural religion, then, entails the rejection of the notion, involved in most conceptions of predestination & election & the like, that God wills a selection from humanity. The implications of this go a long way: it seems at present to reverse Barth's doctrine that to reject natural religion is to reject the *analogia entis* [analogy of being]. [NB 3.34-5; RT, 17]

As a student said: sacrament is the occasion but not the cause of grace. If it were the cause, it would be a magical system, not religious at all. [NB 21.515; RT, 236]

Grades. Part One (1-4): Approaching; Part Two (5-6): Surveying. Part Three (7-10): Examining. Part Four (11-14): Considering. If I can bring it off, someday there will be students given those four grades. [NB 21.343; RT, 204]

Grammar. Nobody can say "I am a wise and good man" without suggesting that he clearly is not: compare Jesus' dislike of being called "good." The reason is...grammatical: wisdom and goodness simply won't fit any statement beginning with "I am," because they're not qualities of an ego. Similarly of course with Milton's God. Hence Buber's "I-Thou" dialogue needs revision: in those areas you can't tell where I stops and Thou begins. Of course anybody can talk to himself: the genuine form of such dialogue is apocalyptic, one that cuts off the ego entirely. As I said (but didn't say in *The Great Code*), everybody has a lost soul, and should make sure that it gets good and lost. But the lost soul is perhaps the only one we have, the *psychikos* body, unless it's the material for the forming of the spirit, as the phrase "lost soul," meaning that there's nothing left to form spirit with, seems to imply. [NOTES 52.50; LN, 2:429]

Great Books. What is the literary importance of the monumental literary object: the leather-bound sets of the great classics, the plastic counterparts of these contributed by the book-of-the-month clubs, the monumental systematic theology or philosophy in a clergyman's study? Plainly it is in part an object of reassurance: contemporary philosophy, on the other hand, distrusts the book as a literary genre. The latter feeling goes with specialization & with the existential: Austin's bits & pieces, or Wittgenstein's, remind one of *Sartor Resartus*. Similarly with the distrust of the epic & narrative in poetry. [NB 19.56; TBN, 14-15]

The Greatest Book Ever Written (at Oxford). I'm in Oxford now, & from my point of view the greatest book ever written at Oxford is the *Anatomy of Melancholy.* [NB 11F.261; RT, 132]

The Greatest Book in the Bible. Genesis. [NB 50.404; LN, 1:337]

The Greatest British Monarch. King Arthur. [NB 52.927; LN, 2:598]

The Greatest Creative Mind of Modern Times. Shakespeare. [NB 8.29]

The Greatest Critic of His Time (potentially). If Hopkins could only have got rid of his silly moral anxieties, his perpetually calling Goethe a rascal and Whitman a scoundrel and the like, he'd have been the greatest critic of his time. [NOTES 54-13.26]

The Greatest Eros Poet (English). The greatest Eros poet in English is probably Marvell. [NB 11F.283; RT, 136]

The Greatest Eros Poets (Non-English). Dante & Plato are the world's greatest Eros poets. [NBS 45.109, 6.4]

The Greatest Example of Linearity. The response of medieval Christianity to the Bible was typically a linear, step by step response, the sacramental disciplinary *habitus* of which the greatest illustration is the interlocking march of Dante's *terza rima* from one end of the chain of being to the other. [NB 21.538; RT, 240]

The Greatest Fiction Writer of the Century (potentially). God, I wish D. H. Lawrence had some sense of real satire: if he had he'd have been by long odds the greatest fiction writer of the century.
[NB 50.332; LN, 1:322]

The Greatest Form of Prose. The Utopia. [NB 50.746; LN, 1:404]

The Greatest Form-Shaper. Dante is an analogical visionary & stands opposite the Scripture, the "paradox" involved being that the greatest of form-shapers turns out to be the supreme analogist or reverser of the Word (Logos). [NB 7.2]

The Greatest Historical Novel. *War and Peace.* [NB 50.761; LN, 1:407]

The Greatest Imaginations. Defeated nations have the greatest imaginations. [NB 21.244; RT, 185]

The Greatest Impersonator in History. There are three kinds of geniuses: imposers, imposters, & impersonators, & I may be the greatest impersonator in history. [NB 34.25]

The Greatest Literary Genius after Blake. The greatest literary genius this side of Blake is Edgar Allan Poe. [NB 44.290; LN, 1: 165]

The Greatest Masterpiece of Experimental Prose in English Fiction. *Tristram Shandy.* [LS, 63]

The Greatest Moral Virtue. Jesus speaks of hypocrisy, which may be a vice in the gospel context but is the one absolutely essential cementing force that holds society together. Morally, it is the greatest of all virtues. [NB 50.69; LN, 1:270]

The Greatest Number of Demonic Images. The book with the greatest number of demonic images in it I ever read (the *Inferno* of course doesn't count) was *Melmoth the Wanderer.* [NB 91-36-11H.21]

The Greatest Occasional Writers. The occasional writing, of which the supreme example is the epistles of Paul, & the greatest English example probably Burke, needs more development. [NB 33.48]

The Greatest Play of Shaw. *Saint Joan.* [LS, 180]

The Greatest Poet for Shakespeare. Ovid [NB 24.171; TBN, 315]

The Greatest Protestant Poet of the Pathos. Bach [NB 5.22]

The Greatest Shakespearean Comedy. *The Tempest.* [LS, 158]

The Greatest Symposium Writer. Plato. [NB 52.667; LN, 2:552]

The Greatest Thanatos Poem. The *Iliad.* [NB 14.1]

The Greatest Titanic Spirit in Literature. Hamlet himself is the greatest example in literature of a titanic spirit thrashing around in the prison of what he is. [NB 27.60; LN, 1:13]

The Greatest of Vices. Pride is the greatest of vices partly because it is the most futile of vices: man has nothing to be proud of. [LS, 87]

Greatness. In reading Goethe, or reading about him, I have often been disconcerted by a certain vulgarity and tawdriness in his mind, his ideas, even his personal life. I can't help wondering whether this isn't simply because he was a "great man." The same thing is much more obviously true of Victor Hugo. Some renunciation of "greatness" seems essential to the highest intensity, that intensity being the revelation or kerygma which is what literature points to. "Greatness" is linked to the heroic, of course: these two fit Carlyle's "Hero as Poet" category, but Shakespeare doesn't, nor does Nietzsche, whose real "greatness" is in his renunciation of greatness…. The hero as poet, like all other heroes, is a tragic figure working out the dialectic of the divine and the human. The tragic unites the heroic with the ironic: the ironic residue, so to speak, is the *poète maudit*. The ability to write very well very easily may lead to Kierkegaard's disease: the esthetic barrier against the kerygmatic. Shakespeare was saved (perhaps) by the fact that he couldn't be a great man or public figure, yet even he wrote the *Merry Wives of Windsor,* which, no matter how much can be found in it (I found most of it) is basically crap. Dante & Milton are closer to being genuine (whatever that means) hero-poets, but of course they stuck to the kerygmatic source. [NB 50.425, 428; LN, 1:341-2]

One of the chief difficulties in the interpretation of any art is that the eye sees more than the heart knows, & what the artist sees as an artist is always more comprehensive than what he believes as a "man." The whole romantic conception of genius is balls to start with: there is no such thing as a great man; it's only that some men can do jobs well that we think important, & greatness always relates to the job & never to the man. Again, genius is a knack & nothing more: everyone agrees to call Beethoven a genius, but no one who had studied his life carefully would maintain that he was an unusually good man or wise man or even intelligent man: he was only a man with a knack of writing music, & equipped with the distortion of character that such hypertrophy brings. Well, we are always being tempted to interpret the great artist in terms of the ordinary man he also was. [NB 8.41]

The "Great Way." I don't think I'll read much more about the Great Way for a while. I don't like the sort of thing it does to me: it rouses the priggish child in me & makes me keep saying "Am I like that?" "Should I be doing this?" even when it's an exhortation to forget the I altogether. I think I'll look up the Zen Buddhist, who decided that the best way to follow Buddha was to tell him to go to hell. [NB 3.59; RT, 26]

Group Monologue. The discussion of controversial issues is group monologue. Like a Chekhov play, everybody talks to himself & the beams in the roof, and nobody listens. Nobody, performer or viewer, budges an inch. There must be better ways: what I call the critical communion is one. [NB 11F.121; RT, 99]

Guilt. The flood is the logical result of the theory of objective guilt, & a God too stupid to have reached the idea of individualized guilt. (It isn't *just* stupidity, of course: we're back to it in our "society is responsible" clichés). [NB 21.443; RT, 221]

Gum Chewing. Here I am, loathing the radio, yet boring myself to madness by an insistent reiteration of six badly-garbled measures of a Bach Toccata. One of the roots of my madness is there, surely, & from the point of view of mental hygiene I'd be far better off chewing gum with a vacant mind. [NB 34.44]

H

Hallucinatory Forms. I have a notion that a prolonged period of solitude & fasting would produce hallucinations, & that these would be mandalas and such: they would be the essential *forms* in which "outer" perceptions are organized. [NB 18.23]

Handiwork of God. In one quarter of Jerusalem there were signs up everywhere telling "daughters of Jerusalem" that the Torah obliges them to be modest & cover up their lousy female bodies. The Israeli lassies wear thin dresses without slips, so that in the bright sunshine a fair amount of the actual handiwork of God does get advertised in spite of these angels of darkness. Nothing, of course, is morally objectionable except the signs. [NB 23.39; RT, 372]

Harnessing Sentimentality. Jung would classify me as an intuitive thinker, which means that my sensational feeling is undifferentiated. Certain emotional stimuli have a way of making me emotionally seasick: I start weeping to myself when I think of that passage in *Religio Medici* as a teacher's confession of faith. This is sentimentality, not bad, but undeveloped & undifferentiated emotional power that has to be integrated & harnessed. [D 49.47; DNF, 68]

Harvard English Department, 1950. I think it's a good thing that there's no "best" English department & no center of English studies, but I also feel that the Department of English at the University of Toronto is not so damn bad a place to be. I must find out more about this: at times, in my delusions of grandeur, I wonder if the world of English scholars isn't waiting for someone, maybe me, to give them a lead. Here at Harvard the best man is Bush, an excellent man in his own somewhat limited way, then there's Sherburn, obviously a stuffed shirt, Ridley, an Oxford cast-off, and that poor lunatic Magoun to sustain the magnificent linguistic tradition of fifty years ago. Spencer & Matthiessen are dead, Ellmann leaving, & Levin's in Comparative Literature. It doesn't add up to anything very impressive. [D 50.501; DNF, 417]

Haunted House. The demoniacs of the Gospels are in a sense the lucky ones, because they know they are possessed. The demonic core is called the ego by Buddhists and the state of pride by Christians. It's Blake's Selfhood & Jung's false ego center—familiar enough, but the variations on the haunted-house theme of the soul are innumerable. The Book of Wisdom speaks of spectral forms (the plagues in Egypt) and the contrast between the dark house and the one lit up by the candle of the Lord is central in the Gospels. [NB 11E.46; RT, 328]

Haydn. If I had such a thing as a favorite composer, it would be Haydn. I think it's Haydn anyway. I'm going to write something on him someday. More and more I find myself turning to Bach & Haydn, which means more & more away from Mozart. Mozart's a skeptic & Haydn's a Christian. Haydn has everything. He has all that Schubert does. [NB 5.15]

Hebrew Handwriting. Curious Hebrew tendency in my handwriting; when I go over it again to make it plainer, it's almost always the vowels that need attention. [NB 11F.197; RT, 119-20]

Hebrew Tragedy. It is a commonplace of Old Testament scholarship that Samuel is made up mainly of an early source, fresh, lively, attractive, setting forth Saul as a rightful King & a national hero, & a late source, bitterly opposed to Saul, to monarchy, to everything that isn't priestcraft. He's small-minded to the verge of spitefulness, & yet without him we'd never have the unforgettable portrait of Saul as one of the greatest tragic characters of literature, the man who can't do anything right. It's typical of tragedy that circumstances, including the wills of gods, are stupider & more malignant than the characters they overpower. The episode of hewing Agag in pieces, & Samuel's insistence that God will *never* forgive Saul for being decently humane (the only place in that part of the Old Testament where God is totally unforgiving), shows with a greater depth even than Greek tragedy the dilemma of a hero caught in the squalid pseudo-logic of superstition. [NB 21.441; RT, 220-1]

Hegel. If Hegel had written his Phenomenology in *mythos*-language instead of in *logos*-language a lot of my work would be done for me.
[NB 44.410; LN, 1:192]

Hegel, more particularly *The Phenomenology of the Spirit,* appears to be the grand philosopher of *anabasis:* one goes upward through morality, art & revealed religion to pure reason. Perhaps he's the reversed St. Thomas, in the way that Goethe attempted to be, at least, a reversed Dante. His scheme however appears to be based on the assumption that there is no difficulty about, and no limits to, the informing power of words. He wrote before the sciences became so informed by mathematics that no one could really tackle such a Pisgah vision without wondering how far words are a reliable ladder, or at least whether concepts aren't displaced images. I suppose the vision of an upward metamorphosis away from alienation is what caught the Marxists, the existential rather than the poetic Hegelians. [NB 19.395; TBN, 89-90]

Because I'm fascinated by the spiral-staircase shape of Hegel's *Phenomenology,* I'm immediately described as a Hegelian. Partisanship is even more automatically assumed in philosophy than in literature.
[NB 50.361; LN, 1:361]

Hegel thought that Christianity was a mythological anticipation of the real truth of his own philosophy; that makes him at least an honest philosopher, or rather theologian: all theologians attach belief only to their idioms. [NB 50.519; LN, 1:362]

The rush of ideas I get from Hegel's *Phenomenology* is so tremendous I can hardly keep up with it. [NOTES 53.97; LN, 2:631]

Helen Frye. This is not a diary, but Helen is dead. Not of cancer: she died in peace, I was told. Her Alzheimer fantasies were already turning her against me: she seemed to feel I could get her out of hospital if I only wanted to. It's better for her to go now than to go through the final Alzheimer cycles, and it was very like her to slip out of the world so unobtrusively.... But they say there are helpers, and for so gentle and pure a spirit there must be. My hunch is that grief of survivors, being so largely self-pity, distresses, perhaps even impedes, progress to a world that makes more sense. I know that she would forgive me my sins of indolence and selfishness in regard to her, and therefore God will. I hope only that she knows now that I genuinely loved her very dearly, so far as human frailty permits. God bless, protect, and keep her among his own. I hope to see her again; but perhaps that is a weak hope. Faith is the *hypostasis* [substance] of what is hoped for, the *elenchos* [evidence] of the unseen. The one thing truly unseen, the world across death, may, according to my principle, be what enables us to see what is visible.
[NB 44.170; LN, 1:137]

It was, as we say, "the best thing that could have happened," that Helen should have died when she did. Why is it that an event which shows the care and the mercy of God would be the most hideous and insensate of crimes if I had taken her life instead? One of those questions so obvious that we forget even to ask it: it's not as easy to answer as all the automatic answers that come pouring out suggest. Is it another dimension to God as scapegoat, bearing the sins of mankind? I suppose "vengeance is mine" is in a similar category. [NB 44.173; LN, 1:138]

My suggestion that grief for the dead impedes and disturbs them may of course be the grossest and crassest of superstitions: one has to try out such things to see if they have any resonance. But grief emphasizes the pastness of the past, and so works against the mythical imagination. Helen was— that's the beginning of tears and mourning. Helen is. What she is, perhaps, is a central element in the unseen which will clarify my understanding, if such clarification is granted me. My whole and part conception may have a link with this. It is right to pray to God, because God is the unity and totality of all this: but the perspective can reverse into millions of presences —the saints, in short. Helen would smile at the notion of being a saint, but I suspect that sanctity is something created by love, not necessarily some kind of essence.

> *Christ leads us through no darker rooms*
> *Than he went through before.*

[NB 44.175; LN, 1:139]

The judgment & trial legal metaphor of the Bible comes from the impossibility of reshaping the past after death. My indolence all too often made life much duller for Helen than it should have been: when I realized this I tried to "make it up" to her, to reshape time into a more comfortable context for her. Death puts an end to all that: never again can I do anything for her in this world, and the fact rebounds on me as a judgment. With her Alzheimer broken will and my own spinelessness leading us both to deadlock, we were both in a sense marking time. Perhaps every death has something of divorce about it: the kind of inevitable parting of ways that is parodied by suicide. On a more cheerful side, the last "m'amour" fragment of Pound reveals (though Pound may not have known it) the profundity of Blake's "emanation" conception: the objectivity one identifies with, with the woman one loves as its incarnate center. [NB 44.188; LN, 1:142]

How tedious is death. Death and his brother sleep. Sleep for me is a series of dreams in which Helen is alive and we're talking and planning things together. Then I wake up hearing reason say "You will never see her again," without bothering to add "in this life." Reason makes the rest of me puke. Love is strong as death: now that makes sense. I take pills, of course, but a drugged stupor is not sleep. Nor is a spirit with a cremated body dead. Ay, madam, it is common. [NB 44.198; LN, 1:144]

Since Helen's death I've felt my love for her growing increasingly beyond the contingencies of the human situation. I begin to understand more clearly what Beatrice and Laura are all about. If the relation is reciprocal there is nothing to regret beyond the inevitable mechanisms of regret. [NB 44.203; LN, 1:145]

I've said that I have hope about another life, but I don't have faith, in the [Book of] Hebrews sense of a *hypostasis* [substance] of hope. The furthest I can get is a negative faith: I do *not* believe that those ten squalid and humiliating days in the Cairns hospital is the total end of a lovely and lovable human being. (Total for all practical purposes: Butler & others would talk about surviving in the memory of others, but miserable comforters are they all.) But when people talk of recognition scenes & such I can't commit myself. She's in heaven, [my friend] Catherine [Runcie] said: but I don't know where (or what) heaven is, or whether the word "where" applies to it. All I can do is define my hope. I didn't want her to go on living her way through the Alzheimer. I don't want her back with *that:* I'm not sure that I'd even want her back in the frailty of the human condition. The Helen I now love is someone whose human faults & frailties count for *nothing:* the word "forgiveness" I shrink from, because it implies that I'm in a superior position. I think (with Keats) that life may be purgatorial in shape, only I'd call it a vale of spirit (not soul) making. I think of her as someone for whom the full human potential is now able to emerge. Perhaps my love and the affection so many had for her helped to do that for her, being the same kind of thing that the Roman Catholics, with their mania for institutionalizing everything, identify with masses & prayers for the dead. If so, then she's an angel, not to be worshipped, according to the New

121

Testament, but an emancipated fellow-creature. Martyrs don't necessarily believe in rewards for martyrdom, but they behave *as* though they were citizens of a bigger multi-dimensional world than their persecutors. [NB 44.214; LN, 1:148]

It's a good thing this notebook is not for publication, because everyone else would be bored by my recurring to Helen. What do I want? I *don't* want the poor lamb back with her Alzheimer condition, or at all in any world she'd have to be dragged back to. I just miss her, and the miss is a blank in nature. I've accused myself of murdering her, at least to the point of understanding what Eliot was getting at in *Family Reunion.* Like Harry in that play, I have to learn to accept the Furies as Eumenides. But I find all my ideas regrouping around her in a way I can neither understand nor explain. The sermon ["To Come to Light"], for example, was all about her, & so will this book be if I write it. She's now a Court of Love mistress, like the dead Laura or Beatrice. I think the judgment phase may be over for me, at this stage anyway. I helped murder her, but she was, I think, happier with me than she would have been with the other men interested in her. And perhaps I love her now in a way that I couldn't have loved her before she died. I don't want her to come back to me, unless she has her reasons for doing so, but if/when I go to her it will be all right. (It's still hope, not faith. I don't even know if it's right to say "help thou my unbelief," because that could lead to self-hypnotism. The Holy Spirit has to take charge here.) Meanwhile, some of my letters advise thinking about our happy days together: that's like advising a starving man to remember that wonderful meal he had three months back (Job 29). [NB 44.223; LN, 1:150]

I may be heading for the grossest kind of illusion here, but I still wonder about Helen's functioning as a Beatrice: it may be nonsense for a man of 75 to talk about a "new life," but all I want is a new book. With God all things are possible. Beatrice was mainly a creation of Dante's love; my love recreates Helen in the sense of recognizing that if a world exists that she's now in, she's an angel. Her human frailties, as I've said, are now *nothingness:* only what she really was remains. (My own weaknesses & guilt feelings, of course, have greatly increased.) She didn't read my stuff, of course, & didn't need to, but she respected what I did very deeply. So although both of us were physically infertile for many years, perhaps another Word can still be born to us, like Isaac. [NB 44.236; LN, 1:153]

God, if I have a book here, help me & guide me in the writing of it: if what I have is a pretentious fantasy, guide me into something genuine as an offering to you and a memorial to my lost love, who I hope and trust is lost to me only and found by and in you, and by me again later. [NB 44.254; LN, 1:157]

Well, I've entered the Elizabethan age [that is, married Elizabeth Eedy Brown]. Not one atom of my feeling for Helen has changed: neither is my feeling that we're linked somehow in the spiritual world. But my notions of spiritual union may have clarified: there is no spiritual marriage because marriage has to be ego-centered and a mutual possession. In *that* world all books lie open to one another. [NB 44.468; LN, 1:204]

One very widespread myth (ancient Egypt, the Orient) is that the psyche consists of several elements, which break apart at death. Let's follow out the Oriental version for a bit. Everybody has, I've said, a lost soul, and should make sure it gets good & lost. When you bust up, the crucial question, as with multiple personality cases, is: which one is the real you? When Helen died, the real Helen became an angel in heaven. There was also a sulking and egocentric Helen, who would become a *preta* or unhappy ghost, and wander around Cairns for a few hours and then disintegrate. Lycidas was a Christian angel, a pagan genius, an absence, and a drowned corpse. Helen was a pile of ashes, an absence to me, and an angel: perhaps she's a genius to me (or anyone else who loved her and is still living or not living and still confused). [NB 44.747; LN, 1:254]

Hell. The traditional hell is the one where we're in the company of fallen angels but keep projecting as other powers, hence as torturers and executioners. Once you identify with them, and have pushed self-imprisonment to its limit, you discover that the Spirit must have the Word (*alchimie du verbe*). [NB 27.218; LN, 1:39]

If one believes that the soul is *by nature* immortal, with Plato, a doctrine of hell seems logical, because after death an immortal soul would go into the state it had itself created, or helped to create. But if man is mortal by nature, & is made immortal only by the power of the Word of God, then hell implies a supreme maliciousness in Jesus, who raises people from the dead simply to stick them in hell. The dumbest person can see that he should of left them lay [sic]. [NB 24.54; TBN, 284]

Hell and Heaven. Aucassin says he'd rather go to hell because everything that makes life in the least worth living is quite obviously headed for there, whereas nobody wants heaven except a bunch of old crocks who are good for nothing else. The gossamer-light humor doesn't conceal the fact, or alter it rather, that many of the author's contemporaries would have said practically the same thing in grim earnest. [NOTES 52.671; LN, 2:552]

Hesse. I started reading *Steppenwolf*…in the sixties, when every fool in the country was trying to identify with Steppenwolf, and abandoned it after a few pages. I couldn't stand the self-pitying whine of someone totally dependent on middle-class values but trying to develop his self-respect by feeling hostile and superior to them. I was hearing that whine all around me at the time. The next stage, also obvious in Hesse's text, is when you try to raise your opinion of yourself by despising yourself. Like the wrestler: "I got so fuckin' tied up all I could see was a big arse in frunna me, so I takes a bite out of it, and, Christ, it was me own arse." [NB 44.437; LN, 1:198]

Footnote on *Steppenwolf:* what I said about it [before] was utter crap, and I didn't abandon it after a few pages: I read it through, and, as my marginal notes show, with appreciation. Funny how screen memories work:

I resented the student hysteria so much in the sixties, and some of them (at Rochdale, e.g.) made a cult of Hesse. So the remark about the wrestler biting his own arse comes home to roost. Not that I think now that *Steppenwolf* is really a great or profound book, but he's aware of his own irony. [NB 44.442; LN, 1:199]

Hierarchies. Hierarchies create local order, they say: so a universal church would have to get rid of such things. I think hierarchy also goes with postponements: you stay in the place God put you or else. Maybe one day there'll be a cosmic tearing apart into life and death, but that's not your business: you stay where you are. Why were the Gnostics and Neoplatonics so obsessed by this kind of language? I know they had a more mobile notion of ascent and descent; you fell a long way and had to scramble back up again. But all ladders and staircases mean degrees, and rationalize a degree-ridden society. So whenever I say that a cycle is a failed spiral I'm falling in with the same habit of thought, spirals being hierarchical degree structures. Creation in the Bible isn't a gradual or hierarchical process: it begins with turning on a light. New or re-creation must be the same kind of thing. [NOTES 52.148; LN, 2:451]

Historical Interpenetration. Criticism also has a tradition that gives a consensus to all the disagreement, including, not impossibly, all the blather and stock response. Because, as I've said from the beginning, even the bullshit documents a history of taste. The bullshitters, of course, are always chasing donkeys' carrots (or bulls' tails), looking for a final reconciliation of all disagreements in the bosom of Marx, S. Thomas, the Great Mother, or what not. The correct form of this is the "God exists in us and we in him" formula of Blake, Juliana of Norwich, and many others. This was the vision of historical Interpenetration I got from Spengler, without for many years knowing what it was I got. [NOTES 53.151; LN, 2:641]

Historical Process. July 14 / 89. [Frye was born on Bastille Day in 1912.] The same ambivalence about the French Revolution that there was in the days of Fox and Burke. In my student days it was assumed that Bastille Day was the opening day of a new era, and that the terror was not really even regrettable, because it was so essential an incident in an evolving drama. There is a historical process, but tracing it brings me around to that silly man DeWitt's "evolution of the unintended" in another context. Everything dramatic in history is bungled—well, there are some completed ones, like the Spanish Armada, but the rule holds—the historical process is never contained in the drama of history. Historical literature shows this negatively: the greatest historical novel, *War and Peace,* shows how utterly chaotic & haphazard the productions of the historical dramatist Napoleon turned out to be. The historical process is guided by the arts & sciences. [NB 50.761; LN, 1:407-8]

Historical Redemption. History redeems: there's a process within history that isn't at all what Marxism calls the historical process, but relates to the cultural tradition. People denounced or martyred as horrible heretics in the hysteria of their times later become objects of great cultural interest. The twenty-first century will find *The Satanic Verses* a document of great interest to scholars and critics, but the Ayatollah will be of no interest to anybody except as one more nightmare of bigotry that history has produced in such profusion. One would hope that eventually the stupid human race would get the point. God doesn't create post-mortem hells even for people devoting their lives to cruelty and tyranny, but if he did the Ayatollah would certainly be howling in one of them forever. Anyway, this historical redemption of culture is something Schelling meant by theogony. [NOTES 53.162; LN, 2:644]

History. History becomes organic when two or three are gathered together in the name of a creative act; for *history* to occur there must be the two or three right people. Two or three (four as it happens) in the Fabian Society in the 1880's changed the whole course of British history to an extent we hardly yet guess at; two or three in Dublin in 1890's changed the whole course of English literature. And within the individual one of the great archetypal forms of the character may be realized when two or three events come together, as a lonely bachelor listening to Ravel's *Bolero* on the radio & lying on a bed jerking off with a commercial magazine on one side of him & Henry James' *Turn of the Screw* on the other may suddenly obtain a vision of the modern world, its autoerotic stupor leading to the sterile orgasms of war & financial crisis, its technique of holding attention by a maddening repetition of a theme in advertising & propaganda, its cult of violence without thrill & terror without romance, its sick misery & accusing conscience howled down in a frenzy of auto-intoxication, its sense of being helpless in the grip of an external evil power that revisits and revisits until the dispossessed heart is stopped. Such visions are ordinarily accidental & depend on an accidental sensibility, hence they survive as memories rather than as fertilizing seeds. [NB 3.74; RT, 30-1]

I question whether it is possible to write diachronic history—that is, apart from things like Pepys' *Diary*. To write about history you must stand outside it, in a synchronic ambience. That means that all history has to have some mythical underpropping, "decline and fall" or whatever.
[NB 27.205; LN, 1:37]

Why do people call *me* "anti-historical"? I talk about *myth*, and it's myth that's anti-historical. It's the counter-historical principle, just as metaphor is the counter-logical principle. History doesn't repeat itself: history repeats myth. (It's not simple repetition, though: it's not a *da capo* aria but a theme with variations.) As I've often said, you never get logic in literature: what you get is what Susanne Langer would call virtual logic, a rhetorical illusion of logic. Similarly you never get history in literature: you get virtual history, history assimilated to myth.
[NB 44.285; LN, 1:164]

A Hole for Allah. Rug-weavers in Islamic countries are said to leave some flaw or loose thread in their design: being formal designs, I suppose they could achieve "perfection," which would be a closed pattern of magic, a defying of God. You have to leave a hole for Allah to look through & see what's going on. Similarly, holistic views of perfected art are an opaque & resisting surface of ego: think of all that tedious waste of time in which Henry James revised his novels, refusing to allow them their own lives. Well, refusing to allow *himself* a life: didn't he develop and change styles like everyone else? So he turned a row of novels into a logocentric canon. [NB 50.539; LN, 1:366]

Holism. The interchange of whole and part I've mentioned is an extension of what is called in criticism the hermeneutic circle. How do we understand the wholeness of a work of art? By studying the parts. But how do we understand the significance of the parts? By studying the whole. There is a vogue now for deprecating holism, but it is an indispensable metaphor: if we want education we also want a "university," despite the miscellany of activities; if we look at the stars, we want to feel that we live in a "universe," despite the discouraging number of galaxies. Apart from that, "we are all members of one body" is the extension of holism from literature into life. There can be no sense of exhilaration, no expansion of the spirit, without wholeness. [NB 44.547; LN, 1:207-8]

Holomyth. I started *Anatomy of Criticism* with a hunch that the contrast between centripetal and centrifugal meaning would take me all the way. The latter is often called "referential" meaning. I soon found that there were two stages of the referential: the first was the context of the individual work of art; the second was the expansion into conventional or dictionary meaning. What I then started to look for was not a monomyth but a holomyth, a map of the verbal imagination that would provide a context for individual works. I think the Bible comes closer to indicating what such a holomyth would be like than any other work in our culture.
[NOTES 52.620; LN, 2:544]

Holy Days. Curious how much holidaying consists of running away from holy days. [NB 44.675; LN 1:239]

Honesty. At all costs one should keep out of moral rat-traps. I was recently thinking how clear was Jesus' instruction not to swear, what a miserable dodge the 39th (I think: the one on oaths anyway) Article was, & then I wondered whether I conscientiously take an oath in court. I shall not soon forget the sense of relief I felt when I suddenly refused to have anything more to do with this dilemma or any others of its kind. Again, a certain amount of hypocrisy, of pretending or giving the impression you've read something when you haven't, is inevitable. The self-directed life says: admitting that you shouldn't mislead students or kid yourself, your primary duty is to plug the gaps in your reading as soon as possible & in the meantime avoid distracting your students' attention from their own ignorance to yours. The superego says: your primary duty is to be absolutely honest with yourself & them—a murderous piece of nonsense. Oh well, maybe I'd have sacrificed to idols in Rome—certainly I'd have lapped up the meat offered to them fast enough. [NB 3.23; RT, 11-12]

In Arnold a church is judged primarily by the quality of its worldliness. In the great variety of "denominations" today, there's of course no question but what they all have to be tolerated. To view them all with equal respect would be nonsense: some of them are bloody stupid, & their adherents can only be classified as either dupes or dopes. The most normal standard to take is an educational one. Every religion is a sort of golfer's handicap: the question is, how much intellectual honesty can one attain in spite of it? My own religious attitude is based on a negative answer to the question: is it possible to attain greater intellectual honesty without any religious handicap? Every religion is damn silly in some respect or other, being a product as well as a discovery of original sin. But no attitude could be completely sensible unless some form of religious intuition could come true. [NB 18.110]

Hope. I don't believe affirmations, either my own of other people's. The motto I've chosen for the book (*quique amavit cras amet*) [and those who have loved now love the more] represents a hope but not a faith: I can't pin down my faith so precisely. What I believe are the verbal formulas I work out that seem to make sense on their own, & seem to me something more objective than merely getting something said the way I want it said. I hope (but again it's not faith) that this is the way the Holy Spirit works in me as a writer. [NB 44.200; LN, 1:145]

Hopkins. I've been reading Hopkins & wondering about the kind of morality the literary critic tends to develop about creativity. He tends to assume that it has priority over everything, & that if a poet has genuine talent, it's a sin not to arrange his life so that he produces the maximum amount of poetry. Hopkins' view of poetry as something that one gives up for Lent seems perverted. The creative view modulates into a view of the healthiness of the release of inhibitions. Hopkins stands by a discipline, or psychological class structure, in the soul, which sublimates and represses. One becomes compulsive & hysterical only when one loses, when discipline, through weakness, becomes anarchy. But the release of inhibitions is *always* compulsive & hysterical, because the emotions have nowhere to go when released. They're like caged birds who, let out of the cage, are not free but merely homeless. [NB 11F.75; RT, 86]

Horror of Animals. I don't know why I have such a horror of animals. A recurrent nightmare is badly hurting an animal and then stomping it furiously into a battered wreck in a paroxysm of cowardly mercy. And that is to some extent what I'm like. Any intimate contact with any animal I dislike, & their convulsive movements give me panic. If I go to hell, Satan will probably give me a wet bird to hold. For one thing, they're afraid, & fear is something I'm an abnormal conductor of. There's a pigeon sitting outside my window now giving me pigeon-flesh. [D 42.31; DNF, 14]

Huckleberry Finn. People get the end of *Huckleberry Finn* wrong: they think it's a Katzenjammer Kids comic strip with a dishonestly happy ending. Tom Sawyer is portrayed all through this book as a Quixote figure driven out of his mind by silly books. But if he were only that he'd be a pathetic figure, and he's not: he's a calculating person, intercepting his aunt's letters with a psychotic's casualness and knowing all the time that Jim was legally free. He wanted the adventure of it, he says, but Jim takes all the risks; he doesn't really, even if he does get shot in the leg. In short, he's exploiting Jim like any other slave owner, but on a level of cruelty so refined that Jim (and Huck, who's also being exploited) can't understand what's going on. I read somewhere that Mark Twain planned a story in which Tom sells Huck into slavery, which shows, if true, that he quite realized what an utter creep Tom Sawyer was. [NB 50.515; LN, 1:361]

Human Aggressiveness. I keep having a vision of a guide or preacher or some professional haranguer standing in front of a war cemetery in Flanders with a million crosses behind him and explaining how human aggressiveness has such essential survival value.
[NOTES 54-1.64; LN, 2:678]

Human Consciousness. Is the world beautiful because it is beautiful or because we've been conditioned to see it that way? That's an either-or question, and consequently is wrong in its assumptions. The human consciousness has three forms of adaptation to the environment for survival value available to it. One of these is the will-adaptation, exploiting nature and using consciousness as an instrument of power. It's produced the technological world, and remains essential even though it's nearly buggered us —may do yet. The second is the adaptation of the intellect, seeing the objective world as a field of study and comprehension. The third is the emotional adaptation that produces the imaginative or created world.
[NOTES 53.14; LN, 2:615]

The Human Form Divine. I can take no religion seriously, for reasons I don't need to go into here, that doesn't radiate from a God-Man, & so Christ & Buddha seem to me the only possible starting points for a religious experience I don't feel I can see over the top of. Hinduism has the complete theory of this in Krishna, and perhaps Judaism in the Messiah, but I'm not satisfied that even Hinduism is really possessed by the God-Man they understand the nature of so clearly. Now in Christianity & Buddhism I reject everything involved with the legal analogy, the established church, & so cling to Protestantism in the former & Zen in the latter. I'm just beginning to wonder if Protestantism & Zen—not as churches but as approaches to God-Man—aren't the same thing, possessed by the same Saviour. [NB 3.110; RT, 46]

The individual is part of the body of all Man, & if you want to call that God I don't see where you contradict any religion that accepts an *incarnate* God. [NB 3.152; RT, 61]

Every Christian feels the enormous paradox of trying to hold to the identification of the Christ who is the divine element of every man with the historical Jesus who was a specific man, & looked like this & not like that. That's I suppose why the Gospels keep Jesus within a discontinuous mythical framework, avoiding everything that the Sunday schools do. [NB 21.69; RT, 152]

When God defines himself to Moses as "I am," surely one implication is that he's also the I am of Moses, though still capable of dialogue with Moses. Prayer is this kind of dialogue, & so is really…an attempt at self-knowledge that doesn't come through introspection. I suppose Buber's point is that if the possibility of this dialogue vanishes, the human being becomes *merely*, or all-too, human. Man's something to be surpassed, by something inside him which is also him. Or he. [NB 21.214; RT, 179]

God made man. God is made man. God will be man. Past, present, future. God's will is to be man. [NB 21.344; RT, 205]

I think I don't believe in the two natures of Christ: I think what he represents is the identity of God and Man, in which the part of man that isn't God, symbolized by Judas, goes to his own place. This is straight Blake,

& so isn't new, but the context may be, & anyway the obvious always comes last in my muddled head. But of course Jesus, the second Adam, follows the withershins rhythm of human life. In Blake the Holy Spirit represents the identity of God & Man that man starts with, the imagination or Poetic Genius in him, & which works against the Selfhood or death-principle. [NB 12.544; TBN, 262]

In popular Christianity, there are a lot of complaints about the amount of suffering a good God permits & about the fact that prayer is a most unreliable method of getting something for nothing. In other words, it is hard to give up the infantile projections of an all-powerful Father floating free in objective space, & hard too to grasp the conception of an incarnate God, working under human conditions & through human instruments. Similarly, in reading Euripides, we take the metaphors of objective beings quarrelling with each other & keeping an absent-minded but suspicious watch over their tributes, too seriously. We forget that those creatures are primarily states of the human mind. [NB 13.97]

Human Heritage. I'm still in search of a genuinely "charitable" vision of spirit that can unite everybody. My "arrest of the mind," the intensifying of consciousness that grows out of the imaginative response, is, I recognize, a bourgeois-liberal conception: a Marxist could say: your poets may talk about primary concerns, but what do they do about forming a social order that actually does something about them? I know the standard answers, the first being that the moment you start doing so you get involved in ideological postponements & excuses, & the end disappears in a labyrinth of means. However, that's a negative and, worse, a merely counter-ideological answer. There's still the gap between belief & rejection of the entity of God, identified with everything "spiritual" by Christianity. To me, God means the unlimited nature of the human heritage. [NB 50, 165; LN, 1:288]

Humanism. Humanism is a cult of an élite, Toynbee's creative minority, neither dominant (Urizen) nor conspiratorial (Orc), but informing (Plato's symposium). Its genera are the *cena* discussion (pure community), the formal epistle (individuals separated but dramatizing a community), and the rhetorical defence (individual before the general public). Its educational program is the encyclopaedic one of concern, & its central conception is the social effectiveness of words. [NB 11F.211; RT, 122-3]

Humanity of Christ. In Adam all die because Adam was all humanity: every man in his situation would have seized the apple. In Christ's death all are condemned because every man would have done what Pilate & Caiaphas did. *All* the disciples forsook him & fled; the winepress was trodden *alone;* Peter, the cornerstone of the Church, denied him. It is this *separation* of all human nature from the humanity of Christ that gives the written record autonomy & destroys the "monologue with itself" claim of the Church. I'm not clear just how, but the humanity of Christ is set over against human social structures, and attachments & commitments to the latter must be tentative. [D 49.66; DNF, 76]

Humour. For many readers of *Paradise Lost* the contrast between the domestic, highly cultivated atmosphere of Eden and the nudity of the inhabitants seems grotesque, like Manet's picture *Déjeuner sur l'herbe.* But Milton's approach to his subject is thoroughly consistent with his view of the human state, and it is by no means humourless: in fact a careful reader of *Paradise Lost* can easily see that one of the most important things Adam loses in his fall is his sense of humour. Humour, innocence, and nakedness go together, as do solemnity, aggressiveness, and fig leaves.
[LS, 86]

Hymns. The other day at the hymnal conference I said that the basis of the impetus to produce hymns in Christianity was the apocalyptic perspective. I think this is true: it isn't the sense of "another world," but of this world as open-ended, as opening up into the presence of God. Without that perspective, all hymns become either derivative or miserable.
[NB 19.291; TBN, 66]

Hypertrophic Distortion. All men are distorted & crippled by their social function, by the hypertrophy that what they *do* forces on them. All women are too, whether their careers are those of nuns or housewives or tarts. The more socially acceptable the career, the less we notice this, but it's always there. Hence our dream of the complete or workless man, whom our aristocracies try to produce. The versatile man, who can do anything, and the entertainer or actor, who can pretend to be anything, are proximate dreams of the same kind. [NB 19.269; TBN, 61]

Hypocrisy. I used to say that hypocrisy was really a virtue, meaning it as half a joke. But when our worst impulses start clamoring that they're our "real" feelings, we realize how debased reality can be even when it's real. [NB 44.636; LN, 1:232]

Hypocrisy is believing one thing & professing another: it therefore takes considerable analytic power to be a consistent hypocrite. The next stage of degeneration is to make the professed belief symbolic of the real one: the next, the attempt to make the true inner reality of the belief consist in the symbolic form given it by the professed. [NB 4.51]

Hypostasis. The attempt to translate the metaphors of transubstantiation and Trinity into conceptual language got philosophers stuck with that unlucky notion of *hypostasis* or "substance" that they've been trying to wriggle out of ever since. [NB 21.504; RT, 233]

Hysteria. Note the hysteria in Proverbs & Ecclesiasticus: teach the way of wisdom to your son, and beat the shit out of him if he doesn't listen. [NB 11F.183; RT, 116]

There has to be revolt, against the preposterous anxieties and legalism of the communion. I pass a small building labelled Foursquare Gospel or something and think how pleasant it would be to drop in on a group of people engaged in a genuinely communal spiritual enterprise. But of course I know that there'd be nothing inside but hysteria and glazed eyes and are-you-saved-brother and I'd have to run screaming out again. Methodism provided an absurd denatured world of soft drinks and playing cards without suits and walking dances: fortunately something in mother refused to believe all the gunk she'd got from her father, though she thought she believed it, or ought to believe it. [NB 46.50; LN, 2:697]

I

Ice Stilts. Discussion of obscenity…among critics has all the graceful & easy assurance of a man walking over uneven ice on stilts. [NB 33.3]

I Ching. I once consulted the *I Ching*, using toothpicks instead of yarrow stalks, saying I didn't want an answer to the specific problem but general advice about what to do and be. I got, without qualification or "moving lines," the second or K'un hexagram, meaning, I suppose, that I was to be a "feminine" or receptive writer. [NB 27.6; LN, 1:4]

Ideas. An idea presents itself at first as a crystallization of experience, as something created out of the duality of knower & known. Many creators of ideas stick at the miser stage of development, and spend their time playing with them. Or rather, we distinguish here between accumulators of ideas…and those who produce their own but have reverted to the original miserly impulse to play with their own excreta. But the idea is not really an idea as long as it retains the taint of objectivity in relation to its creator: it has to become a power of the soul. [NB 3.11; RT, 7-8]

We speak of fruitful & sterile ideas, & it is perfectly true that ideas beget & reproduce like everything else alive, but it isn't just a linear Orc-reproduction: we want novelty, but we want too a consolidating form, a family appearing as a single Man. And while one shouldn't be a Thel, & should haul our ideas out into Generation & write books & take the bushels off our lights, still what really happens is simply a growth *in* our minds, a turning from a center to a circumference. Hence, really, all ideas are unborn. If there is no death there is no birth either, and of course no life. [NB 3.71; RT, 30]

There can be no such thing as the revelation of a mystery, and everyone knows that perfect simplicity is the only way of expressing complex and original ideas. [NB 3.13; RT, 7]

Identity. The life of Christ is presented discontinuously in the Gospels, but it would take a fairly extreme Docetic to believe that it was actually discontinuous. This is connected with the fact that the only form of A-is-B identity that I can grasp is the child & the man—that is, identity can only be achieved in time by a single life. The identity itself demands discontinuous presentation, but achieving it is the one achievement of continuity. [NB 21.470; RT, 225-6]

I'm not sure what I mean by identity, but one of the things it means is: a state of being where there's nothing to write about. That is, where one *contains* all subjects as potential, instead of being subjected to events. The "and-then" aspect of narrative is the passive, or purely sequential, aspect; the "hence" is the mentally contained aspect; there's a third, or full imaginative containment where it's in the outward shadows of possibility in the state of regained innocence. The *contact* at the point of cognitio—in *Fearful Symmetry* I call it a jumping spark—is the first stage of escaping from the cycle. The cycle is in time, therefore its beginning & end are *never* the same: they're the same only above. [NB 10.28]

One way out of the prison of Narcissus is to reverse the Narcissus operation: in other words the self-recognition of Eliot's *Marina*. This brings one to the uniqueness of the New Testament's Moebius strip: Christ as the true individuality in man, part of the individual whole; Christ as the totality of which we are parts; the Other as the Father and not Nature; otherness as the final discovery of identity. I doubt if any sacred scripture has that except the Bible: such things as the Lankavatara don't teach a doctrine; they teach a technique for breaking up and escaping from doctrines. Beyond that they don't go. [NOTES 52.517; LN, 2:526]

Identity With. I've often said that a man's religion is defined by what he wants to identify himself with. I was speaking in social terms, but what I most *want* to identify myself with is my own second self, the kind of person I wish I could be, desiring this man's art & that man's scope. There are two levels of this. One is the straight reincarnation one—what would I do differently if I could do it over again, the same situation but with the present perspective? This is the bull-in-the-ring-for-the-second-time situation, where the bull could kill any toreador. (Note that this isn't exactly reincarnation, because the shadow of the dial would move back to 1912 again.) Well, I'd have a much happier & fuller life & would be able to avoid some mistakes, but it wouldn't be ideal. For an ideal, I'd want to get a much better deal from nature physically, without losing the mental intensity I've developed partly out of compensation. Yet again the shadow of the dial would have to go back: the social context of such an ideal would still be early twentieth-century Canadian white middle class. One's risen body is still rooted in history & a specific culture. I'd want to be an excellent pianist & composer, but in terms of twentieth-century music. This speculative faculty is of a type that's run through culture from the tenth book of the *Republic* to the Eliot *Quartets*. I note that my ideal or perfected self would *not* be a saint: that I've never been able to grasp as a personal ideal. And I'm not sure that the real key to the fantasy is the rose-garden: the Eliot return to childhood with the might-have-been glimpse of Eden informing it. I do notice a large antithetical or compensatory element: I'd want first rate physical coordination & a strong practical sense, the opposite of what I have, without losing what I have. This is the Yeats mask, & indicates both a strong positivistic & will-to-power streak in my writing.
[NB 24.91-3; TBN, 293]

Ideological Allegory. Why are Marxist & Freudian approaches to criticism so sterile and so quickly exhausted when Marx & Freud themselves are so endlessly suggestive and illuminating? I suppose because the center of gravity remains in Marx or Freud and turns all literature into an allegory of Marxism or Freudianism. (I think something similar is true of feminist criticism, even if it has as yet no comparable third figure.) So I ought to know how silly it would be to turn my book into any sort of Biblical or Christian allegory. [NB 44.473; LN, 1:205]

Ideology. Ideology is original sin, and is not got rid of by any dunk or sprinkle. What is not ideology is manifested by the constancy of the martyr in the disguise of a counter-ideology. That's why his beliefs are not important. (Would I maintain this for IRA terrorists?). [NB 27.294; LN, 1:52]

The worst governments are those with double ideologies, where a political doctrine is backed by a religious one, as in Iran. Israel is better, but I'd hate to live even there. But South Africa's apartheid is buttressed by a remarkably dismal Dutch Reformed creed, and fifty years ago the word "Christian" in the name of a political party meant "Roman Catholic Fascist." [NB 27.500; LN, 1:91]

Ideology and Story. After thirty years, I'm back to page one of the *Anatomy*. My opposition to sociological criticism is based on the principle that mythology is prior to ideology, the set of assumptions being always derived from a prior story. The story *says* nothing, and *you* say nothing: you listen to the story. Criticism often assumes that the ideology goes all the way: that there's no point at which the literary work stops saying things & keeping open the possibility of answer. If it's obviously moving from statement to myth, well, that's because of certain social pressures the writer had to conceal as well as reveal his meaning, had to be oblique instead of direct. Nonsense: obliquity is fundamental: it's the core (psychologically, anyway) of revelation. [NB 27.394; LN, 1:72]

The *Iliad*. I find immense difficulty in reading the *Iliad*, & have to get over it for personal as well as critical reasons. The age of childhood is the age

140

of wrath, of aggressive rebelliousness that takes a conventional form. In my childhood I dreamed of the battles of red & blue toy soldiers, which I watched, directed, & determined victory for the red side. I also had dreams of a vast physical prowess I knew I didn't possess. So my resentment against the immorality of the *Iliad* is based partly on my own resentment at outgrowing my dreams of belligerence, which I didn't really outgrow but was forced to give up. I hate all those gut-cut scenes; I'm a violent Trojan partisan; the appalling creatures they worship & their conceptions of an after-life horrify me; their social hierarchy outrages me; and so on. Give me the *Odyssey* every time, I say. [NB 19.247-8; TBN, 56-7]

The *Iliad* must always have been a shocking poem. Religiously shocking, because of its contemptuous treatment of the gods, as it was to Plato. I suppose it was about the same time that Elijah in Palestine was mocking the priests of Baal with "Perchance he has fallen asleep, or is on a journey," which is precisely what Zeus does in the *Iliad*. Historically (or chivalrically) shocking because…Homer's compassion embraces the victor: most of us can sympathize only with losers, hence poets from Virgil to Shakespeare have ennobled the Trojans and vilified the Greeks. Morally shocking, because of the class-conscious bias—even the courteous Hector is reproached by Polydamas for assuming that only the brass can speak. Ordinary people are just there to get chopped up by heroes: they have no other function. And the insistence that there is no immortality worth anything darkens the poem as though the Styx instead of Oceanus ran around Achilles' shield. [NB 7.258]

Illuminations. In the summer of 1951, in Seattle, I had an illumination about the passing from the oracular into the witty: a few years later, on St. Clair Ave. I had another about the passing from poetry through drama into prose. They were essentially the same illumination, perhaps: the movement from the esoteric to kerygma. Any biography, including [John] Ayre's [*Northrop Frye: A Biography*], would say that I dropped preaching for academic life: that's the opposite of what my spiritual biography would say,

141

that I fled into academia for refuge and have ever since tried to peek out into the congregation and make a preacher of myself. That's why I'm taking this preposterous assignment [lectures for *The Double Vision*] so seriously. [NOTES 53.43; LN, 2:621]

I've spent nearly eighty years trying to articulate intuitions that occupied about five minutes of my entire life. I don't mean intuition in my practical life, or anything connected with it: that kind of intuition is as often wrong as right. With me (I'm not an intuitive type), more often. [NOTES 53.127; LN, 2:636]

This world is usually called "timeless," which is a beggary of language: there ought to be some such word as "timeful" to express a present moment that includes immense vistas of past and future. I myself have spent the greater part of seventy-eight years in writing out the implications of insights that occupied at most only a few seconds of all that time. [NOTES 53.267; LN, 2:663]

Illusion. To call religion an illusion or communal neurosis, as Freud does, says nothing either: we create all our reality out of what begins as illusion, and living under social discipline is itself a neurosis. What Freud said of religion was, in effect, precisely what Karl Kraus said of Freudian therapy; that it is the disease of which it professes to be the cure. [NB 27.208; LN, 1:37]

Imagination. The crystallizing drop of the imagination is what causes the chaos of events to take a symmetrical shape, and symmetry means something taken out of history. This I dreamt, July 14/89 [Frye's birthday]. [NB 50.766; LN, 1:408-9]

Imaginative Arrest. The moment of consciousness is a withdrawal from being, but as that it tends, when persisted in, to project a dead world. The imaginative arrest is rather a revolt against the habit of being, which includes a habit of perception. Shelley is the first to stress the imagination's revolt as what Wordsworth had called a recollection but which Kierkegaard saw, more accurately, to be a repetition. The effect of it is that the familiar world bursts into strangeness, a brave new world which is a picture, hence *ut pictura poesis,* & needs brave new words to describe it. [NB 12.157; TBN, 168]

Immaturity. In the course of being Principal [of Victoria College] I've often thought about the curious affinity between high intelligence and a curious kind of social immaturity. It's the quality that makes the "intellectual" so often socially irresponsible. Partly introversion, partly living in an over-simplified Euclidean universe. This latter gives the immaturity a curious ferocity—Blake was right in associating cruelty and abstraction, the preference of mechanical extensions of the body to the body. It comes out in me in the panic of travel worries: when I change place I want to withdraw completely. Other things too, of course: I'm no exception to my own rule. My students are mostly extroverted, more mature than I socially: I worry about their intellectual immaturity, but admire the same combination in the "practical man." One confusing feature of it is that good taste is so often a social rather than an intellectual maturity. [NB 18.143]

Immortality. What is immortal is not the life we are going to live after death, but the life we have lived. The Resurrection must be *retrospective.* [NB 11F.98; RT, 92]

Impotence. The impotence of the Word in passion corresponds to the impotence of Providence before the order of nature. [NB 11B.32; RT, 354]

Imprinting Small Certainties. Adele Wiseman says, referring to her Winnipeg schooling, "many teachers are teachers because they can't bear to have their small certainties disturbed, and want only to imprint them on the unresisting young." That would apply to others besides teachers: she never had to endure the appalling series of parsons I was dragged off to

143

by mother—or perhaps I'm just being romantic about rabbis. (Mother was deaf—a blissful advantage—but she could see, & what she saw was a symbol of her father.) [NB 44.459; LN, 1:202-3]

Imps. I can understand why devils are usually conceived as a swarm, but to reduce them to definite number (seven traditionally) is a stage in advance, & to make that number one is still another step. I believe in the real (i.e. the mental & present) existence of Poe's perverse imp. Nothing else accounts for my going into a pub by myself or reading a detective story (what on earth have I to do with reading for relaxation?) or any other form of an inconspicuous consumption of time. It's easy enough to catch the imp in operation. I hear a clock tick. If I will not to hear it tick, perversity instantly appears. [NB 3.82; RT, 34]

Incarnation. Incarnation includes creation in the sense of realization or physical embodiment. It includes all imaginary constructs, of angels, the spiritual world, & the like, which can be embodied, in works of art or whatever. Thus *1984* is an incarnation of the doctrine of hell, & "pollution" an incarnation of the construct of original sin. The Old Testament narrative shows a progressive incarnation of myth in history.
[NB 21.458; RT, 223]

The religious displacement begins with the distinction of mechanism & organism. The oldest myths are organic: the world comes into existence through sexual activity and as a total seasonal cycle. This is really a female or mother-centered conception. Then along come Plato & the Hebrew Priest, father-centered, impressed by the "design" or "purpose" in nature, thinking of it as something made by a divine artificer. This creates God in the image of conscious, detached, subjective, aggressive man: it places him up in the sky, the abode of order; it makes the human soul female & submissive. What we do now is not, like Graves, to go back to mamma, but to realize that the conception of incarnation has surpassed the notion of creation, beginning as it did with kenosis. [NB 19.296; TBN, 67-8]

Art repeats incarnation by making the construct concrete. As for science, I'm sure there is a connexion between religion which accepts incarnation & the development of a science founded on the repeatable experiment. [NB 21.462; RT, 224]

Indefensible Theory. Once we have understood the self-imposed limitations of Elizabethan music and realized that its whole spirit is domestic and intimate, that it is Marvell but never Milton, Vermeer but never Tintoretto, Jane Austen but never Tolstoy, we shall accept it for what it is and not indulge in evolutionary reveries. Evolution was a theory of history and literature long before it got mixed up with biology; and ever after it took Darwin's name it remains a sloppy, illiterate and indefensible literary theory. We have dropped it in literature: we no longer say that poetry has "improved," that Dryden found it brick and left it marble, or that Pope or Tennyson or anyone else represents centuries of "development." We know now that poetry never improves; it only alters. But musical criticism, owing to the illiteracy of most musicians, has a way of lagging a century or two behind literary criticism, and while the general outlook of *Lives of the Poets* is dead, that of Johnson's friend and contemporary Dr. Burney is still alive. Hence it is generally accepted that everything in Elizabethan music is a crude and unformed beginning of what later composers progressively improved on. [NB 5.28]

Infantilism. If I see a sign advertising a four-square gospel church, I don't go in, because I know what I'll find: infantilism sustained by hysteria. Infantilism, which is part of what I mean by an intellectual handicap, is, I suppose, the negative side of the preserving of the eternal child that Christ talks about. [NB 19.392; TBN, 89]

Inferno. I hate the *Inferno,* because Dante so obviously believed, not only in a substantial & objective region of torture that never ends, but in all the legal quibbles that entrap divine "love" into sending people there, such as failure to have been baptized. It's too easy to work out the imaginative

aspect of it, the symbolic reasons why Virgil can't be saved & a perfunctory Christian can be. One still remains stupefied by the perversity of the human mind. Dante saw everything in hell except the fact that to create an imaginative hell and then suggest that it's real is an act of intellectual treachery to the God in man lower than that of Judas, who may conceivably have acted from better motives. I can't help feeling that there *is* some development in literature, for all I say to the contrary. George Orwell's *1984* presents a real hell, not just one we happen to be more scared of, & his book is morally an infinitely better book than the *Inferno*. Surely this moral superiority has some relevance to critical standards.
[D 50.41; DNF, 229-30]

Information. The A to B notion of communication survives in the phrase "flow of information." Anybody in a field like mine—literary criticism—knows that most of the information available to him is actually misinformation, & the trick is to get rid of it, not to absorb it. [NB 11F.117; RT, 98]

In Medias Res. Every story begins in the middle, because it is always possible to ask "What happened before?" Hence "once upon a time" means "despite this fact, I'm beginning." [NB 27.29; LN, 1:7]

All stories begin in the middle, because it's impossible to think of a beginning of time. There's this guy, see, and there's this dame, okay? From there there are always two questions: what's going to happen to them, and how did they get there? So even the opening verse of the Bible is a vertical slash down the temporal continuum. [NOTES 52.46; LN, 2:428-9]

Intellect. The sacrifice of the intellect is an abomination to God.
[NB 21.434; RT, 220]

Intellectual Handicap. All religions constitute an intellectual handicap: the *worth* of a religion depends on the intellectual honesty it permits. It's silly to respect all religions: Anglo-Israelitism, for example, is pure shit, and cannot be accepted without destroying one's whole sense of reality. The Mormons, the Christian Scientists, the fundamentalists, increase the handicap to the point of crippling the brain. Some handicap, probably, one must have: to accept a crippling one in any field (e.g. the Shakespeare didn't write Shakespeare boys) is neurotic. [NB 18.133]

Intellectual Mongrel. I love Victoria [College]: I'm a long, rangy, flop-eared intellectual mongrel, and, to curdle the metaphor, I flourish best in a smug and sterile soil. [NB 4.40]

Intensifying Consciousness. The awareness of language may begin with the awareness of ordinary consciousness, but it soon becomes clear that language is a means of intensifying consciousness, lifting us into a new dimension of being altogether…. There are many techniques of attaining this more highly structured awareness: there are the yoga & zazen & Sufi schools of the East, & various Western psychologies of psychosynthesis, individuation, peak experiences, cosmic consciousness, & what not. I have been somewhat puzzled by the extent to which all this activity overlooks the fact that all intensified language becomes metaphorical language, & that literature is the obvious guide to whatever passes beyond language, just as Dante's obvious guide to states of being beyond life in 13th-century Italy was Virgil. [NB 11H.31-32; LN, 2:717]

Intercourse. Tolstoy says there should be no intercourse after conception, that being the kind of thing Tolstoy did say in his dotage. But I wonder. Helen's [Frye's wife's] doctor, who is enough of an old woman to have a pleasant mixture of superstition & ancestral wisdom mixed in again with her medical knowledge, says the same thing, & remarks in connection with that that the loveliest babies are often those borne by unmarried mothers whose onlie begetters have cleared out after their discharge. That rings a bell in folklore, & seems to point toward the union of a virgin with a spirit of life that produced a perfect man. One can't imagine the Holy Spirit hanging around, so to speak. [NB 3.68; RT, 29]

Interpenetration. The First Spirit is the spirit of unification & therefore to some degree of exclusion; the Second Spirit is the spirit of interpenetration, in whom all the spectres of the dead are awake. [NB 11E.4; RT, 319] .

That God may be all in one: that's the text for interpenetration. I notice that Jung misquotes it as *one* in all, because he thinks of unity and reconciliation as the end. [NB 11E.99; RT, 339]

The conception of interpenetration is that of natural inclusion. We are in God; God is in us. Therefore there are two worlds, as at the end of *Paradiso,* one the other turned inside out. My consciousness of things put those things inside me, but whatever is conscious has me inside them. I fell over this years ago in dealing with art & nature: in art nature is turned inside out. But I didn't see it as interpenetration, or an aspect of it. Perhaps this mutuality of awareness *is* identity. My memory holds my past selves in me; my growth, or body of fate, or what the hell, holds my future selves. [NB 12.503; TBN, 253]

Love is interpenetration, but it has to extend beyond the sexual interpenetrating of intercourse. Every act of hostility is penetration with a threat, with a desire to dominate or acquire for oneself. Love means entering into and identifying with other people and things without threats or domination, in fact without retaining an ego-self. [NB 44.501; LN, 1:209-10]

The "subject" swallows everything objective to it: hence the pan-historical critics of today, the Hegelian pan-philosophical absolute knowledge, the pan-literary universe which only three people understand: Blake, Mallarmé, and myself. The *final* answer, naturally, is interpenetration.
[NB 44.717; LN, 1:247]

The end of the journey is interpenetration, or perhaps the hologram model. It's the recognition scene of proclaiming word & responding spirit.
[NB 50.693; LN, 1:395]

works must have some roots in the world external to the inventor. So we invent our text, in a mood of Leibnitzian optimism that the words being used in it are the best of all possible words. [NOTES 52.391; LN, 2:501-2]

I.Q. Tests. I've been wondering if the I.Q. test measures anything more than the degree of mental vigor, a sort of brain temperature. Surely health & energy have everything to do with the speed of response, which seems to count for a great deal in such tests. I feel that my reflexes have slowed down a good deal. Whack me on the knee & look for a kick in the balls anytime within the next three days. I have no doubt that my I.Q. would be down 20 points from what it was at 19. But I'm so much wiser than I was then: slow & controlled response is wisdom: lightning automatic flashbacks are evidence of gigantic I.Q. & very limited intelligence, if intelligence means insight. Intensity of vision delays the automatic apparatus of response: the pure contemplative can't respond at all. So I.Q. tests, a cult of youth & a respect for the kind of "intelligence" that really just means a conditioned reflex & is produced by motor energy, go together in a mechanical civilization. [NB 3.107; RT, 45]

Irony. All literature is literally ironic, which is why humor is so close to the hypothetical. If you don't mean what you say, you're either joking or poetizing. [NB 18.22]

Irritability. A weak body & a hypertrophied development of it (I am an intellectual chiefly because I was born cerebrotonic) led me through an unhappy adolescence into a state of chronic irritability, a neurotic fear of being bullied by vulgarity, and a deeply-rooted "sissy" complex. The result is a constant sense of spinsterish outrage fostered by panic & laziness, & fended off only by a relatively comfortable life. Here again is the perverse imp: I dislike a noisy radio not because of it but because of a personal resentment directed at the vulgarity of the person operating it. When I am told the irritating things that most people dwell with most of the time, excessive irritation is inspired in me because the creator of that irritation blends into a resentful memory of the bully I ran away from & wish to hell I'd beaten up. (I never scored a victory, as many children do, & in fact never rose to an occasion: cowardice was bred in me, as it is regularly, by premature, over-active & perverse imagination.) There's no point in detailing confessions, I find: self-knowledge can do without that; but a habit of suppressing irritability & of resisting irritating stimuli (brooding over a slight or a bad review) is the first stage of Yama, & will give what I think is a natural cheerfulness a chance to emerge. A strict mental censorship over sterile & harmful fantasies has to be established. [NB 3.80; RT, 33]

I have just had an itchy and uncomfortable eczema skin eruption all over me. I suspect a partly "psychosomatic" factor: I'm the most irritable and irascible of men; I'm aware of the folly of expressing this in front of innocent people, so the irritability comes out in this form. To compare small things with great: were Job's boils his body's protest against his patience? If so, something in him agreed with his wife. [NB 50.753; LN, 1:405-6]

Isms. Isms, feminism & Marxism most obviously, are plate armor for the second-rate: people with nothing to say can always spout their line. But the established religions aren't much different, except that a cooling of pressure in an ideology gives the more flexible individual more of a chance to emerge. The whole business of the individual emerging from a solid mass social conditioning needs to be handled very carefully. The whole principle of ideology is that everybody spouts some kind of line: it's the personal examination of it that matters. [NB 50.194; LN, 1:294]

J

Jealousy. In a recent experience of mine all the screaming demons of accusation and insecurity came to me, in a form I described as "jealousy." It would be very pleasant to say that I faced them and fought them down, in the metaphor of the heroic dragon-killer. But of course I didn't face them; they faced me. Now I think I understand a little more clearly something that's always puzzled me in Dante. Three beasts appear to him: they face him, but he doesn't dare face them; he turns away, and the whole inferno-purgatorio-paradiso journey is the result. You only gain your vision by running away. [NOTES 54-3.5]

Jehovah. The Jehovah of the Old Testament...is not a theologian's God; he an intensely humanized figure as violent and unpredictable as King Lear. He does silly and vicious things; as a human being we wouldn't let him into our front parlors.
[NOTES 54-1.22; LN, 2:668-9]

Jesus. Jesus was without crime, though considered the worst of criminals by society. But he can't have been sinless: that's a sterile conception. You can't live in the devil's world without making friends with the mammon of unrighteousness. Even in Job the presence of Satan in God's court is tolerable. If Jesus were sinless he'd have been discarnate. The Crucifixion convicts the entire world of sin, but Christ takes responsibility for the sin. The Virgin Mary can't have been sinless in that context either: that, I gather, is why St. Thomas Aquinas denied the Immaculate Conception.
[NB 27.509; LN, 1:93-4]

Bring in the point about Jesus as a refined homosexual celibate who had a beloved disciple, whose last words to a woman were "don't touch me," and who was so hung up on sexual intercourse & Oedipal trauma that he insisted that his mother was a virgin & his father not his real father.
[NB 21.191; RT, 174]

The Gospels present a mythological Jesus, and out of that an indefinite number of historical Jesuses can be extracted. The notion that "the" historical Jesus would emerge if we only juggled and jiggled the Gospels in just the right way, is an obsession and an illusion. Granted that the Christ-figure was dropped into time as an egg is dropped into boiling water, it remains separate from the water. One book says that the wedding of Cana was the wedding of Jesus & Mary Magdalene, & that Jesus ducked the crucifixion and escaped to Marseilles, where he begot the Merovingian kings—the Bald, the Simple, the Fool and the Fat. I don't find it convincing, but I suspect that if we found "the" historical Jesus it would be so shattering an anticlimax that very little Christianity would survive it. Only a Noah-family of people willing to accept the Jesus we now have, the mythological one.
[NB 44.301; LN, 1:167-8]

The Logos-over-Mythos superstition makes us think that Jesus was a teacher with an original doctrine, who in the Synoptics illustrated that doctrine with parables. The reverse is true: Jesus was original only as a story-teller, & his doctrines are commentaries on the Old Testament, echoing those of contemporary rabbis. (He was also, of course, original as a healer, but I'm thinking primarily of the literary context.) If the Gospels are inspired at all, they're inspired to prevent us from probing further than that. In John the parables disappear and are replaced by dialogues or discourses of self-definition, not of teachings. Of the thousands of things John 1 means, one is that in Christ Logos and Mythos are the same thing.
[NB 44.302; LN, 1:168]

Jesus was not the world's only saviour or enlightened or even divine man:

his uniqueness has to do only with his being the only-begotten Son of the Father. I don't yet know what I mean by that, but it's important to find out. [NB 11E.27; RT, 324]

Jesus Freaks. It still seems to be true that Christianity has some affinity for stupidity. If I were to see a small church labelled "the foursquare gospel" I'd give it a wide berth, because I know I'd find nothing inside except what I'd call hysteria. Not that they wouldn't be individually well-meaning, decent people, or that a written-out statement of their beliefs couldn't be read without (much) revulsion…. I wonder if Jesus freaks and Pentecostalers and similar totally uncritical Christians aren't saying something rather important: that we all know that we are immortal children of God but keep suppressing and censoring the knowledge. Under the pressure of that censorship there's no refuge except in hysteria: the comfort of a reasonable religion is one thing our age doesn't seem to want. [NOTES 54-5.152; RT, 303]

Judas in the Soul. I think Hera, the bitchiest of the goddesses, is what I call the Judas in the soul, the part of us that gets jealous at anything that seems genuinely divine or imagined. [NB 13.103]

Judgment. My difficulty with Kant's *Critique of Judgment* is, of course, that I don't believe in judgment, except in a very tentative way. It's bound up with teleology: if a lion kills and eats a deer, the deer's notion is that deer exist for the sake of being deer, and that lions are an unwarranted and arbitrary intrusion into their world. The lion's view is that deer exist for the purpose of being eaten by lions. Humanity has been brought up by all its cultural conditioning to believe that nature exists to be exploited by man, and brought up by some of its religions to believe that humanity itself exists for the purposes of God. As we don't know what these are, we can go ahead living our lives in our own damfool way. [NOTES 53.72; LN, 2:626]

Jung. My objections to Jung are not to him but to my being called Jungian:

I'm not much interested in alchemy and I don't want *literature* to be turned into a psychological allegory of individuation. On the other hand, once I move back from literary to existential metaphor I'll come very close to it. [NB 44.138; LN, 1:131]

I hope I don't have to try to crack that infernal Jung book again (*Mysterium Coniunctionis*), though its existence shows how important he thought the theme was. But I don't believe Jung's animus really corresponds to the anima: all humans are symbolically male, and they all have animas. The animus is part of something still residually alienated, like the female in Nietzsche or Paul. [NB 50.381; LN, 1:332]

Psychological constructs like those of Jung are simply the other side of the objective universe. I have to go carefully here, because I seem to outsiders to be close to Jung, even to derive from him, and I have to establish the fact that the aesthetic world or cosmos doesn't derive from the psychological one; the latter derives from the subject-object split. Kant's *Critique of Judgment* is the classical text here, although it's tough going. [NOTES 53.11; LN, 2:614]

Justice and Power. For Socrates the word justice can exist only in a world where such words mean what they ought to mean. *To mean is to acquire power.* So he accepts the challenge of his disciples, and proceeds to set up a counter-world, a society illustrating the meaning of justice. Such a world can exist within the individual, whether it exists within society (or as a society) or not. Modern synonyms for original sin, like "fascism," refer to the isolating of power, holding power without the need of rationalizing it. Socrates, like Hegel, is trying to build a verbal structure that will contain power. That's the bigger irony Plato *is* aware of. [NB 50.41; LN, 1:264]

𝒦

Kami. The Shinto conception of *kami* is useful, because it unites nature-spirits & heroes (i.e. ancestors), & shows how, e.g., Homer can unite the two. Wonder if Christianity would have been better off if it had kept a "pagan" indigenous cult that was simply there, with no theology and no arguments. [NB 11B.13; RT, 351]

Katabasis. To descend is to pass through the chattering, yelling, gibbering world of the demons of repression to the quiet Spirit below. As Eliot says, contradicting the Sibyl, it's not easy to go *all* the way down. To reascend is to bind the squalling demons into a unified creative power.
[NB 27.201; LN, 1:36]

The myth of ascent is a quest for liberty or self-realization; the myth of descent is first of all a quest for equality. Shit and death are democrats. The opening pages of *Moby Dick* are crammed with images of descending into a Charybdis whirlpool, but the first positive discovery Ishmael makes is his human equality with Queequeg. The descent here is the descent of love (including a perspective in which tolerance is love at a distance), where we realize the iniquity of proletarians or excluded groups. Doubtless this could extend, as it does in some Oriental religions, to forms of life other than human, but the extension would take us beyond the range of the normal Western cultural imagination. But that's why religion is the worst possible basis for society, because all communions sooner or later turn their backs on each other.
[NB 50.344; LN, 1:324]

Christianity emphasizes Jesus' repudiation of what he finds at the bottom of the world, which is death and hell; but the quest incorporates the whole Virgilian descent as well, and there must be a treasure there as well as a dragon guarding it. [NOTES 52.155; LN, 2:453]

If there are two kinds of descent, the confrontation with nothingness and the creative descent that finds a treasure, there should be two kinds of ascent, perhaps the two indicated by the doubling in the gospels, resurrection followed by ascension. In resurrection the hero explodes from below with soot on his face; in ascension he simply sloughs off the lower world as an encumbrance. His prototype in ascension (not in resurrection) is Elijah, going up into the sky and throwing down a cloak. Perhaps the death of Moses which was so curiously not a death is a prototype for the resurrection though it's hard to see just how. I think my point about Moses' vision of the Promised Land as superior to Joshua's conquest of Canaan has something. [NOTES 52.165; LN, 2:455]

Keats. A famous English poet tells us that not only are truth and beauty the same thing, but that the knowledge of that identity is all that we need to know. Or, at least, the poet was contemplating a "Grecian Urn," which most scholars assume to be a chunk of Wedgwood, and the Wedgwood told him that. One wonders why so distinguished a poet should venture on so preposterous a statement. If we take historical truths only, practically all of them are quite unbearably ugly, and practically all beauty is based on an illusion of some kind. Then again, both words have become tarnished in the course of time: beauty is a most suspect word now, and truth is pragmatic, what seems to be approximately true for us now. [NOTES 53.57; LN, 2:623-4]

Keeping up To Date. At Princeton I bought four books to keep me up to date with the mid-50s: Maritain's [*Creative Intuition in Art and Poetry*], Malraux's *Voices of Silence*, Auerbach's *Mimesis*, and Curtius on medieval literature and Latin. At that time Curtius was the only one I could read with any real profit: *Mimesis* was all very well but I was working out an anti-mimetic theory of literature; Malraux said a few excellent things but was full of bullshit; Maritain, as I said, kept busting his skull against this preposterous "Art and Scholasticism" thesis, insisting that critical theory just had to come out of St. Thomas, who cared as much about the arts as I do about basketball league playoffs. [NB 44.705; LN, 1:244]

Kerygma. Kerygma is *spiritual* rhetoric, rhetoric delivered from ideology by being on the other side of myth. The gospels contain the teachings and parables of Jesus: they're "logocentric," but they come to us in continuous (to some extent) written form. The kerygma is—and I use the term advisedly—the *resurrection* of the living speaker from the written myth. Or rather, the living word. The Sermon on the Mount isn't a harangue. To choose a text for a sermon makes a myth into kerygma. Kerygma is the completion of the personal possession of the written word: it's linked with mantra, but without the "vain repetition" that often goes with that. It's the actualized form of the "myth to live by," assuming that the real life is a spiritual one, delivered once for all from all ideologies or rationalizations of power. [NB 50.254; LN, 1:306]

There's a famous passage in William James' *The Varieties of Religious Experience* (which would be an almost definitive book on its subject if it hadn't used those absurdly tendentious "healthy-minded" and "sick soul" categories) where he says that on coming out of nitrous oxide he was aware of parallel worlds, some so close as to be entirely recognizable. The world of Jaynes' "hallucination" is one such world: a world where God speaks. That's where the kerygmatic voice comes from: a hell of a good universe next door. Or sometimes, just hell. My own kerygmatic anthology would include *The Marriage of Heaven and Hell,* some fables of Dostoevsky and Kafka, the opening of Buber's *I and Thou,* some Rimbaud & Hölderlin. *Zarathustra* I should disqualify for trying too hard. This is a purely subjective list of no value: I made it because it shows that *no* kerygmatic canon will ever be drawn up: it would be impossible to find a committee to agree on the selections. [NB 50.537-8; LN, 1:366]

Key / Keys. For at least 25 years I've been preoccupied by the notion of a key to all mythologies. [NB 21.311; RT, 198]

Consider the possibility of starting with a set of "keys," a Tarot pack or alphabet of forms, arrived at inductively from a series of analyses, as in my myth course. The point of epiphany is one; the point of demonic epiphany another, & the cycle a third. Then there are *nekyia* [descent to the underworld] complexes (monster-swallowing; cycle-projecting, etc.), unborn world complexes, & so on. The thing is that I mustn't tackle another book without getting at least the *Iliad,* the *Odyssey,* the *Aeneid* & the *Commedia* firmly into my noddle. [NB 18.45]

Kierkegaard. I'm trying to reread Kierkegaard now: I don't find him an attractive personality, because he seems to play the same cat-and-mouse game with his reader that he did with poor Regina—and that God played with Abraham and Job. He's a trickster writer, in short, and interests me because a literary critic sees him as doing the opposite of what he thought he was doing, obliterating the barriers between the aesthetic, the ethical, and the religious. That is, he's clearly a "metaliterary" writer, like Dostoievsky, Kafka and perhaps Nietzsche (well, Mallarmé too).
[NB 50.517; LN, 1:361]

Kierkegaard's *Repetition*…is basically an anatomy, I think, but of course an existential genetic 19th-century anatomy would have to be a confession too, so it's the *Sartor Resartus* hybrid. The trouble is that Kierkegaard disguises the confession & approaches the anatomy quizzically, so it's hard to figure out just what the hell he does mean. Like his Victorian contemporaries in England, he has a stentorian censor at his elbow ready to roar down any irony it doesn't feel it can control. By that I mean that one has to distinguish irony within a convention from irony that threatens the convention. Or humor, perhaps, even more than irony. One can recognize humor in Wagner's *Ring,* for instance, in such things as Mime & Alberich, & yet simultaneously realize that the Ring is fundamentally humorless…. So with Kierkegaard: he's a great humorist, like Carlyle, yet his final sympathies are anti-humorous. I think the fear of subversive humor is clear even in Dante. However, this *Repetition* book deals with my epic circle idea, that the essential quest is cyclic, but returns, not to the same point, but to the same point renewed and transformed. As opposed to recollection, it's the Protestant justification by faith as opposed to the Catholic sacramental repetition of substantial presence. At least I think it is: whether he knows it or not is another matter. [D 52.68; DNF, 488-9]

King Arthur. Myth is the language of religion *and* the structural principle of literature. No discussion of mythology can leave out literature. Take King Arthur. All sorts of mythical patterns can be seen in the literature about him, but so far as I know no archaeologist has ever discovered a shred of evidence connecting him with specifically religious things like a cult or statues or temples or beliefs or shrines. So in connexion, say, with Arthur, we have three things: an imaginative life in literature (flourishing), a cult life in religion (possible, but no trace remaining), and a historical existence. This last has the very casual relation to the myth that all history (apart from the Christian myth of Jesus) has. He was apparently a British leader who effected a temporary rally against the invading Saxons, who of course won in the end. As such, he is far less of a "great man" than Alfred, but he does have a conceptual core in his myth: in the Geoffrey legend he conquers the Roman Empire & his parallel in romance is Charlemagne, so he's the prototype of the Holy Emperor, the defender of the faith. [NB 10.76-7]

Kitten-in-the-Ball-of-Yarn Principle. I have always wanted to write a book that would sit there while I worked on it. My ideal for this book is a general overall scheme clear enough for me to fill in, in an unhurried fashion, whatever details my current reading suggests. Every other book I've done has been done on the kitten-in-the-ball-of-yarn principle, every new piece of reading suggesting a new idea, every new idea revolutionizing the whole structure, the whole making an obsession that had to be given every priority possible until it was off my hands. I can never read library books, partly because I work with marginalia on books I own, perhaps because every book out of sight is also out of mind. If I could only get a firm enough doodle for my controlling scheme, so that the book could gradually evolve! Not just a mechanical filling in of a design, like a hooked rug, but with something like that principle. [NB 12.318; TBN, 209]

Knowing the Truth. Confronted by the mysteries of birth and death, one may feel (*I* may feel) I wish I knew it all. It may be that it's unknown because it's not an objective body of knowledge to be known: perhaps it's a process of being realized out of an illusion. It won't be known until we've finished working at it: the simple way to interpret "finished" is to identify it with physical death, but maybe it's a bigger process than that. I wish John had reversed the syntax he assigns to Jesus: the truth is what makes you free, *and then* is known. Cf. Jung's notion of sermons addressed to the dead, as though they had something to learn from the living as well as the other way round. [NB 44.446; LN, 1:199]

Knowledge. Knowledge is cyclical: the sun goes over your head; what you learn is the last thing you've learned, & you attach it to the other things you've learned; nothing is new *under* the sun. [NB 27.9; LN, 1:4]

My point that knowledge has the power of veto over value in criticism has a lot of implications, including theological ones. More knowledge (or wisdom as potential knowledge) has the power of veto over everything founded on present knowledge. This is especially true of faith, which cannot be a virtue except insofar as it grows with knowledge & wisdom. Or is it faith that grows with knowledge (i.e., with the dialectic of doubt) and hope that grows with wisdom, out of the dialectic of despair? Love, perhaps, grows with vision, out of the dialectic of wrath. I've said all this: I really should write out my sermons. [NB 21.468; RT, 225]

Knowledge Contract. Western philosophy for some reason got bogged down in a contract of knowledge: "subject & object & the nature of reality." Here we are, & there it is: how did we get in contact with it? What right have we to know anything? What *guarantee* is there that we know? [NB 11F.220; RT, 124]

Koans. Two recent koans of mine: that nothing happens in the world except the education of the people in it, and that knowledge is of the actual and leads to wisdom which is of the potential. [NB 24.204; TBN, 324]

Kook Books. For years I have been collecting and reading pop-science & semi-occult books, merely because I find them interesting. I now wonder if I couldn't collect enough ideas from them for an essay on neo-natural theology. Some are very serious books I haven't the mathematics (or the science) to follow: some are kook-books with hair-raising insights or suggestions. [NB 11H.9; LN, 2:713]

The Koran. In my Religious Knowledge course is a clever & plausible remark about the Koran: suras arranged in order of length only means that if the Koran is the Word of God, God doesn't give a damn about narrative sequence. Hence the rise of narrative literature and of causality structures (science) in the Christian culture founded on the Bible. There may be still something in this; but it may be balls too. After sura 1, an obvious opening invocation, sura 2 outlines the same old fall-exodus recapitulation, sura 3 adds Christianity to it; sura 4 deals with points of law like Leviticus, and so on. It's just possible that the length-order is the right one, moving from a sort of *East Coker* laying down of the law, in roughly continuous prose, toward a shower of lyrical apocalyptic sparks, charms, riddles, curses, etc. [NB 11F.69; RT, 85]

The repetitiousness of the Koran would drive a reader out of his mind if he were reading it as he would read any other book. But for a Mohammedan, brought up from infancy to learn it by heart, to attach the greatest possible reverence & weight to what it says, it does exactly the job it should do. It gives the impression that while man's will bucks & plunges in all directions, God's will is steady & unyielding, incessantly coming back to the same point, until the horse is broken in, so to speak, & has learned to move with a direction and a will that are not his own. [NB 21.294; RT, 195]

Kundalini. I'm reading a book that impressed me, Gopi Krishna's *Kundalini.* The introduction writer says we in the West need a new vocabulary for spiritual reality. Even the commentary is rewarding, though it's by a Jungian. (Note: during the war I had racist prejudices against Germans, feeling that there was nothing so dumb as a dumb Kraut. When Jung started talking about Jewish consciousness and the dangers of entering into Oriental attitudes, the farts of a dumb Kraut polluted the air: I think he outgrew that, at least in that autobiography, but (as with Spengler) I distrusted the dumb Kraut for a long time.) Anyway, Kundalini woke up in him accidentally and almost literally buggered him: I wonder whether prayer, the sacraments and the like aren't really forms of *sedation.* Masturbation too, considering where she [Kundalini] is. [NB 50.479-80; LN, 1:353]

Kundalini is the ouroboros, the serpent coiled up chewing her tail. She's also the coiled-up seed, the seed of the spiritual body. According to Gopi Krishna & others, if she wakes up without warning she'll kill you or drive you nuts, because she's going about the city & seeking her beloved, who's in that mysterious cranium chamber. She may wake up in a near-death experience; she may be locking up gently without one's knowing it. [NB 50.497; LN, 1:357]

Kundalini symbolizes the *power* that comes out of nature, viciously evil if it goes up the left side: if it goes up the right side it goes through wisdom (lower), and thence through love (lower) into the *chakras* of higher wisdom & love. [NB 11H.39; LN, 2:718]

L

Ladder of Being. Pierre Bezuhov in *War & Peace* asks why the ladder of being should stop with him. We all wonder…why the level of personal reality should go up to man and stop, even if we can't raise much interest in the nine orders of angels. But the atheistic argument (Sartre) that if we admit the existence of God we're "dependent on" God and thereby lose our "freedom" (whatever that is) is bloody stupid.
[NB 44.484, 498; LN, 1:206, 209]

Laforgue. I don't know why I've spent so much time on Rimbaud and Mallarmé when it's so clearly Laforgue who has all the answers.
[NB 44.191; LN, 1:142]

Language. Whorf's metalinguistic discoveries, suggesting that we allow the grammar of our language to structure our world, are interesting and important, but they're not decisive. For example, Hebrew did not have a past-present-future tense system of verbs and Greek did, but it was Hebrew and not Greek that developed a religious vision based on a historical past and a prophetic future. The simplest way to get out of this bind of letting one's grammar structure one's world is to turn from prose to the figured language of poetry, where you have to come to terms with the opposite problem, the inadequacy of the world to meet the structuring demands of language. The "is not and yet is" side of metaphor is what's important here.
[NB 27.372-3; LN, 1:66]

As language is concerned with the symbolic transformation of the split world, it never is fully capable of expressing the categories of that split world. Tense, for instance, is never primarily an attempt to express time: the fundamental distinctions in tense are into the perfect & the imperfect, the conception of the Become & the Becoming, the dead & the alive. Philosophers nowadays demonstrate with many triumphant grins & axe-swinging iconoclasm what literary men have always known, & what philosophers could have always known if they had read their Plato without skipping (*Cratylus,* e.g.): that metaphysics is a function of language, & follows the curves of the grammatical conceptions of the language in which it is composed. [NB 33.14]

Language Learning. Why can't I learn languages? Because I can't bear to read anything unless it contains potentially something I can base a critical judgement (no) aphorism on. You can't find such material in the opening pages of a Russian grammar. In other words, pure vanity.
[NB 44.658; LN, 1:236]

I wonder what sort of people find languages easy. Any I ever tackled let me in for fearsome complications of paradigms, idioms, irregular verbs, & syntax, followed, if at all, by looking fifty thousand words up in a dictionary. But then I'm bad at languages anyway: too careful & panicky—a curious combination, but it exists. [D 42.18; DNF, 10]

Last Judgement. The miserable bureaucratic parody of religion that says that all those who are not good enough for heaven must be bad enough for hell, when it's so obvious that nobody is fit for either. Something here that blocks up the doctrine of immortality. No serious person will listen to such nonsense. The creation is not in the past; the Last Judgement is not in the future; we must get a proper view of creation that isn't a projected sexual or artefact myth: when we get it the Last Judgement conception will clear up, & when that clears up there shall be a way open for a conception of life without birth & death that isn't either before birth or after death.
[NB 11F.29; RT, 77]

Law. Jesus says that the "law" is more permanent than heaven or earth: if this means that 635 precepts about not seething a kid in its mother's milk & the like will outlive the subsiding of the universe into entropy, the statement is obviously bloody nonsense. I think that when heaven & earth pass away, the old alliance of moral & natural law is dissolved, which means that the "law" becomes something very different. It's the light, or the clue, that we carry with us when we descend to the labyrinth of the dead. The true witnesses are the martyrs, who go down into the silence alone with their vision, & come back from the grave with the body of the redeemed. The false witnesses (here of course I'm back to Blake) are the Watchers, the "spheres that testify," as Baruch calls them, who form the body of the Covering Cherub. [NB 11F.197; RT, 119]

Law depends entirely on its two foci: what it meant then and what it can possibly mean now. The laws in Deuteronomy about stoning a woman if the tokens of virginity are not found in her and cutting off a woman's hand if she grabs one of two fighting men by the balls belong to a (speaking mildly) barbaric age: hence they have either to be junked or rationalized on some "oh, well, it doesn't really mean that" basis. What then does it mean? Something that can be squeezed into the acceptable. Contemporary conscience is the arbiter. [NOTES 53.66; LN, 2:625]

The Leader. The leader, nowadays, is treated with Messianic rituals suggesting that he's going to do this & that, & is required to make promises to that effect. But actually he inherits a tradition & tries to continue it. If he's a leader in a very great power, he has power to destroy, but almost no power to innovate or create. This is connected with the fact that many things are technologically feasible that will not be done unless there is some powerful economic or political motive to do them. [NB 11F.77; RT, 87]

Learning. Attachment is ignorance, & knowledge disentangles us from the grip an unreal world has on us. A city man lost in the woods finds bondage in his ignorance of woodcraft: an experienced woodsman can detach himself from the woods by his ability to maintain himself independently of the clutching branches, tripping roots & stalking animals. Once we think of learning as a disentangling & relaxing process, we think of ideas tending toward wisdom, or the growth of a free spirit, instead of to more & more learning. [NB 3.114; RT, 47]

Leisure. Work is a curse, & the pursuit of wisdom has to begin in leisure & spread out from there. The great mass of people, whether rich or poor, suffer from too great a lack of leisure ever to develop much wisdom. This lack of leisure has two causes: one, the amount of time compulsively spent in uncreative work; the other, perverse dither. Wisdom would normally begin in real leisure as opposed to work, in real thought as opposed to action. That's why the law about the Sabbath is so fundamental. From there the spirit of leisure & wisdom & thought should irradiate & inform the rest of one's time. Blessed be he who has found his leisure, as Carlyle did not say, and has made his work the outward projection of his leisure. Now work is natural, & the product of a state of nature: it's ritual, the humorless customary basis of life. Reflection (literally) is thus linked with holidays. But leisure is profoundly unnatural, & hence most people fear it & put work or work substitutes (= dither) in its place. The history of the world, of course, is the class struggle of workers & ditherers. Leisure begins by repairing the tissues: dither develops wild tissue or cancer, frantic efforts to be entertained by something non-progressive. Practically everybody, & this goes for me too, has enormously greater leisure than he thinks he has. The connection of this with the foregoing is that the goal of leisure is to develop a sense of time, to develop a creative rhythmic beat on one's time, to subdue the Spectre of Urthona by Los. [NB 3.117; RT, 48-9]

Life after Death. So many people are repelled by the idea of a life after death that if there *is* a life after death a lot of people are going to be damn mad. But then a lot of people are damn mad about having been born into this world, though few of them, and those mostly suicides, get to the point of formulating it in those terms. [NB 21.293; RT, 194-5]

Literary Education. Twenty-five years ago, when I started expounding my views, I met with the most strenuous resistance from my students; today I have the feeling of battering down an open door. The reasons for the change are of great significance. In the last generation, we were all in the grip of a writing culture. There could be no truth except truth of correspondence conveyed by simple & accurate description. Their questions were loaded with value-assumptions: is it all just a myth, only a myth, nothing but a myth? They had been educated the wrong way in literature, by educators who disliked & feared literature & trained them first in "communication arts," then circled cautiously over to prose, & ended by surveying poetry as Moses did the Promised Land, dividing it into allegorical themes or topics. What poetry had been taught them had been metered gabble of the Longfellow-Whittier kind, on the theory that this would be the kind of poetry that would connect with their ordinary experience. The result was that when they collided with genuine poetry in the university, with Yeats or Rimbaud, they did not think of such poetry as a direct, forceful, natural, even primitive form of utterance, but as something wilfully & perversely obscure & difficult. Educators today seem to be as silly & ignorant as ever, but they can no longer cripple their victims to such an extent. Young people educate themselves today, partly through films & television, media that are capable of great symbolic concentration, partly through listening to folk singers & rock & roll music which introduces them to what is, for all its obvious limitations, a more normal poetic idiom. As a result mythical habits of thought seem natural to them.
[NB 11F.4; RT, 73]

Literary History. For a long time I've been obsessed by the notion of writing a definitive history of English literature. I'll never do that, of course; but why should the idea fascinate the author of the *Anatomy of Criticism?* Could it be that there's a possibility of writing a history, based on but not confined to English, that would have the form of an incredibly complicated fugal structure? Themes from Irish myth going through Grail romance, *Tempest, Comus,* to Eliot & Yeats & Joyce. Biblical typology organizing the whole damn scheme?... Now could I just die & get reincarnated in somebody like me & take about eighty years off to do the job? [NB 18.132]

Literature and Life. One of the stock responses to me is that I try to separate literature from life. But of course it's the people who go in for documentary criticism, whose first impulse it is to relate literature to the non-literary, who really make the separation. [NB 11F.148; RT, 107]

Little Jack Horners. I was criticized for not separating myself from Blake [in *Fearful Symmetry*]. I started with the assumption that I was addressing people who would be interested in Blake & not in me, & that if I undertook to explain Blake my primary duty was to get the hell out of the way so that the reader could see Blake. I do not understand why the statement that the reader cannot see me for Blake is intended as a complaint instead of a compliment. What do I matter? The important thing is what is in Blake, not what the professor has finally had the sense to see. I know that criticism is full of self-congratulatory Little Jack Horners, but I have no desire to be one of them. [NB 7.19]

Location of God. All thought is talking to oneself. All prayer is talking to God. The difference between thought & prayer thus depends on one's conception of where God is. If you accept the Thou Art That doctrine, prayer is controlled & directed thinking. Similarly the difference between grace & inspiration depends on the location of God. [D 49.242; DNF, 148]

Logocentrism. If I'm old hat because I'm "logocentric," I want to know why I'm that, and not just be that because I'm ignorant of the possibility of being anything else. The New Testament certainly defines faith in logocentric terms, as a *hypostasis* [substance] and an *elenchos* [evidence] — the latter, it is true, only in an existential context. [NB 27.127; LN, 1:23]

Looking Up. What we look "forward" to gradually fades out as it is transmitted to posterity and renounced for ourselves, & finally disappears altogether. The essential thing is something to look "up" to, until we begin to realize that there is also a misleading factor in the metaphor "up": i.e., it is not necessarily out of our reach. [NB 44.475; LN, 1:205]

The Lost Chord. I'm beginning to feel that I really am the man who's found the lost chord, somebody who really can, on the basis of literature, put the Tarots & alchemy & cabalism& the rest of it together into a coherent speech & language. [NB 11F.156; RT, 109]

Lost Leaders. I can still remember the sense of outrage & betrayal when, as a young student facing the world of the depression & of Hitler & the great Stalin neuroses & looking to the writers I most admired for guidance, I picked up [T.S. Eliot's] *After Strange Gods.* I had to learn the hard way that all leaders are lost leaders, like Moses in the wilderness. [NB 13.57]

Lost Souls. I can see that some lives, lives given up to destruction & cruelty & massacres, could be conceived as lost, that is, not as tormented in hell forever, but as forming no part of the risen body of Christ. But *victims,* the slaves & the downtrodden & oppressed, can hardly be lost souls: they form part of the resurrection because their lives have been part of the divine agony & endurance. Job, of course: but doesn't this give them a *future?* [NB 11F.99; RT, 92]

Paul's "Christ in me" is not "I am Christ," but its exact opposite. The latter is the demonic parody of the former. The ego is a lost soul: this means that everybody has a lost soul, and should make sure that it gets damn well good and lost. [NOTES 52.731; LN, 2:566]

Love. If love is not a feeling but a capacity of acting, the *jnana* road to love is through the inexpressible comprehension of what a created thing is. I see a person as a whole being; I see utterly what he is; nothing I say about him can be an adequate expression of any part of my understanding of him. My idea of him is my power of grasping his entirety, a power which

is incommunicable. I suppose that's what Gestalt psychology is about. But such "love" depends on knowledge, & it's a love that only a novelist could have for his characters. In real life such understanding goes with love in the sense of interested attached feeling, such as I have for Helen [Frye's wife], whose face is vaguer to me in her absence than that of many casual acquaintances. One has to develop, for everything to which one is not attached, something of the novelist's total act of knowledge, the divine comprehension which has sympathy but not affection, wrath but not resentment.
[NB 3.53; RT, 24]

The difference between love & lust is, of course, that the former is personal & particular, & the latter impersonal & general. Marriage is prompted by lust, desire for the body of *a* woman, more or less any woman capable of slaking the desire. Love develops the universal out of this particular, & transforms the woman picked more or less at random from a large possible number into the emanation, the only woman in the world, the personal response from what one loves. Romantic love & orthodox marriage are both the opposites of this love, & that's why they merge so readily into one another. Neither gets its mind above the gutter, the physical union which is the foundation of marriage & is therefore not the superstructure. Love is not for the only possible woman at first, as the romantics claim: the state of being in love is the sense of the infinite possibilities of what is to come. And not until the woman really is the only possible woman has the marriage been consummated & the two flesh become one & all the other things that Christianity is talking about, none of which apply until then.
[NB 3.65; RT, 28]

Love is the only virtue there is, but like everything else connected with creativity and imagination, there is something decentralized about it. We love those closest to us, Jesus' "neighbors," people we're specifically connected with in charity. For those at a distance we feel rather tolerance or good will, the feeling announced at the Incarnation.
[NB 46.45; LN, 2:696]

Luminosity. Maybe I've just been hypnotized by the lucidity, almost the luminousness, of my *Critical Path* essay. I feel that a sequel to it that was the Huckleberry Finn to its Tom Sawyer, so to speak, would be something fairly definitive for our time. [NB 11F.173; RT, 113]

M

McLuhan. McLuhan has of course enormously expanded my thesis about the return of irony to myth. His formulation is hailed as revolutionary by those who like to think that the mythical-configuration-involved comprehension is (a) with it (b) can be attained by easier methods than by the use of intelligence. Hence everyone who disagrees (as in all revolutionary arguments) can be dismissed as linear or continuous. But there are two kinds of continuity involved: one is the older detached individuality, the other the cultural and historical continuity of preserving one's identity and memory in moving from one to the other. The issue here is a *moral* issue between freedom of consciousness and obsessive totalitarianism, plunging into a Lawrentian Dionysian war-dance. [NB 12.61; TBN, 145]

Madness. It doesn't matter if the poet "is" "mad"—the quotes indicate how irrelevant this is. Madness is a social judgment by a mad society. That society can protect or seclude those who are helpless or dangerous to it, but it can't judge madness as such. The prophet is invariably mad, and society has no criteria for distinguishing the prophetic standards, the mantic from the manic. [NOTES 52.638; LN, 2:547]

Magic. Magic implies mechanism: you pronounce a name and the entity designated *must* appear and do things. A primitive building a boat will use technology, but will also mutter magic spells to take care of the intangible factors. I suppose computers are the physical realization of magic, just as the television screen is the physical realization of ghosts.
[NB 44.262; LN, 1:159]

Consciousness is a magician who controls the demon of the will. Like other apprentices, it gets automatic with control, & so anarchic. Blake's Spectre of Urthona. Prospero was a magician of the old school, a Magus: he controlled a spirit of the elements and then let him go. [NB 44.296; LN, 1:166]

Magnum Opus. Stevens' "great poem of earth" probably can't be written, because the narrative has to end with a vertical vision looking up & down. Even *War & Peace* ends with the contrast between those two states (*Mir* in Russian means a lot of things besides peace). Mallarmé's "great work" certainly wasn't written, but maybe a comparative study of the Bible and the literature we have may give critics, *in critical terms* only, some notion of what it would be like in outline. [NB 44.538; LN, 1:216]

Mahler. I find Mahler very pleasant & easy to listen to—the theme of the *Funeral March* haunted me all day—but I certainly don't find the profundities in him that I gather I'm supposed to find. Or, if they're there, they're romantic & introspective profundities only: no objective plumbing into the world. [D 50.109; DNF, 257]

The Majority. In a democratic society the will of the majority must prevail: and the majority in any society are dead: *Migravit ad plures* [joined the majority]. [NB 42.10]

Making. Over the triad of the good, the beautiful and the true, there overarches the category of making. The good is how we ought to act, the beautiful how we ought to feel, the true how we ought to think. Ought, ought, ought. My ass. All these categories are aspects of how we ought to make. [NOTES 53.59; LN, 2:624]

Male Love. I have never myself felt any physical basis to my affectionate feelings for other men, but there must be one, and it seems to me as pointless to speak of all male love as buggery as it would be to speak of all marriage as legalized whoring. When Marlowe said that the beloved disciple was Christ's Alexis, he wasn't just being a bad boy: the sense of his remark is that Christ's love, being human, must have had a substantial quality in it. I think—I'm just guessing—that our sentiment against the open physical expressions of love among men—embraces, for instance, and remarks about a boy's shape—may have made "normal" male relationships needlessly abstract, and forced all the "abnormal" people to become a separate caste of fairies. However, I'm so strongly "normal" in emotion myself that I don't really feel this. [D 52.8; DNF, 465]

Male Virgins. It's bloody confusing to read in Revelation that the redeemed are all male virgins, never "defiled" with women. Not that anyone ever took it—well—literally:… Its demonic parody is Genesis 6:1-4: the Revelation bunch are sons of God who stay where they are, & don't go "whoring" after lower states of being. [NB 50.453; LN, 1:348]

Malignant Observation. When I got scooped on Blake by Schorer my feeling that his book is a soft, silly, second-rate book was correct; my feeling that the people who preferred his book to mine were fools was to that extent correct. If I were actually a person of no greater ability than he, I should feel his limitations as strongly as ever, & be just as right. The fact that I am actually a far greater critic is my way of escape from this particular rat-trap: it seems like taking an unfair advantage of the people who are helplessly caught in a hell of malignant observation, besides being very like thanking God that I am not as other men are. The fact that comparisons are relevant only to inorganic quantities and that all qualitative units such as human souls are incomparable takes a long time to get over.
[NB 3.167; RT, 66]

Mallarmé. But it's Mallarmé who will take me through the third great crisis of the birth of the spirit out of the depth of fallen spirits. (Victor Hugo of course saw the primary importance of the theme, but was too much in love with his own rhetoric to do more than talk about it.)
[NB 27.232; LN, 1:41]

Mallarmé really does talk sometimes as though he thought literature was a "substitute" for religion, though of course no "substitute" can have more than an *ersatz* reality. I suppose he would say, if he were using my terms, that literature is the antitype of what religious symbolism hazily points to. This is a defensible view in itself, but criticism has further to go than that. [NB 44.372; LN, 1:182]

Valéry, writing of Mallarmé: "Language thus becomes an instrument of 'spirituality,' that is to say, of the direct transmutation of desires and emotions into presences and powers that become 'realities' in themselves, without the intervention of physically adequate means of action." The whole paragraph is very important: Valéry can certainly write when Mallarmé is telling him what to say. [NB 50.108; LN, 1:278]

Mallarmé is very heroic in the way he tries to sink himself in myth & metaphor so completely that the kerygmatic will speak through. "The pure work implies the disappearance of the poet as speaker, yielding his initiative to words." That's the regular rhetoric-poetic distinction: don't let the ego quack: let the words come. But it also echoes Jesus' advice to the 70 not to rehearse what they're going to say, which means that kerygma is *on the other side* of the poetic from rhetoric.
[NB 50.241; LN, 1:303]

Mamalujo: Eastern Version. The Man of intellect (Jnāna-Yoga); the Lion of emotion; the Bull of sensation (Hatha-Yoga), the Eagle of intuition (Bhakti). These carry the everlasting gospel over the world, and their return to the ark is revelation. [NB 21.197; RT, 176]

Mammer. Ovid [and] Virgil...both end in deifications of Caesar, the type of Antichrist. Churchill said he didn't want to preside over the disintegration of the British Empire, but he'd have been an infinitely greater man if he had: Gorbachev is a later example of a leader whose essence is renunciation. Perhaps Hadrian, with his cult of Terminus, is a corresponding figure in Roman times. I'm yammering, I know: it doesn't matter, or mammer. [NOTES 53.117; LN, 2:634]

Man-made World. When man gets to the point of saying "God made the world" it means that man sees a structure of order in nature. He's not saying "I make the world by observing it." But he is beginning to interpose a man-made world between a nature-made world and God. This man-made world is made ultimately out of human quarks—words & numbers. These become metaphors for God. [NB 11H.19; LN, 2:715]

Maoism. I know this sounds like an obsession, but for anyone living in 1967, the thought of millions of Chinese yelling their guts loose & waving the little red books of Chairman Mao's thoughts in the air ought to be pretty central. Anything can happen, but one thing that certainly can happen is that China will unify itself around the "thought" of Mao, & become strong enough to wipe us out with the back of its hand in a very few years. An old & sophisticated bourgeois civilization like ours thinks in terms of the variety of its ideas, of the intensity of criticism, and above all, of the fact that to be intellectually weak & open to criticism is to be ineffectual. Great is truth & will prevail. For any bourgeois intellectual it would be a miserable impoverishment to confine oneself to the thought of Chairman Mao. Nobody's thoughts can be all that good: words can only do so much. But China is probably enjoying a more intensive & widespread intellectual activity than we are. It doesn't matter whether the thoughts are vulnerable to criticism, including the criticism in your own mind. It doesn't matter how true they are if a powerful social will is determined to make them principles. Eventually, of course, the Chinese myth of concern will complicate itself & become critical too, but that's much later. [NB 19.408; TBN, 92-3]

Marble Game. As a child I had a board with 33 hollows for marbles, the central one empty. The puzzle was by jumping over marbles & removing them from the board to leave one in the middle. There were four side areas to be cleared. This game has the solution to my projected book on an *I Ching* or model of augury. I record this because anyone reading these notes would assume that they were the work of a psychotic, so I may as well furnish the definitive proof of the fact. [NB 12.251; TBN, 192]

Martial Music. The only kind of martial music that ever impressed me as being more interesting aesthetically than carpet-beating is the *Last Post*. I wonder if equivalents for this—unconsciously great art not conceived originally as a work of art—could be found in literature or painting? [NB 4.25]

Marxism. I've been reading another Marxist essay by someone outside a Marxist dominated country, very anxious to dissociate himself from "vulgar Marxism." The trouble is that Lenin was a vulgar Marxist.
[NB 27.418; LN, 1:76]

It's ironic that Marxism, which tried to define ideology as the rationalizings of non-Marxists, should have turned into the one movement of our day that absolutizes ideology. [NB 44.28; LN, 1:107]

I have often asked myself what it is in Marxism that I find so irrelevant to my own interests. The core of the answer is in the total inability of Marxists to incorporate the tradition of literature, or to show any correlation whatever between literary centrality and political centrality. They talk about using drama for their purposes, but before Chekhov (and even he's a doubtful case) there is only one play, by Lope de Vega—a remarkable play, it's true, but still a fluke. Literature is all about something totally different.
[NB 19.347; TBN, 79-80]

It's ironic that Marxism, which began by pretending that it had no ideology and that ideology was something only the bourgeois had as a rationalizing defence, turned out to be in our world the great absolutizing of ideology. Such people as Walter Benjamin say, quite consistently, that myth is an oppressive dragon about to be slain by some ideological knight of the classless society vision. [NOTES 52.621; LN, 2:544]

179

Marxism and Christianity. I'm not interested in the cliché "Marxism is really a religion after all," but in the fact that the religious-secular, theist-atheist antithesis doesn't make sense anymore. It restates the old business about the resemblance between Biblical & Classical myths. The paranoids said the heathen fables were all devil's parodies; the reasonable people said they were the natural man's counterpoint to revealed truth. Today there are thoughtful people in Latin America and elsewhere who realize that Christianity and Marxism sooner or later have to kiss & make up: there are paranoids in Marxism yelping about "ideological contamination" and now I see the Vatican bureaucracy has come out with a no-you-mustn't admonition to politically radical priests. [NB 27.278; LN, 1:49]

Masterpiece. Masterpiece and classic don't mean inherent formal qualities but a locus of social acceptance. Perhaps they emerge when acceptance becomes recognition, a vision of form irradiating it. [NOTES 58-8.13]

Such words as "classic" or "masterpiece" cannot refer to any inherent or structural qualities. They refer to a certain locus of social acceptance, and this acceptance is a loose amalgam of the critical and the popular, the traditional and the contemporary. Perhaps the nearest one can get to an internal criterion would be the possibility of recreation by the reader. But once this is understood, we should understand too that there is no basis to the conventional view that criticism is second-hand creation. A creative act of response is essential to allow the creative work to exist. Until that, the greatest work of literature is still wrapped in eternal silence far from enemies. [NOTES 54-10.4]

Mathematics. When we begin mathematics we expect it to follow the outlines of & comment on the physical world: arithmetic & geometry at this stage are counting & measuring physical objects. When we pass into algebra & trigonometry mathematics begins to get "useless": that is, it becomes an autonomous language, a form of mental comprehension of reality which interprets reality within its own system: it is no longer a second-hand illustration of the second-hand illustration of the reality which we know as physical nature. [NB 3.133; RT, 53-4]

Meander-and-Descent Patterns. Graves says nothing prickles the hair in poetry except the white goddess. That's his mamma fixation. Everybody has a fixation. Mine has to do with meander-and-descent patterns. For years in my childhood I wanted to dig a cave & be the head of a society in it—this was before I read Tom Sawyer. All the things in literature that haunt me most have to do with katabasis. The movie that hit me hardest as a child was the Lon Chaney *Phantom of the Opera.* My main points of reference in literature are such things as *The Tempest, Paradise Regained, Milton,* the *Ancient Mariner, Alice in Wonderland, The Waste Land*—every damn one a meander-&-katabasis work. [NB 19.336; TBN, 76]

Meaning. It may be thought that the very question "What does a poem mean?" is illegitimate, like asking what a flower means. But, first, this contradicts our experience, for we do try to grasp (allegorical) meaning when we read. Second, a flower in a crannied wall also has meaning, though a meaning derivable only from the whole horizon of reality it's in. So Tennyson's statement is a quite simple & literal one. Third, there's the related question, "What is a poem (flower)?" which can only be answered by seeing it as an individual of a class. [NB 12.95; TBN, 154]

Mechanized Phoenix. One should have bigger & better conversions every day, like a mechanized phoenix. [NB 21.495; RT, 231]

Medium and Message. I have never understood why that blithering nonsense "the medium is the message" caught on so. Apparently the terms "medium" and "message" are being aligned with "form" and "content" respectively. And while it would make sense to say that form and content are inseparable, a medium is just that, a medium. It's a vehicle, a transmitter, a means of communicating words and sounds and pictures. It is not and never can be a form. The form of a verbal message is as verbal as its content. The content of a musical message, say a Mozart quartet, is a musical form. It may be heard in a concert hall or over the radio or read as a score in a book, but such varieties of media touch neither form nor content. On Magritte's pipe principle, the content of a picture is not the objects it represents, but its form or pictorial organization. But painting itself is not a medium: painting cannot be a means of transmitting painting. [NB 44.651; LN, 1:234-5]

Memory. The memory selects, rejects, rearranges, condenses and displaces. In short, it *mythicizes* our history. [NB 27.211; LN, 1:38]

Blake's "imagination has nothing to do with memory" is about the least helpful comment he ever made. I wish he had said, "imagination begins in reversing the current of memory." Memory progressively dematerializes images and rearranges them into a Narcissus-mirror of ourselves: imagination (as Blake meant it) goes in the opposite or presenting direction of *ut pictura poesis*. In memory the metaphorical context is formed by association; in imagination it is formed by an assigned context. If not narcist, memory simply follows the conventions of tradition: this is what bothered Blake. Yeats in *A Vision* was pursuing images back into the Great Memory. [NB 27.357; LN, 1:63]

In my speeches I often speak of earlier moments of intensity. They were usually not moments of intensity, but only look so when I remember them. In a sense, therefore, I'm simply lying. But perhaps this is what the memory is for, to bring to life past moments. If so, the memory, like the sensory apparatus, is selective & exclusive. Screen memory is the only memory. Nietzsche says that when the memory says "I did that" & pride says "I didn't," the memory gives way. I wish to hell mine would, & that I didn't remember so many silly & humiliating things. Maybe it's a disease that it doesn't, & it should. Perhaps that's the meaning of Lethe, losing the memory of sin, in Dante. Of course an old man in complacent dotage, with a battery of stories showing him in a good light, isn't exactly the noblest work of God. But memory is the key to identity. And perhaps (as Coleridge once suggested) the key to resurrection too. My own memory, employed in this way, brings an almost intolerable weight of nostalgia with it: I want to go back to an earlier & simpler time when all those people were alive. Maybe, as Vaughan says, we go back to heaven & not on to it. [NB 11F.158; RT, 109]

I was wandering the streets of Moncton [New Brunswick], thinking how, in the course of time, memory tends to distribute itself between waking life & dream life. Some of my most vivid dream settings have been on Moncton streets. Streets are, of course, a labyrinth symbol, full of Eros: they recapture not past reality but my reality, reality for me. I wish I knew what I meant: something eludes me. Cf. Joyce's hallucinatory Dublin, the name Dedalus, the Count of Monte Cristo. [NB 12.148; TBN, 166]

My "recluse" existence is not wholly laziness & inertia. My work depends on a good memory, & the way to keep a good memory is not to make too many waves of experience in between. The hours I spent in [the Merton College] Mob Quad reading about Old English literature are as vivid to me still as the hours I spent last week at a CRTC hearing, & of course I remember the content of those hours far better. [NB 24.229; TBN, 330]

My memory of past experiences becomes more intense all the time, yet much of it never happened, happened otherwise or in a different sequence, or with a very different emotional harmonization. (It's this last that makes the present so much less real than the past: as in art, an imaginative recreation lifts them clear of the dithering of time.) I think the real memory is the habit-energy that is, perhaps, our real selves, that is, perhaps, the only thing we could take into another world. It's what we consciously remember in reverse. [NB 21.605; RT, 253]

Mendelssohn. I have a great theoretical respect for Mendelssohn. He was the only romantic who did anything serious with Bach's forms of oratorio and fugue, and the only one who contributed to Bach's instrument, the organ. But while I have a great theoretical respect for Mendelssohn I can't stand any of his damned music, which is rather hard on my tendency to transcendentalize art-forms. He may be from that point of view the only connecting link between Bach and Cesar Franck, but that doesn't give him what they've got. [NB 5.1]

Mental Subway Tracks. Thinking, of course, is not something I do: it's something that happens where I am. It gets done in spite of what I do: everything I "do" is mental automatism, running along prefabricated tracks that look like a map of the London subways. There's the black sado-masochist line, consisting of remorse (in the literal "agen-bite of inwit" [remorse of conscience] sense) over the past & stewing about a future invented for the purpose of stewing about it. There's the blue line of all the good things I've written or said in the past and am going to write or do in the future (the future part of this is the only one I feel as voluntarily assumed self-indulgence). This is the anecdotage line: I might call it the Narcissus line, except that Narcissus was a comparative realist: the image he fell in love with really did resemble himself, & wasn't one invented out of mainly imaginary qualities. Whenever this line stops at a station, we instantly transfer to the black line. Then there's the inner circle, or what Beckett calls the Belacqua line, of diddling & twiddling & meandering around what is in front of one. I resent other people's automatisms excessively because they run over the same lines, & delay or impede mine. [NB 12.280; TBN, 199-200]

Mercy. Easter, 1980. God is very merciful. Praise to his name. [NB 11B.81; RT, 359]

Metaphor. There are three phases of metaphor. Phase one, the "lunatic" phase, is that of the Bacchantes, the shaman's journeys to upper & lower worlds, the totemic identity with the totem, the identification stages of mysteries and initiations. Phase two, the "lover" phase, is the ideal of one soul created out of two bodies in the sex act. Phase three is the "poet" phase, where metaphor passes out of the "ecstatic" stage. The progress to a fourth phase is a recapturing of the ecstatic. In Elizabethan poetry it was assumed that the poet started as the lover of a disdainful mistress & was driven to poetry by frustration. [NB 27.292; LN, 1:52]

"The Kingdom of Heaven is within you." We may disagree on what that means, but we all agree on what it does not mean: it does not mean, "literally," that the kingdom of heaven is inside us in the sense in which the food we have just eaten is inside us. Consequently all discussion of the meaning of the sentence has to start with the interpretation of a metaphor. It is the same even with doctrine: Christ is God & Man; his body & blood are the bread & the wine, are doctrines expressible only in metaphor. It is the attempt to translate them into "literal" or reasonable language by such concepts as *hypostasis* [substance] that is not simple.
[NB 11F.2; RT, 72-3]

Every one of the standard figures of speech, except the metaphor, draws attention to the fact that it's "just" a figure. The simile has its reassuring "like," the oxymoron draws attention to its self-contradiction; the hyperbole to its excess; the synecdoche to its deficiency; the metonymy to its "signified." Only the metaphor says "This is {not}." Juxtaposition of two images suggests identity, whether asserted by "is" or not; the fact that there are two images to be juxtaposed suggests the "is not" counterpoint.
[NB 44.319; LN, 1:171]

The word with power is the metaphor. Metaphors normally have two units, tenor & vehicle, & so are word-phrases, positive & negative magnets. But many metaphors, like "way," are single-multiple words.
[NB 44.420; LN, 1:194]

Metaphor is the language of immanence; metonymy of transcendence.
[NB 11C.21; RT, 347]

The sense of identity in Palaeolithic cave-drawings with bisons and the like is pictorial metaphor, but it modulates very quickly into acquiring the quality of the animal, not just being identified with it. The totemic set-up is pure metaphor; the sorcerer or shaman with a beast mask is moving in the direction of *techne,* manipulation, magic, doing things with the identification. To manipulate things is to deprive them of will. [NOTES 52.522; LN, 2:527]

Metaphor is the attempt to open up a channel or current of energy between subject and object. It begins in ecstatic metaphor (Stone Age painting and "primitive" music), and literature develops in proportion as the sense of a split between subject and object becomes habitual. The link with religion is there because metaphor creates a "Thou" world between the "I" and the "it," and the god is the stabilized metaphor. This "Thou" originates probably in the sense of the mother, and hence the "white goddess" aspect of poetic imagery takes its rise. Theseus on the lunatic, lover and poet: the lover has to be there because Eros is the original inspirer of the poet and because sexual love is a throwback to ecstatic metaphor. But of course the actual union of two bodies in one is possible only in Oedipal fantasies. [NOTES 52.569-70; LN, 2:537]

Metaphor and Myth. Metaphor starts out as magic, half creating and half perceiving, as Wordsworth says, elemental spirits, totems, local gods, & the like. The Biblical opposition to "idolatry" involves renouncing the magic and sublimating or internalizing the verbal metaphor. So metaphor is the arrest of magic and of logic; myth is the *arrest* of history and dialectic. [NB 27.59; LN, 1:12]

Metaphorical-Game Tradition. There's a slight but significant body of writing, connected with what I've called the anatomy.... This is the writing that explores the metaphorical and diagrammatic bases of second-phase writing, and so turns its constructs into a kind of metaphorical game. The word game is linked to the fact that its center of gravity is that

186

mysterious area I've talked so much about, where the oracular and witty seem different aspects of the same thing. Boehme is one of the greatest writers in this tradition, and the one that impinges most closely on the response to the Bible. Carlyle's *Sartor Resartus* is a very typical example; others are Poe's *Eureka,* Butler's *Life and Habit,* Lawrence's *Fantasia of the Unconscious.* It's really allied to the oratorical tradition, I suppose; it clearly has links with occultism, which is essentially a schematic way of thinking about nature, and so is closer to a linguistic basis. Regarding the metaphorical-game tradition: I have a certain affinity with this tradition myself, a fact that has put off a number of my readers. It's hard to know whether one is "serious" or not in this tradition: cf. Samuel Butler especially, whose prose style is one I greatly admire. Similarly with the sane bits of Lawrence, such as his lively analogy of the bicycle. The owlish solemnity of *Eureka,* the hysterical parts of Lawrence, and the affinity with occultism generally, which hasn't much humor as a rule, may be over-compensation.
[NOTES 54-5.144, 146; RT, 301, 302]

Metaphors of Emotional Concern. I was recently taking part in a social-science discussion on values when it occurred to me that there is perhaps one set of criteria—a dialectic set—which we use in different contexts, with different metaphors, the standard of difference being the amount of emotional concern we feel. Ordinarily we discuss values in the metaphors of mechanism, & talk of functioning & breakdown, because there emotions are at a minimum. If we're a little more concerned, we shift to organic & medical metaphors, & talk of health & sickness, or, if we do say breakdown, we mean by it something more like disease or neurosis. Confronted with southern segregators, we step up our concern to moral metaphors & talk of the bad or the wrong. Confronted with lynching or the Nazi persecution of Jews, we feel that only the religious categories of evil & sin & the judgement of God are appropriate. As Burke says, there's a point at which the mistaken theorist becomes the bad man (in the intervening medical stage, we ask, not if the argument is valid, but: what's the matter with a man who wants to argue in this way?). [NB 33.59]

Middle Class. The word "bourgeois" is practically synonymous with creative man: the middle class has produced culture and civilization alike. One can find exceptions, just as one can find women composers; but just as it is true that men & not women have composed the world's great music, so it is true that the middle & not the upper or the lower class has produced culture & civilization. A worker of genius instantly moves into the middle class; an aristocrat of genius embarrassedly condescends to what he well knows is a middle-class activity. The middle class is the Aristotelian mean & the Hegelian synthesis Marx was looking for at once, & the only truly human class. The other two, being parasitic, are primarily animal classes, & the cult of idealizing them is part of the united front against reason. Culture & civilization wither at the coming to power of any other class, & we very coarsely mean today by "democracy" a dictatorship of the bourgeoisie. All this can be found in any sensible Victorian political thinker, before the self-destroying & self-accusing idealistic conscience of the middle class addled its brains. Yeats as an Irishman (Ireland, like Spain & Russia, is a poor country with a weak middle class, & so tends to revolutionary upheavals) thinking of the bourgeoisie in terms of England, was in a hopelessly false position from the first. [NB 31.8]

There are only two branches of the human race: those who belong to the bourgeoisie and those who wish they did. There is no such thing as a proletarian consciousness. [NB 44.533; LN, 1:215]

Mind. I wonder what it would really be like to get one's mind completely clear of the swirl of mental currents. It would be like walking across the Red Sea to the Promised Land, with walls of water standing up on each side. [NB 3.184; RT, 71]

Miracles. Perhaps the miraculous & the natural are really two modes of perceiving. There's no such thing as a miracle in the sense of an event having *no* explanation within the context of reason & ordinary experience. But of course such things as life can be seen as miraculous by a simple change of mood. Similarly when phenomena explained rationally by a scientist are seen as beautiful: there's no beautiful thing that isn't rationally explicable, but the shift in the *mood* of perceiving it is important. A miracle in the sense of a simply incredible or impossible event is, doubtless, not an event at all but a symbol. There's an element of projection here: just as beauty is in the eye of the beholder, so perceiving events teleologically is projected, as in the providence views I've mentioned. But the rational perception is also projected: the problem is not to choose one & reject the others, but to coordinate the possibilities. The miraculous as something that *mocks* reason is all wrong. [NB 21.369-70; RT, 209]

In one of the stories of Buddha, Buddha is represented as ridiculing an anchorite who after 25 years of austerities had learned to walk across a river. Quite right, but if Jesus condescended to walk on water it's not a wholly despicable feat. I imagine that the imagination in the void, wholly detached from any particular stunt, is capable of turning around and performing a great number of such stunts. Within limits (for even Blake distinguishes possible & impossible miracles, and I imagine that the faith that removes mountains is apocalyptic) I suppose the emancipated imagination can do what it likes, what it likes to do being conditioned by an organic will, as above, & as in Samuel Butler. I want to see what men—wise men, of course—who have looked into the matter would be willing to concede the imagination in the way of miraculous power, because of the way the Gospels seem to insist on its relevance. And of course I feel that one should read the Gospels with Christ in the reader, not outside him doing tricks. Miracles are assigned to the disciples in any case. Perhaps all creative people have potentially miraculous powers only of a type appropriate to their character. The important thing is that the outward life of a miracle-worker would be the same as that of an ordinary person, as no one wants to do tricks for newspaper reporters. But while magical powers are thus wholly neutralized, I'm not clear that all imaginative efforts are expressed in the world of art, as I used to infer from Blake. How far were the Evangelists newspaper reporters? Hardly at all, I'd say. In short, I suspect that everybody is capable in some degree of performing miracles which are only intensifications of aptitudes, though, because miraculous, appearing in unrecognizable forms; & that these miracles are connected with a process of creative evolution, though not in any obviously biological way. [NB 34.51]

Missionaries. A missionary hymn of my childhood began thus:

> *Far, far away, in heathen darkness dwelling,*
> *Millions of souls forever may be lost.*
> *Who, who will go…*

If the word "psychotic" means anything at all, it means the state of mind that can excrete this stuff. And yet, I can't honestly say it's as bad as racism, or even inseparable from imperialism. Missionaries in Fiji stopped cannibalism & widow-strangling. They brought writing & some elementary hygiene: they did a lot of positively good things. In the West today yogic Zen missionaries are trying to save our souls from damnation. They (and we) don't call it that, but the benefits of cross-pollenization are clear enough. [NB 11E.61-2; RT, 332]

Möbius Strip Paradox. The Möbius strip paradox, as I call it, that Paul can speak of "Christ in me" because Paul is a particular whole of which Christ is a part, while Christ is a universal whole of which Paul is a part, belongs with the point…that wisdom cannot be predicated of "I am." Thus "Christ in me" is the opposite of "I am Christ." [NB 27.27; LN, 1:7]

Morris. I don't know why I have felt, ever since I started to think seriously about the matter at all (since sometime around 1944, I think, when the dense Blake fog began to clear up) that William Morris, with his left-wing political views, his late 19th-century flourishing period, and his vast collection of epic & romances, was a guide to what I now think of as the Adonis world. [NB 14.2]

Mother Nature. I don't think it's coincidence or accident that feminism and ecology should become central issues at the same time.

[NB 44.495; LN, 1:206]

Music. Music, says Oscar Wilde, "creates for one a past of which one has been ignorant, and fills one with a sense of sorrows that have been hidden from one's tears. I can fancy a man who had led a perfectly commonplace life, hearing by chance some curious piece of music, and suddenly discovering that his soul, without his being conscious of it, had passed through terrible experiences, and known fearful joys, or wild romantic loves, or great renunciations." This seems to me a wonderful insight, with overtones that go far beyond music, true as I think it is of music. It verges close to my notion of myth as what really happened, as distinct from history, which is only what we'd have seen happening.

[NOTES 54-5.69; RT, 285]

I've been resisting playing the piano for so long that I will perhaps never get any skill back. I don't know why, but instead of relaxation it's become a mechanism for churning up the gibbering monkey's recital of embarrassing memories. My adolescent interest in Classical music (I could never hear anything in popular music but an unpleasant noise) was obsessive, a reaction against Monctonian, parental, & school environments. I was never very good: my sense of rhythm was poor and I have always been too lazy (and weak) to play up to speed and volume. I had dreams of being a great composer but never worked at them as I worked at my writing. Why this furtive scurrying approach? Far worse, I can't play in public because the same gibbering monkey sits at my ear and says at intervals "all right now, it's time for you to make a mistake." I always really wanted it this way: I wanted to read everything and scurry over the top of the keys. This caused conflicts when I finally did take lessons.... My mother's feeling that she had only one son and that I was a second-rate substitute for him (God provided the substitute, but God can be a pretty blundering fool in evangelical minds) may have affected me in some ways. Fortunately I was always too indolent & selfish to make silly efforts about it, trying to "prove" myself and the like. [NB 44.660; LN, 1:236-7]

Mutilated Bodies. "He that hath suffered in the flesh hath ceased from sin." For me, a certain awe, a certain sanctity, a certain visitation of the spirit of the crucified Lord, attaches itself to all people whose bodies have been mutilated by other men, for almost any cause. That is why we must not torture Nazis—they must not be allowed to drink of the cup of Christ. [NB 3.55; RT, 24-5]

Mystical Experiences. I have never had the sort of experience the mystics talk about, never felt a revelation of reality through or beyond nature, never felt like Adam in Paradise, never felt, in direct experience, that the world is wholly other than it seems. I don't question the honesty, or even the factuality, of those who have recorded such experiences, but I have had to content myself with the blessing to those who have not seen & yet have believed—if one can attach the word "belief" to accepting statements as obviously true as the fact that I have seen New York. The nearest I have come to such experiences are glimpses of my own creative powers— Spengler in Edmonton and two nights with Blake—and these are moments or intervals of inspiration rather than vision. I'm not sure that I want it unless I can have clarity about other things with it. What are all the miracles and divine visions of Bernard of Clairvaux to me when I know that he preached vehemently in favor of crusades? I had rather been impercipient all my life than preach a crusade. And much as I admire the clarity of structure in the religious thought of Eliot or C. S. Lewis, I don't want it if it's inseparable from the controversial one-upsmanship of *After Strange Gods* or the 16th-century history. And I won't have a morality that violates my own moral principles, that tells me, for instance, that my physical love for someone is merely adulterous when I know that it must be a part of God. I feel I must have God on my own terms, because God or somebody else's terms is an idol. God of course would act on his own terms, but he would respect my own imaginative needs if he were a genuine Father, as

I would my son's. The vision of nausea is very important, & the vision of moral nausea or conviction of sin or sickness unto death infinitely more so. But this kind of nausea is phony if it comes at second hand: if I become nauseated by my love for someone because I'm married to Helen, that's only because I'm accepting a moral code as a ready-made substitute for the real object of nausea in myself that I wish I could kill: something silly & masochistic & infinitely tedious, the very essence of tedium itself, which I want to kill in self-defence, because it wants to kill me.
[NB 19.265-6; TBN, 60-1]

Mysticism. If Plotinus & Eckhart & Sankara are mystics, one begins to see in what sense Plato, St. Thomas Aquinas & Dante, who all get extensively quoted in any serious study of mysticism, are also mystics. Here the term mystic tends to mean that large & more powerful comprehensiveness of mind (*and* speech *and* soul *and* all the other words) which makes a poet a Dante & not a Shelley, a composer a Bach & not a Wagner, a philosopher a Plato & not a Descartes, a contemplative a St. Theresa & not a Guyon. Now one can illegitimately confuse these meanings….. Or one can unite the partial to the total, & see the complete mystic way as one of a group of means of developing the soul. I feel that this perception, this ability to see the whole process in perspective, is the true Raja Yoga, which differs from all others in being the power of perceiving other approaches as Yogas.
[NB 3.31; RT, 16]

I've been called a mystic as well as a myth critic, because some people think that's an even more contemptuous term. If myth is really mythos, story or plot, then mysticism is being initiated in the mysteries. The mysteries historically were rebirth experiences, and as such they belong to what Jesus tells Nicodemus is central to spiritual life. The connection with shutting the eyes and above all the yacking mouth (turn off the fucking chatter) takes one from the world of convention and tradition that's always sure it's going somewhere into the inner world of before birth and after death and thrownness and vision in between. Jesus entered synagogues, even preached in them, but he also talked of going into a closet and shutting the door. This is the world of the individual experience that isn't just subjective and egocentric. It's also the nothing-world out of which nothingness grows into creation. [NOTES 53.153; LN, 2:642]

Myth. Some archaeological bugger has just "discovered" that the Exodus is a myth. Well, it's central to the Bible, and everything in the Bible that isn't a myth is an excrescence. *When* will people learn that the Bible approaches history *from above*, that it's subsumed in myth? The purely historical belongs to experience: every event is unique. The purely mythical is simply repetitive, & belongs to knowledge and conscious memory. Practice or habit memory, in its social aspect, develops the repetition of myth into the crisis or kairos of history. It was this perception of "historical process" that has made Marxism so powerful a movement in this century. But the belief in historical process has spawned some horrible superstitions in our time: it can't seem to manage the vertical lift that would take it out of the future and put an end to history. [NB 50.501; LN, 1:358]

Myth and Ideology. I shouldn't have to say that I am not postulating a golden age of pure myth with no admixture of ideology; but because of the extraordinary adherence of some readers to such inferences, I do have to say it. Such an age is like the Garden of Eden, not a description of anything that happened in the past, but a postulate that makes what follows more intelligible. That raises the question of the function of postulated myths, which will bear thinking. [NB 44.105; LN, 1:122]

Myth Criticism. There are practical and theoretical recreations of myth: the practical one is literature, the theoretical one the criticism of literature which has to expand into a theory of myth as a whole. At present, myth criticism is regarded as an antiquated and minor subdivision of criticism: it's actually criticism itself, as critics may come to realize after they've exhausted every conceivable variety of Trivial Pursuit.
[NB 27.379; LN, 1:67]

Reception of Blake: accustomed to it as I am, I am still not clear why mythological criticism evokes so powerful a resistance. [NB 11H.29; LN, 2:716]

Mythical Thinking. The fact that there is no dialectic or power of distinction in mythical thinking is something I have to face as a principle. It explains a great deal of fuzzy analogy-thinking, as in Bayley's *Lost Language of Symbolism,* which degenerates into playing around with resemblances in words (the thing is that there probably isn't a universal language, whereas there could be a universal language of myth). There's no doubt a feminine link here: ideas indefinitely extending themselves by analogy. "Stubborn" facts & "hard & fast" distinctions are male metaphors.
[NB 19.318; TBN, 72]

Myth of God. I have been writing about the devil-myth ever since my undergraduate days: if I could establish its opposite, the myth of God, which is a myth of identity, I'd have cracked a tough nut.
[NB 19.303; TBN, 69]

Mythographers. All good mythographers have two characteristics: one, they sound like cranks or nuts (not typical of the humanist pose, of course); two, they show a great respect for the "wisdom of the ancients."
[NB 11F.177; RT, 114]

Mythology. The disinterested imaginative core of mythology is what develops into literature, science, philosophy. Religion is applied mythology.
[NB 21.101; RT, 158]

Myths. Myths are constructed out of personalities assimilated to nature as ordinary experience sees nature: whimsical, unpredictable, liable to tantrums sometimes, to serenity sometimes, sometimes bursting with life, sometimes dying or dead. [NB 44.306; LN, 1:169]

N

Nakedness. The statement that Adam & Eve were naked and unadorned was too much for the commentary-stuffers. In the History of the Rechabites (II, 457) we're told "But we are naked not as you suppose, for we are covered with a covering of glory; and we do not show each other the private parts of our bodies." (The next sentence says this was true of Adam & Eve before the fall.) [NB 44.74; LN, 1:115]

Narcotic Necessity. For that relaxation of the spirit which is wisdom some kind of narcotic is essential, I think. It disturbs routine existence enough to suggest the infinite. Teetotallers are often cultural go-getters & over-rationalized. Their rhythm is all wrong. In the Middle Ages everybody was stewed in beer all day long. [NB 4.95]

Natural Aggressiveness. I said fifty years ago that the doctrine that man is by nature good does not lead to a very good-natured view of man. Communism apparently failed because it assumed that man could become naturally cooperative, whereas man is naturally aggressive and competitive, and becomes cooperative only when he becomes also fully matured individual. Hence all the retrograde steps, as a Marxist would consider them, "back" to competition and the deified open market and all the rest of it. But East Europe wants these things because they lead to the emancipation of the individual and his primary concerns, and only after that can we talk about producing for service instead of for profit. When man becomes critical of the competitive and aggressive aspect of nature, instead of regarding it as a means of justifying his own shittiness, he begins to recreate nature. Nature isn't by itself much more than what man makes of it: that's why there has to be this third factor of a spiritual kingdom, where alone the providence of God can operate. [NOTES 53.245-6; LN, 2:659]

Natural Religion. The reason why natural religion is a red herring is that one can learn from nature only what is natural, just as one can learn from history only what is historical. (This last is why I call it "illiterate" to believe "in" (accept as historical) what breaks the pattern of history, like the Virgin Birth or the Resurrection.) What "natural religion" obfuscates is the emerging descriptive power of language (which couldn't really develop until the sense of its limitations had also developed). Humanity was being differentiated from animals *and* God, not simply placed on a chain between them. I wonder if this is connected with Foucault's idea that "man" is a post-17th-century conception. After all, it's part of the same chain-break as the Copernican revolution.
[NB 50.467-8; LN, 1:351]

Nature. Flying over the Rockies recently I thought how human civilization cuts into the continuum of nature, which is really doing something else, with another rhythm & dimension from another world. From the perspective of that world, nature is "fallen," down under it. There is such a thing as creation, something that neither evolution by mutation nor any revolution that starts with a *culbute* [social overturn] can explain. How did we get to warm-blooded animals? How did we get to consciousness? All the links are missing. [NB 12.240; TBN, 189-90]

Nausea. I recently saw a spaniel sniffing with great concentration at a little girl's wet diapers, & reflected on the fact that although, as Smollett says, we snuff up our own with great complacency, still we regard that type of experience with nausea, & the nausea must be (as I think nausea always is, from Sartrean existentialism to sea sickness) the result of panic. Being just a bit "above" that, we feel dizzy in contemplating a plunge back into those depths. Now, why is smell below us? Does the great mystic take a

similar nauseated view of sight & sound? (Actually he'd presumably lose the nausea, with regard to smell too, because he wouldn't panic.) We tolerate smell only in sublimated forms. A woman can put perfume, usually derived from animal excreta, on to excite sexual appetite, but such perfumes are significantly described as "essences." Taste seems to be just teetering on our present level: we can only just tolerate the gourmet if we concentrate on the objective aspect of eating: but if we applied aesthetic theories of empathy & *Einfühlung* [sympathetic understanding] to taste we'd promptly get nauseated again.
[D 50.407; DNF, 376]

Navel. In the Song of Songs the word "navel" to describe one of the beloved's charms has been said by many authorities to be a euphemism for the vulva. But the passage begins with the bride in "sandals": if she has her shoes on she's more likely to be dancing than in bed, and in dancing the navel is, so to speak, called to the lover's attention. It seems to me that all sexual union in this poem is hypothetical and subjunctive, postponed until after the poem. [NOTES 52.163; LN, 2:455]

Ned Pratt. It is difficult if not impossible to write biography & criticism at the same time: I discover when trying to review a book by a personal friend that what I know of his personality is at once immediate and irrelevant, & confuses the criticism. Yeats' doctrine of a mask or antithetical Self helps a good deal, but oversimplifies. Thus a poet (I'm thinking of Ned Pratt) may take his initial imaginative experiences from the grimness & terror of Newfoundland; this becomes a mask only because he builds up an anagoraphobic love of symposiums against it, the "apocalyptic dinner" in the winter solstice or just before dawn. Then the grimness of the mask frightens him, and he varnishes over his tragedies of waste (nature's prodigality being a parody of his own) with epilogues postulating a cosmological cosiness. And yet if there weren't this intersection between "will" & "mask" the personality would fall to pieces. It would be like the drunk who, because his own mind is dulled & slowed down, assumes that everything has brightened & speeded up, & sees himself as the Socrates of a wise & witty symposium where everyone else sees only a slobbering bum. [NB 3.73; RT, 30]

Negative Capability. The moment of illumination, the flash of Chik-hai Bardo, the instant that Satan can't find: that's the anastasis that arrests the time-rhythm of original sin, the Karma of being dragged involuntarily backwards. That is apocalypse: that's what each life leads to as its own fulfilment. Nobody can move toward it: inspiration, providence, instinct, intuition, all the metaphors of involuntary accuracy, including grace itself, are groundswells carrying us along in a counter-movement, forward to the moment. We go by relaxing ourselves, & trying to put ourselves in the organized receptivity, the "negative capability," of being ready to listen to or look at whatever comes along. If it never comes, that's not our business. If death brings it, as the Tibetans say, that's the point about death. But to have something shown you & then refuse to admit that you saw anything of the kind: that's the sin against the Holy Spirit of inspiration which is not forgiven (i.e. makes it impossible for you to arrive at release or anastasis) either in this world or the next (Bardo). You can't expect something, or you'll find an oracle in every spiritual breeze that passes over you; you can't expect nothing, or you'll have in yourself no principle of escape. [D 49.223; DNF, 140-1]

Newman. "Lead kindly light" is a hymn I have a peculiar dislike for. Not because it's doggerel in shaky grammar—it could be that and still be a memorable or even great hymn. But choosing and seeing one's path is not pride: it's what God wants us to do. Otherwise we get the dangers of spiritual gravitation. The whole point of Newman's journey over crag and torrent was that the Roman Catholic Church was at the bottom, ready to end the journey. I suspect that Newman never *really* wanted to become a Roman Catholic, but once he got into this "lead Thou me on" routine he couldn't avoid falling into it. [NB 50.790; LN, 1:412-13]

Newspaper Names. Many newspapers are called the Star or the Sun; but you never hear of one called the Moon. Something in our symbolic subconsciousness never thinks of the moon as a watcher. [NB 1.68]

Next Tuesday. While undoubtedly many of the early Christians thought of the Second Coming as simply a future event which would take place for the benefit of the faithful, perhaps next Tuesday, I think a rather subtler conception of time than that is involved in both Jesus' teaching and in the mind of the author of Revelation.
["SYMBOLISM IN THE BIBLE," LECTURE 11; RT, 503]

Nietzsche. The phrase "God is dead" may have made some sense in the Nietzschean context, but as a slogan it's sheer idiocy. It is far more likely that in the twenty-first century the birds in the trees will be singing "Man is dead, thank God." What really is dead is the antithesis between a subjective man and an objective God. Nietzsche, by the way, was a power and will worshipper, and because everything man *does* goes in a circle, he *had* to wind up with his identical-recurrence horseshit.
[NB 50.291; LN, 1:313-14]

The way Nietzsche talks about himself in *Ecce Homo* is wrong in fact, but not in conception: it's the way a Communist would talk about Marx, so it isn't impossible. Given ever so slight a list to port, the history of the future might have gone through Nietzsche instead of through Marx. By the future I mean his future, our present. But still Nietzsche had no sense of dialectic incarnation: he couldn't organize or produce the form of the Pauline or Leninist epistle, hence his views about his own historical importance are a *post hoc propter* hoc fallacy. That is, he's not a genuinely existential thinker, but a hypothetical one who thinks he ought to be.... I suppose one of the things Nietzsche was trying to say is that if man could only think of God as an enemy he might get interested in him—the point behind a good deal of the anti-Nietzschean too, such as conviction of sin and Barth's *ganz anders*. [D 53.13; DNF, 591-2]

Non-Being. Naturally, one of the themes involved is: what sort of being has non-being? That's part of the old pun on nothing as not anything and as something called nothing, as in Stevens' *Snow Man*. The revolution of consciousness I've been connecting with plays, where the notions of reality and illusion you bring into the theatre with you get reversed, is certainly relevant. The reality of non-being is linked to the reality of a dream, and to the dream-reality reversal. Most of what we call reality is the debris of previous human constructs, that is, the blockage of the past, the voice of memory and the accuser. The alien vision of the sun brought into the flickering shadows of the cave. [NOTES 52.17; LN, 2:423-4]

Notebook Obsession. So the anagogic book would be aphoristic, obviously, and all my life I've had the notebook obsession manifested by what I'm doing at this moment. Writing in notebooks seems to help clarify my mind about the books I write, which are actually notebook entries arranged in a continuous form. At least, I've always told myself they were that. [NB 44.326; LN, 1:172-3]

There has been a very long interval between this note & the last one. I get periodically bored with notebooks, because so much of what I put into them is just a form of masturbation: an empty fantasy life making the scene with beckoning fair charmers who don't exist. However.
[NB 24.240; TBN, 332]

Why do I try to keep notes like this, when forty years of experience shows they don't do me any good? [NB 33.80]

I keep notebooks because all my writing is a translation into a narrative sequence of things that come to me aphoristically. The aphorisms in turn are preceded by "inspirations" or potentially verbal *Gestalten*. So "inspiration" is essentially a snarled sequence. Many of the nuts and cranks who write me letters are inspired, but can't get to the verbalizing stage. Some of them are nuts because they accept the pernicious Shelleyan fading-coal fallacy, and think they're descending to commonplace when they attempt sequence. [NB 44.591; LN, 1:226]

I think in cores or aphorisms, as these notebooks indicate, and all the *labor* in my writing comes from trying to find verbal formulas to connect them. I have to wait for the cores to emerge: they seem to be born and not made. Because of this, continuity is associated with moral duty, as in Coleridge. This is old stuff. But *is* there a kerygmatic style? What's confusing me just here is the Kantian "the critical path is alone open," which historically means that the conceptual idiom is now permanently aware of a fully matured descriptive idiom contemporary with it. This quality of awareness recurs in the distinction between the genuine rhetoric that respects conceptual and descriptive integrity and the mob rhetoric that howls them down. It doesn't have to be conscious awareness: usually it's better if it isn't. [NB 50.529; LN, 1:364]

Nothing. In public school my teacher was demonstrating a vacuum with a suction pump, & said it was a big vacuum. I said "What would there be if you got *all* the air out?" He said (impatiently, to a silly question) "There'd be nothing there, of course." I'd asked the question because it had suddenly floated into my 12-year old mind that I couldn't take in the notion of nothing. Something with nothing inside it was still something; "a vacuum," being a noun, is something; even if I say with Gertrude Stein "there is no there there," I'm talking about something. Empty space is something, namely space; the act of perceiving it is an event in time. No matter. I suppose all Zen "koans" are really about that.
[NB 11F.163; RT, 110-11]

We start out with things like "nature abhors a vacuum," which is a metaphor. As metaphors are for practical purposes the elements of language, they can't be broken down into more elementary units: they can only be rearranged. One rearrangement is "God made the world from nothing." What was God before he made the world? Boehme says "a nothing longing to be something." At least that seems to me what his Urgrund is a metaphor for. This is one of the metaphors of the *via negativa* that extends from John of the Cross to Taoism with its *wu wei* notion: by doing nothing everything is done. [NB 44.373; LN, 1:183]

The dialectic to which the cyclical imagery of the Bible leads is the separation of all reality from nothingness. Nothingness is that which cannot be transformed into negation. [NB 11B.74; RT, 358-9]

Among the ambiguities of "nothing" ("there is nothing to be afraid of" and Heidegger's "dread reveals nothing") there is the supremely terrifying "there is nothing to stop you." Hitler & his like hear only the first half of this, until it's too late. [NB 50.510; LN, 1:360]

Whatever nothing is, it's the goal of time, which is why every surrender to time, like death, leads in the direction of nothingness. Is that why the *axis mundi* is so central; because it's the *dead* pillar of the risen body set up as an emblem of resurrection, of refusal to surrender? I've been wondering where my way & journey stuff went: "there" is always an illusion, the end of the promising rainbow. [NB 50.580; LN, 1:375]

Nothing to Be Done. The staircase among other things is a symbol for or metaphorical expression of a spiritual awakening in which, as St. Thomas says of the Holy Spirit, there's no intervening space between being-there, or Heidegger's *Dasein*, and being *there*. The upward metamorphosis of the transfiguration in the gospels is again symbolic: note that Peter's proposal to stay "there" is explicitly condemned. The Zen and Taoist view that there is nothing to be done, and that that nothing is the same thing as everything, may be right in theory. [NOTES 52.149]

Numbers Game. I think a metaphor connected with my numbers game is important: there are twelve zodiacal signs, or symbolically twelve stars: these surround a thirteenth, the sun. The twelve stars are visible at night

when the sun is invisible; the sun is visible by day when the stars are invisible. Similarly with my 78: that's the number of cards in the Tarot pack if
we count the Fool one instead of zero. As zero, it's the essence of all the
others. This metaphorical interchange between the unity and the variety
of identity may turn out to be important.
[NOTES 52.180; LN, 2:459]

Recurrent numbers, seven & twelve & the like, are elements of design only:
they represent no hidden mystery or numinousness in things. Not even the
trinitarian three or the Jungian four. There are twelve signs in the zodiac,
but it would be equally easy to see nine or eleven or fourteen and a half.
Only fractions seem so *vulgar*. [NB 44.255; LN, 1:157-8]

O

Objects of Reassurance. What is the literary importance of the monumental literary object: the leather-bound sets of the great classics, the plastic counterparts of these contributed by the book-of-the-month clubs, the monumental systematic theology or philosophy in a clergyman's study? Plainly it is in part an object of reassurance: contemporary philosophy, on the other hand, distrusts the book as a literary genre. The *latter* feeling goes with specialization & with the existential: Austin's bits & pieces, or Wittgenstein's, remind one of *Sartor Resartus*. Similarly with the distrust of the epic & narrative in poetry.
[NB 19.56; TBN, 14-15]

Oedipus. Humanity is only a criminally insane Oedipus with only two aims in life: to murder his father God and rape his mother Nature.
[NOTES 52.36; LN, 2:427]

One-Hundred Chapters. Oh, God, I could be ecstatically happy for years if I could work out the scheme of a 100-section book so that I could work on the total scheme in my head. In fact it would make me so happy that I've simply got to have one. Question: will it be a real or simply a mnemonic one? Never mind that now. 100 sections with an occult meaning for every damn one; patterns of repetition connecting them; climactic sequences 27-33, 60-66, 90-99; prime numbers after 50 perhaps philosophical. Odd numbers cyclical, especially 7, 11, 13 & 17; even numbers dialectic, especially 8 & 16; five & decimals mixed, that sort of thing. It isn't *just* childish, either: Dante & Joyce do it. It probably won't work out, but God, it would be wonderful to have a scheme one could work on as women do with knitting. A hundred big filing cards, to be played with like a Tarot pack. Every other piece of writing I've done has been a spider-string filament strung painfully from my own guts: a straight line in the work has been to keep it from becoming a web. A pattern sufficiently discontinuous—oh, well, there's no point going on & on about it. Can I do it, & if I do will it be normal scholarship or specifically creative? Or is it only one of those creative farts I've let from time to time? [NB 11F.254-5, 257; RT, 131]

Opening Sentences. The famous opening sentences of *Pride & Prejudice* & of *Anna Karenina* are vestigial conventions deriving from the exemplum convention: one can trace it back to the *Decameron,* where every story is preceded by general statements which the story is supposed to illustrate. *Rasselas;* the first chapters of the books of *Tom Jones,* etc. [NB 18.84]

The Oracular World. Anybody who's ever read a book on spiritualism or kindred subjects realizes that the oracular world is a damn confusing place. No definite individuality; nothing but bits and pieces of personality floating about, some of them apparently separate from the medium, others part of him. It's in this world that all the guesses about a life after death… keep trying to fix on definite things. [NOTES 54-3.16]

Oral Poetry. In poetry, whatever Derrida may say, the oral takes precedence over the written, because poetry is being referred back to an original performance. The personal poet has to be represented by somebody, however remote from the poet or however silent. But, of course, the poem is not a direct address, but broadcast like a radio program.
[NOTES 52.569; LN, 2:537]

Orange. If I were to say to an orange what a beautiful orange you are, and if the orange could talk, it would say: orange is the one thing I'm not, the one color I totally reject. That's why you see me as orange: it's the color I banish from myself. If you could see me as I really am I'd be more like blue.

Now *there's* a color. I wonder how far this principle could be extended to, say, how we see other people's characters.
[NOTES 54-5.155; RT, 304]

Organized Religion. The effect of organized and institutional religion on society, for the most part, is evil. It isn't just reactionary or superstitious; it is evil, and stinks in the nose of God. One has to remember this when thinking of the easy conquests of secular revolution over it. They, of course, become evil in their turn. [NB 12.347; TBN, 216]

Original Pettiness. It isn't original sin that makes one feel sardonic so much as original pettiness. Take Plato, with his idealism soaring up to the moon like the Tower of Babel. Yet the climax of the *Symposium* is the great news that when he's in bed with another man Socrates will cuddle but not bugger. [NB 23.42; RT, 373]

Ornament and Imitation. Ruskin's distinction of ornament & imitation is fundamental to painting. Imitation is extroverted & phenomenal: ornament is abstract, introverted, & concerned with what is transcendental in the Kantian sense: the *categories* of form & design. In our day we go from extreme abstract expression around behind to an anti-painting based on the principle of the fetishistic (ornamental) aspect of the *objet trouvé* [found object]: this began in photography, & develops through types of futurism, surrealism, dadaism, like the pop art currently fashionable.
[NB 19.47; TBN, 13]

Other Worlds. What I'd like to find is a real hypothesis, if there is one, underneath all the priestcraft and political exploitation connected with other-world beliefs. [NB 11E.35; RT, 325]

Ozymandias Complex. Most civilizations have tried to make their definitive cultural achievement some kind of stone monument—the Ozymandias complex. Especially Egypt, where the association of stone & death seems to be so strong. The Hebrews entrusted their achievement to the most brittle & fragile product of the ancient world, thereby following the rhythm of life itself, which is equally fragile, & yet more endurable in its repetition than the hardest unrepeatable substance.

[NB 21.336; RT, 203]

$\mathcal{P}$

Palaces of Criticism. If there's no real difference between creation & criticism, I have as much right to build palaces of criticism as Milton had to write epic poems. My whole and part interchange works here too: inside the *Anatomy*, everyone is a disciple & to some degree a captive of Frye—every writer has a captive audience—but surely one can finish the book & then do as one likes, with something of me inside him. If he doesn't have something of me inside him, he won't, at this time of history, have anything of much use to say as a critic. [NB 44.108; LN, 1:123]

I'm beginning to feel that the schematic structure of the *Anatomy* is a key to a much larger principle. People don't have to remain doorkeepers in it forever, as in Psalm 23: they can go out to build palaces of their own. I suspect also that the key to philosophy is the exact opposite of what philosophers do now. It's the study of the great historical systems, each of them a palace and a museum, that's genuine philosophy. At a certain point they interpenetrate into a house of many mansions, a new Jerusalem of verbal possibilities, but that's a tremendous state of enlightenment. [NB 44.110; LN, 1:123]

The Palmer Method. In public school there was an attempt to teach writing by a "forearm movement," starting with the whole arm instead of making twiddly voluntary movements with the fingers. I knew I would never learn to write this way, and as far as my observation went nobody else did either, even the teachers. But they worked out better compromises than I did. What I didn't of course realize was that this was really a "Zen" technique, based on the principle of letting the writing emerge from the arm. Perhaps if I had learned to write this way I'd have become a poet or novelist instead of a critic: perhaps some ability to draw would have emerged, instead of the total inhibition of that faculty which has always mystified me. [NB 44.450; LN, 1:200]

Paradox. Aldous Huxley quotes a Chinese Zen as saying "He (the *guru*) has done all he could for you; he is exhausted—only able to turn round & present you with this iron bar without a hole." "What precisely is the significance of that iron bar without a hole?" asks Huxley. "I do not pretend to know. Zen has always specialized in nonsense...." Well, I know. The road to this kind of spiritual energy lies through paradox, & Huxley has no feeling for paradox. [NB 3.52; RT, 24]

Much has been said of the paradox of the Incarnation, but the paradox of Jehovism is much less conceivable. This is a matter of God's naming himself, of his deliberately limiting his essence to the God worshipped by the Jews. This is the fundamental paradox in the West.
[NB 19.41; TBN, 11-12]

Paranoia. Human paranoia is so great: an earthquake in China, if we're in Europe, doesn't raise any questions, but in the Lisbon 1755 earthquake everybody ran around in circles screaming: How can God let this happen? Man always thinks that if he were Providence he'd do more to earn his keep, interfere more & push people around, in short, create romances.
[NB 11E.31; RT, 324-5]

Paravritti. The opposite of the verbal perception is the presentation, the communicated message, what Marshall McLuhan talks about. Marshall says it's the form & not the content of the message that's important, which is why the nature of the medium is also important. It seems to me that the form has this importance only as long as we're unconscious of it: to become aware of the form as a form is to separate the content. At that point the presentation goes into reverse & becomes a perception: the form comes from us then. Such reversal of movement (*paravritti, wider Kehr*) is of course a hinge of all my thinking. [NB 19.58-9; TBN, 15]

Parents. I think it is normal to hate one's parents, in a rather more literal sense than Jesus had in mind, and not only the parent of the same sex. The point is that they are the visible symbols of the chain of "habit-energy accumulated since beginningless time," the heredity or Karma we are hoping to break. Again, if the child is an undeveloped human being, the parent, the complement of the child, is an imperfect one. Once the child matures, the parent must *qua* parent disappear & either become a personal friend as nearly as differences in age & tastes allow, or incur resentment. Worry over the social blunders committed by parents, a worry which is usually excessive & often created out of nothing, is a frequent expression of this resentment. I have always approved of the weak family feeling among the Fryes: differences in taste should not tie one too closely to the compulsory & conventional affinities of the family. That is, differences in taste should be indulged, not suppressed by convention. I imagine that many Victorian daughters who were stuck by society with an old man & compelled to waste their lives on him on the pretext that he was their father nagged him unmercifully. [NB 3.66; RT, 28]

The ego swallows its parents and puts them to guard the door of the Id. As obstacles, they're Satan & Rahab; as transparent, Los & Jerusalem. The ego, the reality-principle, deals with conflicts of truth & error; the id, the pleasure principle, with conflicts of good & evil. As opaque, the parents are narcissistic, reflecting the ego on itself, & also presenting the pleasure-pain values of the id in terms of a moral law of good & evil. Freud says that the id is inherited & the ego isn't; the superego, being the boundary, is a memory which *may* be a revived inherited memory, Jung's archetype. Anyway, what the ego has to do is swallow its parents a second time, in their second or permanent death, & occupy their place.
[NB 3.149; RT, 60]

My mother was very subject to autonomous appearances from her unconscious: they fascinated her & made her feel that she was especially *en rapport* with spiritual phenomena. Her attempts to interpret her dreams & automatic voices were, as I think, premature, & tended, with her deafness, to shut her in. My father is completely indifferent to all such matters, or appears to be so, though I believe he had a couple of minatory dreams. I trace both tendencies clearly in myself. From early years I have deliberately frightened myself with my own shadow, or hoped to see visions, though I no longer am much interested in the world of *objective* spirits— neither in a way was mother, who despised spiritualism. Yet there are still twinges, & old superstitions still persist: even on this plane the flattering of the ego which is the beginning of magic can be traced. [NB 3.150; RT, 60-1]

Participation Mystique. In the earliest traces of human creativity we can discover, such as the cave-drawings in Altamira or Lascaux, we see pictures of animals, drawn with joy and exuberance under the most fantastically difficult conditions of positioning and lighting. We can isolate various aspects of the impulse to produce these paintings, the most obvious being the magical impulse, to ensure a plentiful supply of game. But no single aspect, magical, religious or aesthetic, brings us to the center of the titanic will to identification with the objects represented. That seems to be what has been called a *participation mystique,* a sense of identity with the object which is not verbal but existential. We notice that some of the figures are those of sorcerers or shamans dressed in animal skins, another aspect of identification. Similarly, the earliest use of music seems to have been primarily ecstatic. Also rituals. [NOTES 52.395; LN, 2:502-3]

Parts of Speech. I wonder just how far the conception of metaphysics as a grammatical fantasy can be pushed. The noun & verb represent respectively the sources of being & becoming, of the ideas of the substantially existent & of the motor-genetic. The universal (this was C. D. Broad's suggestion) comes out of the adjective, & the universe of value springs from the adverb. Note that the universal modifies substance (as in Thomism) & that value modifies manifestation or coming into being. Conjunctions & prepositions are then the source of the essential associative machinery, such as causality, & the pronoun involves the whole question of persona, the person in the substance & standing in place of it. [D 50.145; DNF, 271]

Passion and Indolence. Yeats spoke to Bridges of a young American as having the American passion for ideas combined with the American intellectual indolence (and physical energy; less important). That is about the profoundest remark about the American intellectual I ever expect to hear. It may even be a profound remark about me, but I doubt it: I haven't any real passion for any ideas except my own, & that should be a sufficient antidote to indolence. I occasionally wonder, though, if I'm not the passion for ideas stepped up to a kind of medium. [NB 34.26]

Past / Future. To remember without being bound to the past: to anticipate without being bound to the future. [NB 44.196; LN, 1:144]

The Path. The path is before me, & it is always there: no God puts my application on file & makes me wait until I hear from him. Nor is there any magical spell on it: I may start out & turn back innumerable times, but the path is unaffected by that, though I'm not. [NB 30R.12]

Pattern-Making. I'm often attacked for deliberate pattern-making, but that's how I've learned a lot of things. If A & B have opposites R & S, & A & B are followed by C & D, then these probably are T & U. [NB 24.217; TBN, 327]

Pepys. I've been reading in Pepys, to avoid work. I can't understand him at all. I mean, the notion that he tells us more about himself & gives us a more intimate glimpse of the age than anyone else doesn't strike me. I find him more elusive and baffling than anyone. He has a curious combination of apparent frankness and real reticence that masks him more than

anything else could do. One could call it a "typically English" trait, but there were no typical Englishmen then and Montaigne performs a miracle of disguise in a far subtler & bigger way. Pepys is not exactly conventional: he is socially disciplined. He tells us nothing about himself except what is generic. His gaze is directed out: he tells us where he has been & what he has done, but there is no reflection, far less self-analysis.
[D 42.67; DNF, 28-9]

Personae. The individual man comprises a multitude of other characters —Jung's archetypes are surely only a few threshold dwellers. There is at least a good-sized village inside me. Many are children, some are women, & a few may be animals or even monsters. Some are replicas of other people I know, either in personal acquaintance or in reading. They die, but new ones move in & grow up. All this is not pure whimsy—I'm trying to get at a real fact of existence. Ever since Plato people have talked of the state in terms of the individual: what would happen if one were to look at the individual in terms of a society? Suppose Jung's "anima" were not *a* feminine figure in me, but the aggregate of all the female characters in me? He says himself that the animus is regularly a group or council. So with me: in the course of a day, even a day spent in pure solitude, I should go through a bigger dramatic repertoire than any commedia dell'arte. Pedants, buffoons, comedians, debaters, politicians, hermits, saints, sages, middling-sensual men, suburban bourgeoisie all dispute within me, & everything I do & say is the calculus of probabilities resulting from their competition within me. [D 49.361; DNF, 200-1]

Strange the variety of dramatis personae we contain: we have mockers, accusers, even saboteurs and traitors, and doubtless at the center a judge with a black cap, waiting to put it on. We objectify and project all these things first as gods, then we dramatize them in human society. The extent to which we dramatize is only just beginning to dawn on me. With the death of the king [George VI], press and radio are full of people asserting solemnly that they feel emotions they can't possibly feel. They must be

214

either congenital liars or actors in a play: it's more charitable to assume the latter. The people who acquire feelings after they've been suggested to them, or have emotional vacancies in their lives that need filling, are another matter. [D 52.109; DNF, 506]

Personal Truth. I often have the feeling that my thought is an elaborate rationalization of my own temperament and social attitude, that its profoundest areas are verbal formulas connecting one prejudice with another. I used to worry about this & feel I ought to become more objective and impersonal & what not. But now I think it's only what's true only for me that's really true. That is, it's all that gets into the higher area of personal truth, & thereby becomes absolutely or universally true on the flight-of-the-alone-to-the-alone principle. Impersonal truth is only a drop in the ocean of the petty omniscience of a God who hasn't yet been incarnated. [NB 12.313; TBN, 207]

Pets. I have no love for parasitic fauna of any kind, & I think pets have a bad influence on people, the bigger the creature the worse the influence: look how bad Moby Dick was for Ahab. But while I am not fond of dogs, dogs are very fond of me, & I'm always fending off the embraces of some maudlin yap who's out to show me that he's man's best friend.... Animals' minds are still an unexplored mystery of nature, & hence become a hideout of superstition of all kinds, from anti-vivisection to the popular (because anti-intellectual) beliefs in the mysterious accuracy and insight of animal instinct. *The Reader's Digest,* which seldom makes a mistake about the sort of vulgar error that people want encouraged, runs columns going to prove that every animal is directly inspired by God. The story of the cat who's abandoned two thousand miles from home & eventually turns up with a loyal but reproachful expression on its face is dug out of the newspaper morgue every three weeks or so. I suppose this is all covered in the *Natural History of Nonsense,* but it's a phobia of mine, as animals symbolize something to me: I dream of injuring them. [D 51.17; DNF, 459-60]

Phenomenological Fox. I recently heard of a little boy who drew five horizontal lines on a piece of paper and told his mother it was a picture of a fox hiding behind a fence. The mother said: "I see the fence all right, but where's the fox?" The child protested: "But I *told* you; he's *hiding behind it.*" If I knew the answer to that one I'd know more phenomenology than Husserl, and more of the noumenal world than Kant.

[NB 44.454; LN, 1:201]

Philosophical Problems. The problems of philosophy are not solved, but we do succeed in losing interest in them. We have not solved the medieval realist-nominalist dispute, the arguments for & against the validity of the ontological proof, or the Renaissance controversy over innate ideas; but we have acquired an overwhelming sense of their unreality which is better than a solution. If I hear undergraduates arguing over free will & necessity, I can only sit there in a smug stupor of inarticulate ignorance in which I am as convinced of my greater maturity & wisdom as though I were drunk. My brain beats out a drone bass indistinguishable in sentiment from the intellectual tortoises they're trying not to be: "I don't know what you're talking about; but I have known, and you'll never catch me in *that* rat-trap again." For if you can express your reasons for finding the question unreal you're still arguing about it, & still involved in its illusion of reality. And while the individual is far enough from total understanding to keep himself articulate to the end of his days, total understanding is utterly inarticulate, the circumferential grasp (rather an illogical phrase) in which the understood thing is wholly imprisoned. I suppose similarly the more one knows the more meaningless become practically all propositions about one's knowledge. Perhaps a good mental exercise would be to take a sentence at random & ponder it until it becomes utterly meaningless, as I should think the proposition "there is a God" would be to a really religious man. [NB 3.64; RT, 27]

Physics. Physics started back in the early years of the 20th century with a planetary model, where electrons formed orbits around a proton but could engage in a kind of dance, jumping from one orbit to another. Questions about whether they occupied space or not, whether they travelled in time and space or simply manifested themselves elsewhere, about whether each particle of matter had its counterpart in some opposed world, came up just as they did in scholastic philosophy in a macroscopic framework. The real "spiritual world" seems to have turned out to be subatomic. [NOTES 52.115; LN, 2:443]

Picasso and Braque. What painter has done the most to reeducate our visual associations? Picasso gets the publicity, but maybe Braque did the essential job. [D 50.69; DNF, 241]

Picking and Choosing. The Pope is touring U.S. now [September 1987], trying to tell American Catholics that they can't pick & choose what they will believe out of a dialectically conceived doctrine. The point is that everyone, Catholic and non-Catholic, picks & chooses how he will believe, & that's really what my book [*Words with Power*] is about. In revising the book there should be quite a lot about the difference in charity between a dialectically conceived doctrine and a mythologically conceived one. The latter will never be adopted by my church, but it will be by an increasing body of the public. [NB 50.236; LN, 1:302]

Pious Fraud. One reason why myth always lies is that (as I discovered with Burke) it can't distinguish appearance from reality. What things ought to be is primary; what they are is secondary, & hence a selection must be made, from the things that are, of the things that symbolize the way things ought to be. A sacramental pious fraud. [NB 11F.206; RT, 122]

Platonism. A certain amount of Platonism is inevitable with social institutions: every student, every churchgoer, every voter, has some *idea* of the university or church or government which is not destroyed by the pedantry or stupidity or dishonesty that he finds in the operating institutions. [NB 44.565; LN, 1:211]

Play. The conception of play I got originally from Huizinga, from whom I deduced the principle that work was energy directed toward an end, and that play was the end, energy for its own sake. In society work is a penal effort imposed by society and accepted for the very little amount of play it allows. I imagine Nietzsche has a lot to say about this emancipated energy ("gaya scienza"), though its "will to power" connections are a product of frustration, at least so far as they're aggressive. [NB 50.6; LN, 1:256]

Neoteny: play is the basis of cultural development, and play in animals is a rehearsal for mature serious work. In humans, if we stuck with nature, we'd grow into apes, like that man in Huxley's novel [*Ape and Essence*]; if we transfer our lives from nature to spirit, from the symbolic mother to the symbolic father, play becomes a rehearsal for spiritual life. [NOTES 53.223; LN, 2:654]

Play Thinkers. We still don't know how to deal with the play thinker (like me, dammit), despite Nietzsche's *Gaya Scienza*. Butler is in his grave. [NOTES 52.913; LN, 2:596]

Pleasures. There are two kinds of pleasures that I know of: the pleasure of conquest and the pleasure of retirement. This distinction extends to everything: with me, an unusually hypertrophied (or perhaps integrated) person, both are found in literature and music. The difference in emphasis goes very deep: in general, literature is conquest and music escape, but there are subdivisions, & most of the great classics are conquest & most of the romantics retirement (or relaxation). Dante excites, and Shakespeare: Poe, Bulwer-Lytton, Wilkie Collins, ghost stories & some detective stories relax; Bach fugues excite; Schumann & even Tschaikovsky relax. It seems to me the part of wisdom to ignore neither, but accept both and, above all, align them. I don't feel that Poe or Schubert are secret vices, as many do, or affect to do, and their inferiority to others seems to me partly an accident. I do realize, however, that my fondness (all right, weakness) for corny romanticism, facile supernaturalism, and Gothic horror generally is inspired by a nostalgia rather than the creative response, and as nostalgia longs for the vanished, there is a residue of indefiniteness about it that leads to some dissatisfaction & disillusionment with what one attains. Thus in buying a house I can distinguish, as the builder of Casa Loma apparently could not, between the house I really want & the vast gloomy Victorian barn that a part of me hankers after. [NB 34.2]

Plotinus. I've been trying to read Plotinus (in McKenna) with little success. I don't mean I can't get through him, but he doesn't give me any ideas. The positivistic streak in me is much stronger than I thought—I keep saying this is shit, although I thought temperamentally I was akin to it. I ain't. However. If McKenna's admirable style represents the original, it's an interesting style: discontinuous, easy-going meditative, question-&-answer rhythm, which is partly addressed to a reader & partly not. It's an Avatamsaka rhythm too: each tractate is the center of the system, so that a sufficiently astute disciple could reconstruct the whole system from any one. [NB 18.100]

Poe's Mental Landscape. I'm attracted to this subject because Poe sets down the elements of the imagination, in its introverted or projected dream form, so nakedly. This, as I explain in *Anatomy of Criticism*, is why he has so immediate an influence on our own time as compared with a more displaced writer like Hawthorne. As for the Germans (except Novalis & possibly Jean Paul), the less said about them the better. Most of them don't know what the hell they're doing—I'm not saying Poe did either, but something in him did. [NB 13.84]

Poetics, Part 2. Aristotle's contemptuous dismissal of mythological thinking in the *Metaphysics* is natural historically: it's consistent with the rejection of poetic & intuitional thinking: i.e., what comes up in bits & pieces directly from the mythological universe. It's inconsistent with the second part of the Poetics, but I wrote that, not Aristotle.
[NB 11B.16; RT, 351]

Poetic Vision. The world across death is the invisible world that enables the new creation, that of human art, to become visible. I said that the question whether Yeats in Byzantium is talking about life after death or about the poet's transforming of reality is one of those either-or questions that have to have a both-and answer. I don't think Dante is predicting his own salvation at the end of the *Paradiso:* I think he's predicting the salvation, that is, the guarantee of the reality, of his poetic vision. [NB 44.587; LN, 1:225]

Point of Demonic Epiphany. Celine & Genet are morally significant because they shock & horrify: they help to prevent us from becoming what we behold. Hell is not knowing the difference: it's the world of sub-art and anti-art. But everything that *is* art goes through the point of demonic epiphany and contemplates it. Similarly at the top, where everything that's literature is an analogy or masque of heaven. [NB 6.62; TBN, 121]

Political Analogues. The political analogue of Freud is Marx: what's the political analogue of Jung? There isn't one really: his real goal is the individual who's moved his center of gravity from the ego, so its political vision is a democracy in which the individual is not diminished in dignity by his social contract. The closest approach I can think of is William Morris, but he fell into left-wing hysteria, just as Carlyle, Ruskin & Burke fell into right-wing ones. (So did Jung.) Coleridge stopped at anxiety, but was heading in the same direction, and Nietzsche is closer to Adler. [NB 44.351; LN, 1:178]

Pornography. Everybody has a point at which he can't take a convention: pornography, for example, which sacrifices all the traditional literary conventions for a prodding of reflexes, appeals only to those who like having their reflexes prodded & don't resent it. The majority of people do like being drilled & ordered & told what to do, & pornography does this along with reversing the context & giving the illusion of escape. That day we read no farther, as Eve said. [NB 27.421; LN, 1:76-7]

Portable Beulah. When I was about seven I had a passion to live in a cave, which lasted a surprisingly long time, & if I'd been born in Tibet or early Christian Egypt I suppose I'd have become an anchorite. At eleven I had an equally strong passion for a private study, which I still have. This may be an underground current that breaks out in the form of my recurrent agoraphobia. A psychoanalyst would talk about wombs & foetuses & mothers & of course the everlasting Oedipus: I see it as the necessity for a Beulah or a place of intellectual seed. One should have this, but one of the essential features of the visionary life is a portable Beulah: I approve of the overthrow of monastic & so-called ivory-tower ideals, though not in the interests of the hey-fellas type of herd mind that usually replaces it. American civilization in particular seems unable to get over this elementary dilemma. [NB 34.44]

Posing. I have often despised myself for posing, & I now realize that I was right, but only because I posed badly. The thing is to get a persona or mask that one can really wear. And posing well is important not as a necessary evil, but as a necessary virtue—unless, of course, one is born with the mask attached—is genuinely unaffected, as we say. The first step in all imaginative effort is to concentrate one's faculties, achieve some sort of one-pointedness, charge one's batteries. Religious devotees do it with icons; narcissists with mirrors; in ordinary society those with most distinctive & magnetic personalities are those who have thrown themselves into a part, & who use the strain of acting that part as a means of keeping their batteries continuously charged. The most successful are those who never think of abandoning the part when done; it's those who try to keep slipping in & out of their roles who look like fools. The mere act of charging the batteries is in itself neither good nor bad: Hitler & the man in *The Plumed Serpent* did it for evil reasons; Loyola for reasons considered good in some quarters. And it's conventionally considered good to act alone with the same appearance of self-respect one displays in public. [NB 3.70; RT, 29]

Possession. Most of the occult mafia of our time seem to think that getting taken over by another spirit is always good. (Others may think it always bad, but they're out of fashion.) [NB 11B.26; RT, 353]

Possession vs. Contemplation. In Plato we move from the iconic contemplation of beauty, where it's still objective, to union with it. Union is based on the analogy of sexual union, so it is a sublimation of Eros. In literature a play in the theatre is an iconic spectacle: union with it is possible only through the written text. This links with my experience-criticism point, and perhaps the role of the text indicates how Eros is regained in a Biblical context. I've been calling this possession, which is only the subjective analogy, except for the fact that the subject experiences. Possession is subjective & contemplation objective: union is both, the identity of experience with form which is upward metamorphosis. From the point of view of the text, of course, it's a downward metamorphosis, a series of disguisings and misreadings. Similarly from the point of view of the subject as "real person." There's no person & no text, only an experience identified with the form—you are the music, as Eliot says.
[NB 15.17-18; RT, 315-6]

Posterity. Reading books is a form of necromancy, as no book attains its full meaning until its author is dead & reading becomes a form of communicating with the dead. Milton's conception of the book as the consolidation of a man's soul is true enough, but in time it's his preserved & mummified body. Speaking of a book as a man's soul, I've often wondered if there isn't a real world of creative value withdrawn from our judgement of it. Posterity brings a great deal to light & levels out much injustice, but it's not infallible, & even when it's right its rightness isn't relevant. There must be a world in which every artist *has* the greatness he dreamed of & tried to achieve. The Beerbohm Enoch Soames story is an ironic frame-up: it shows how inadequate the future is as a substitute for eternity. There must be a world in which Benjamin Robert Haydon is exactly the genius he thought he was—the future, like the past, is the mouth of hell, & confirms his own doubts. I wouldn't give the devil two cents for a peep at the

British Museum catalogue in 2049 without a written guarantee that it would be interesting. I'm quite sure that a hope that posterity will recognize the greatness of such books as *Fearful Symmetry* doesn't really support me. I'm so detached from that that it surprises me: it's either the mercy of God or the fact that I have a job & a steady salary cheque coming in. Or a combination of the two. [D 49.199; DNF, 130-1]

Power. Knowledge is still power: what's wrong with our present power is that it isn't *humane*. [Fritjof] Capra & others talk about whole views vs. partitioned ones: that's part of the answer, but the humanities are still the missing ingredient. We study literature in order to possess its powers: it's *not* a verbal icon. [NB 23.62; RT, 376]

Prayer. Harold Bloom asked me what prayer was: I told him I thought it was an effort at self-knowledge that doesn't come from introspection. [NB 11F.171; RT, 112]

If prayer is the attempt of the creature to direct words to his creator, revelation is not merely an answer to prayer but a *counter*-prayer. If the revelation is thought of as definitive, it is the answer to all possible prayers. And if art is the central form of the creature's effort to transform himself into a creator, it makes sense to call the Bible the Great Code of Art, as Blake does. And if I'm right in saying that prayer is self-knowledge not gained through introspection, then revelation, or counter-prayer, gives knowledge of what is not oneself through introspection, the word in the heart. [NB 21.578; RT, 247]

Predestination. Samuel Butler seems to me to take one further than almost anyone else in the mystery of predestination. Our notions of free will & moral responsibility seem to me to be rationalizings of something given, data, données. The possession of beauty or strength is obviously to some extent a datum, & so is intelligence. I glory in my intelligence, & should, yet in me a universal intelligence reaches a certain focus. We back into such questions through our reversed perspective which sees only the Tower of Babel, the ranking pyramid of egos. We like to compare, & ascribe guilt or culpability to those who are compared against. [D 49.162; DNF, 116]

Pre-emption. One curious feature of all my fictional reveries is the prophetic: several times a notion I've had actually turns up in some professional writer. Thus Katherine Anne Porter's *Ship of Fools* has just (April 1962) appeared. This is one of the many reasons why I suspected my Bardo novel is not something to write, but a *koan* to think about and exercise the mind. If I write it I might be snatching the bread out of the mouth of somebody who otherwise would have done it better. [NB 2.18]

Presentation and Possession. Irony, in the sense of the eiron's self-deprecation, is the very essence of courtesy. Making oneself small by certain gestures, such as bowing, are central in social ritual. Attaching minimum value to what one has & maximum value to what someone else has is central in social activity. Religious & moral codes insist on pursuing this into one's habits of thought. You may be great or good; I know I am neither. Modesty is infinitely more than a pose or a convention: as what Eliot calls humility, it's a pre-requisite of both virtue & knowledge. The general principle seems to be: what is presented has the maximum oracular significance to be attached to it, because something may be learned there, like nature in Baudelaire's *Correspondences*. What is possessed has the minimum significance, because there is always something to be learned or added. What's presented may be a work of art, which must be approached as though it were as great as possible, according to my own anagogic principles. The resolution of presentation & possession is identification, where one self is one with something bigger & the possessing or egocentric self cast out. What you identify with possesses you, and operates as an informing principle in your mind. Now if what's presented is, say, a poem written centuries ago in a different cultural context, what's the problem? Historical criticism, establishing as nearly as possible what it meant then, devalues its oracular significance. This devaluing has something to do

224

with the fact that sacred books, approached historically, turn out to be fakes. Arthur Waley says that the *Analects* of Confucius contain few & very probably no authentic sayings of Confucius: it's a statement of what early Confucians believed. The Gospels dissolve into a mass of early Christian *adagia*: everything in Homer or the Mahabharata that's most important for belief is interpolated: the Mosaic code is stuck into a period of history centuries too early. [NB 18.115-6]

Preserving the Group. Caiphas' "It is expedient that one man die for the people" is definitive: it speaks for the entire human race. Everybody without exception adheres to nature & the anxiety of continuity, believing that the individual has to be expendable to preserve the group. Martyrdom & sexual abstinence were two aspects of the revolt against that—Jesus had to die & not only be born of but be a virgin. It focuses the contrast between the Christian myth & the Frazerian dying-god one. [NB 21.631; RT, 258]

Pretty Pattern. I've got stuck in my noddle the two names Prometheus and Hermes, and am beginning to feel that, apparently just for reasons of symmetry, there must be a second cycle incorporating the bulk of the imagery of modern poetry that doesn't get into the Eros-Adonis cycle. I'm putting it in the strongest terms a hostile critic would apply: because I've got a pretty pattern to apply, the facts have simply got to conform to it, and naturally with that attitude I'll succeed sooner or later. I'm familiar with that kind of shit. You can't be original unless you work with hunches and treat them exactly as a paranoiac would do. Of course I find what I want to find in the texts themselves: what else does the double meaning of "invention" mean? [NOTES 52.10; LN, 2:422]

Pretzels. I must proceed to find out (still keeping in touch with all the great Yogins, of course, including the Bhaktis) something about the yogic processes underlying creation. I notice that [Evelyn] Underhill says "In the artist the senses have somewhat hindered the perfect inebriation of the soul." You have to learn to do without pretzels. [NB 3.40; RT, 19-20]

Priests. A priest personifies spiritual fatherhood, but as insofar as he is male he is still involved in a sex war, his body, like that of all shamans, tends to become hermaphroditic. The number of priests with a fat, wide, spectacled, intelligent & yet somehow simplified face in which it is hardly possible to distinguish the male & female elements is startling. [NB 34.50]

Primary Concern. Why was I so fascinated by Frazer? Because he linked mythology with anxiety about the food supply—a primary concern. Why am I fascinated by *The White Goddess,* a wrong-headed book in many ways? Because it links mythology with sexual anxiety, a primary concern. Why did I get so fascinated by that sibyl G.R. Levy? Because she linked mythology to shelter & buildings, a primary concern. Food, sex, shelter, *are* the primary concerns, all grouped around God the Father & Nature the Mother. [NB 27.426; LN, 1:77]

What would a society genuinely based on mythology and primary concern be like? Well, that involves the nature of the contract myth & the Utopian vision—except that all the Utopias we have are ideological. For primary concern, the real outlaws would be the criminals, i.e., the people who violate primary concern by murdering, slandering, stealing & raping. The latter half of the ten commandments. For an ideology the worst "criminals" are always ideological opponents, political prisoners. The people who got burned alive were heretics, coiners & witches, those who threatened or were thought to threaten the monopolies of power of priests, kings & males. "Thou shalt not commit adultery" means, for primary concern, "thou shalt not rape or seduce," because the motive for rape is not sexual but sadistic, a desire to hurt and humiliate. For ideology, of course, adultery means going outside the marriage contract. [NB 27.466; LN, 1:85]

I'm wrong about religion as an ultimate but not a primary concern. Where did I come from and where am I going are primary concerns, even if we don't believe there are any answers. But if only the social institution answers, the answer is ideological only. Maybe that *is* something we learn about only from literature, but God, the digging & burrowing to get at it! [NB 44.103; LN, 1:121-2]

Primitives. Once we accept the fact that human beings at least as intelligent as ourselves have been around for half a million years or so, our perspective on the "primitive" mind changes somewhat. The question is, what were these "primitives" interested in? If they were interested in mythology, they could perhaps construct far better mythologies than we can: more ingenious & complicated, more subtle & imaginative. [NB 11F.177; RT, 114]

Private Judgment. The imaginative world can't be subjective because the self-contained individual doesn't exist as such: the individual is a social and historically conditioned product—also ideologically conditioned. Hence private judgment, acting according to one's inner conscience, and the like, are horseshit. Luther didn't say: "Here I stand, because my conscience tells me to." He said: "Here I stand, until I am convinced otherwise by arguments drawn from the Word of God." [NOTES 53.138; LN, 2:638]

Private Mythologies. All mythologies are private to the poet and it's the critic's business to see that they aren't private to anyone else. The mythology of the Christian Church was doing a bit better when Isaiah saw God in the temple, & when Elijah heard the still small voice, than it ever did when it was able to force millions of people to say they believed it or get burnt alive. The critic proper is to the biographer what law is to history— a spatial cross-section. Besides, it's the dispossessed mythologies—Jewish & Celtic—the despised & rejected ones, that really get there. [D 50.339; DNF, 346-7]

Productive Scholars. There are so many critical schools because of an assumption that everyone employed on a university teaching staff ought to be a "productive" scholar, and the variety of schools provided a prefabricated series of models. Many of these schools, such as feminism, are only temporary ideological trends: I note that even such broken-winded old nags as Yvor Winters and F. R. Leavis are taken out of pasture. The whole notion of "productive" is an assembly-line notion that is now being outgrown. A scholar should take a *creative* interest in his subject, and what will make the "productive" compulsion less universal will be the rise in adult education. [NB 50.575; LN, 1:373-4]

Progress. Evolution gets perverted into "a man is the lord of creation" hierarchy, which even if it's true is a very dangerous state of mind, because of the way it leads to exploiting nature. That in turn gets corrupted into progress, where "civilized" means "better weapon technology" and "primitive" means those who get enslaved or exterminated. The moral horror of progress, however, is less in imperialism than in sacrificing the present to the future, which is precisely what the killing of the divine king is all about. *Do ut des* means: I give now; you repay me later (or you're a cheat, suppressed). The prophets say that God never signed any such damn contract. [NB 50.374; LN, 1:330]

Progressive Articulation. Intuition, what I call literal apprehension, begins all creative activity. Intelligible articulation of this is progressive; emotional reaction to it is regressive, at least in itself. If thinking or creating strikes a snag, the emotions register anxiety or bewilderment: if everything goes well, they register buoyant pleasure. Naturally we try to get to a point which will register pleasure on the emotions, but we cannot pursue the pleasure unless we avoid the possibility of anxiety, bewilderment, even suffering, that comes with progressive articulation. That's why the pursuit of happiness is, in itself, regressive. In thought it leads to the state of mind many theosophists are in, of confusing profound thoughts with pleasure at the idea of having profound thoughts. [D 49.30; DNF, 60]

Prometheus. Prometheus is forethought or ascending wisdom, leaving his shadow-bound brother behind along with Pandora. Pandora is a baggage: that is, she's identical with her box. [NB 50.441; LN, 1:345]

Proof of Eminence. I'd like to get a good book on Scotus Erigena, or a translation of his book on the *Division of Nature....* He got 19 theses condemned by a synod, which proves his eminence as a thinker. [NB 44.729; LN, 1:250]

Protestantism. The medieval Christian Church had the model of a totalitarian state, consolidated by fear of hell. People say very silly things about Protestantism, but no movement except one shaped the way it was could possibly have broken the monopoly of that Church. One feels, reading Erasmus & Rabelais, perhaps even More, that a far greater Reformation was prevented by anxiety & intolerance, but no other Reformation would have been even remotely possible. This means for me that any religious beliefs I hold have to be connected with Protestantism. Because I believe in the revolutionary nature of Christianity: that is, my first belief about the Church is its need of radical reformation. [NB 21.24; RT, 144]

Providence. The will to believe is directed at not God but providence. Because providence is the ghost of nature: it's an extra &, strictly, unnecessary hypothesis added to an event. And just as in fortune telling the tendency is to forget the misses & remember only the hits, so the sense of providence is strongest when you win. The storm that destroyed the Spanish Armada was a providential event to the English, but a natural event to the Spaniards. [NB 21.350; RT, 205-6]

"Providence" is a perspective of the Logos phase of the world, where man is a child under a Father & Mother. It's important to distinguish what's genuine in that phase from what's phony: man must outgrow his childhood & work to rebuild the real temple & Jerusalem, but if he did so the parental nature of Otherness would become clear. [NB 11E.30; RT, 324]

Pseudepigrapha. I've picked up again Mead's three volumes on Hermes Trismegistus: that's always been assumed to be a deservedly forgotten effort of pseudo-scholarship. I think it may be the spiritual vision of that literature: I've read Frances Yates on Bruno, and she's obsessed by the pseudepigrapha side of it; the hermetic literature wasn't written by an ancient Egyptian god or whatever, but, etc. That affects *psychikon* history, not spiritual history: similarly with Jessie Weston's notion of an ancient civilization behind the Grail legends. This is all a part of the Atlantis myth that gets into all spiritual vision in some way or other. What's under the Atlantic is what's inside us: if we uncover it we either find a spring of living water or we get drowned in a new flood just for us.... The whole Bible, from the Genesis of "Moses" to the Revelation of "John," is a pseudepigraph, but no less relevant on that account. [NOTES 53.27, 29; LN, 2:618]

Pseudo-revolutions. The feudal aristocracy was a militant revolutionary group, whose strength was in subduing the internal proletariat (chivalry) & whose weakness was in trying to take on the external one (crusades). Hence not only are Carlyle, Bentham & Marx wrong in attempting to solve class conflict through a dictatorship of one class, but a pseudo-aristocratic revolution (Nazism) cannot produce anything but a race myth, & a pseudo-proletarian one nothing but an anti-democratic one. (The pseudo-bourgeois revolution is that of the "intellectuals," or "natural aristocracy," that attempts to make like the goose that laid golden eggs, but only produces turds.) [D 50.47; DNF, 231-2]

Punch and Wit. The form in which an idea is expressed is part of its truth. If I set down ideas without punch or wit or vivid imagery or a vitally logical connection, & then revise the passage so that it becomes more readable, with more punch & wit & so on, *it thereby becomes more true.* A work on the inner mysteries of profound intellectual disciplines which is dull & hard to read is simply not a true picture of those disciplines. [NB 30N.16]

Puppeteering Teleology. The will of God can't operate in the world that man sets up deliberately to neutralize it. The Taoist conception of *wu wei,* applied to God as well as man, is pretty crucial. But what's its *literary* embodiment? Certainly not romance with its puppeteering teleology: that's another kind of vision. [NB 11E.31; RT, 325]

Purgatorial Quest. My whole conscious life has been purgatorial, a constant circling around the same thing, like a vine going up an elm. I note that I'm repeating even things from earlier pages of this notebook. And "purgatorial" is only a vague hope: maybe I'm not really going up to a final apocalyptic vision but just going in circles, like a senile old man who thinks the two-hundredth repetition of the same old story is new. Perhaps the end is the choking of the host. Well, when it's vertigo to look down and despair to look up, one can only keep going. But there again I'm assuming an up and a down, and assuming I'm going somewhere. Actually I keep revolving around the same place until I've brought off a verbal formulation that I like. [NB 27.486; LN, 1:89]

The purgatorial journey is towards the original place of birth, or earthly Paradise. It goes up a mountain or upstream to the source of a river. Hence the "happy valley" in a mountainous landscape. It's the Israelite wilderness wandering toward the Promised Land; note the paralleling of Virgil & Moses. Similar journeys to rebirth occur in *Ash-Wednesday* & several poems of Yeats. Often the earthly Paradise is a place of sexual fulfilment, but more often the journey is towards the presexual world of "innocence." Dante's ring of fire is like a recognition of a birth trauma. The drive of Menandrine New Comedy is toward a sexual fulfilment which is also a *social* birth. The pastoral world is often innocent (*and* poetic) in the same sense. Freud's Eros-journey is also a recapitulation of childhood, a continuous recognition of blocks with the birth trauma at the end.
[NB 12.4; TBN, 128]

Purgatory. Hindus & Buddhists insist on the revulsion of mind which sees reality as Mind, but generally assume that it takes so long to get to it that one needs thousands of rebirths. The mystics also think in terms of an ascent, a ladder of development, usually to be completed after death— well, that's the Catholic doctrine of purgatory, which seems to me an effort to adapt the doctrine of rebirth to Christianity. If I had to believe in either, I'd choose rebirth, as purgatory as a set plane of existence different from this doesn't make sense—Dante's purgatory is in this world, by the way. The Protestants identify the initial conversion with the final vortex, & I wonder if this Lankavatara Sutra I'm reading, in spite of its traditional guff about a stock of merit accumulated for God knows how long, doesn't point in the same direction. [NB 3.45; RT, 21]

The only conception of an after-life that doesn't identify God with Satan is that of purgatory, a realizing of one's true nature in a process which is still temporal but leads out of time. [NB 21.612; RT, 254]

An otherwise rather bad and lazy book by Hans Küng on immortality says one good thing: "Purgatory is God himself." A death is one's first gasp of "spirit," meeting the Lord in the "air." [NB 44.219; LN, 1:149]

The Purloined Letter. The purloined-letter archetype [is] the thing that sits there staring you in the face while you're knocking yourself out hunting for it and not finding it. Some say it's a clitoris and others that it's a phallus. I think it's the kerygma of God, the verbal message everybody wants to kidnap but can't get hold of. [NB 44.555; LN, 1:219]

Q

Quest. Man is asleep and fantasizing in the ladder, garden and seed worlds. His central activity there is *quest,* the projection of Word into Deed that enables him to go on sleeping. In the fire world he's compelled to wake up, hence the first thing he does is withdraw the quest. *Paradise Regained, Prometheus Unbound, Parsifal,* Tolkien, etc. [NB 27.188; LN, 1:34]

So the quest of this book would be, what the hell is religion?, and it would have three main sections.... In the first the quest would be illustrated by descent symbols in literature; in the second by the Logos-Eros-Adonis complex; in the third by literature itself as the telos of mythology. The abhorred; the adored; the explored. [NB 11F.253; RT, 130-1]

The justifying faith must be something founded on the Ecclesiastes principle of the capacity for enjoyment: the sense that life has a point. All attempts to find out what that point is are religious quests: the accumulation of detail is in vision, not in belief. [NB 21.205; RT, 177]

Quicksand. I think I should hang on to the "science" thesis, because the scientific is the opposite of the systematic. Systems are crustacean & aren't built, like bridges, to stand stress & strain; science is organic, with its skeleton inside. Also, once you start thinking of systems, you get trapped into questions of "How can you criticize literature until?" type. Usually this is filled up with "—you study metaphysics (because of the "assumptions" involved), economics (this is Marxist, & not now fashionable), theology, aesthetics, or anything but literature." Most of these assumptionmarshlights lead you along a path marked "Quicksand" with the greatest plainness. There is a lot of work to be done in criticism and all "until" questions are mere pretexts for not doing it. If we need a word for this attitude, the word "phenomenological" is a good one, because it's an even longer word than metaphysical. Actually all metaphysical questions, as the etymology of the word indicates, follow such work & don't precede it—the same is true of aesthetics, which can't budge an inch "until" more work is done on the theory of criticism in the different arts. Theology is not a science, but (like occultism) a system; science is *incidentally* systematic, & there have been no metaphysical discoveries in our time that haven't (properly) followed scientific discovery. Thomism is the *analogy* of science: I think Dante's sun expresses something of this. [NB 18.48]

ℛ

Rabelais. I've picked up my copies of Rabelais again, as I always do when I get to thinking about a book on the verbal universe. Rabelais is probably the writer who most clearly grasped all the dimensions of language and verbal communication. There's the episode of Panurge speaking every language known, of the Limousin talking a barbaric monkish Latinate in defiance of humanist etiquette; there are parodies of what is now called body language and gesture—there's practically nothing to say about words that he hasn't said somewhere. He seems to have a clearer grasp of my fourth phase of language point than anyone else, even his macaronic contemporaries like Folengo (Merlin Coccaius) and the author of *Hypnero-tomachia*. [NOTES 52.176; LN, 2:458]

Radio. My idea of perfect discipline…, at least in mental production, is not, or rather not only, the terrific concentration that it would be possible to develop in loneliness, but the swivelling flexibility of a Mozart writing out a symphony with his friends around him. I tend to seek streetcars & restaurants when I want this kind of balance, but it's a sheltered sort of balance—a radio destroys it, my glance is cringing & blinded, and above all I want worn paths: I dislike exploring, except in rare cases. The radio is the subtlest attack on human peace of mind yet made, and constitutes a major obstacle, perhaps in many cases an insuperable one, to it. I know that music—often bad music—is continually playing in my semi-conscious, and when I shut it off, which I do with some difficulty, the sense of quiet is startling. I suppose radios incarnate the semiconsciousness of others, and of course increase the mental disturbance they've turned on to soothe.

Note that third-degree tortures—glaring lights & loud radios—merely intensify what we all have to live with most of the time.
[NB 3.16; RT, 8-9]

Ragweed Awareness. We make our language to suit ourselves, & are often unable to frame conceptions because we haven't the words for it. Nature is extraordinarily sensitive to the rhythms of the calendar: ragweed pollen, to take a familiar example, always hits Aug. 15 directly on the nose (my nose) whatever the climate is like. We can't say that the ragweed plant "knows" that it's time to break open, for knowledge means a specifically human faculty: to say that "nature knows" is merely a metaphor derived from a mother-goddess myth. We have no word for this unconscious vegetable awareness of Aug. 15, & consequently feel inclined to brush the question off as "mystical." The awareness is a fact, but knowledge is not based on facts, but on language, and language is variable symbolism. Our awareness of the "fact" that the sky is blue is not knowledge, but a subconscious experience of contact with the environment like ragweed's awareness of the calendar. The knowledge consists in our ability to form symbolic representations of that experience. [NB 3.104; RT, 43]

Readers. One reason why definitive criticism is something no critic would be fool enough to think about is that every poem has a community of readers, and one reader isn't all the others too. Even if it were possible, it would not illuminate the poem but merely replace it.
[NB 27.84; LN, 1:16]

I suppose it is true what I think Roland Barthes says somewhere: that only rereading counts, because all first reading faces not a text but a mirror. But I now feel that there is a very large class of readers for whom a text can never be anything but a mirror, & who will never discover in any page of print anything beyond a reflection of what they already think they think. I used to feel that if people persistently talked nonsense about me it was my own failure to be sufficiently lucid, but now I realize that that is only teacher's masochism. The notion that every "reader" is a potential reader of texts is something I no longer assume. [NB 50.334; LN, 1:322]

Reading. I suppose I should follow my own leads on the question of reading. When I was reading the Charles Pseudepigrapha, I was really onto something: reading in that area is easy for me, so it must be good. Reading comparative mythology is easy; modern poetry is pretty fair; fiction I do a lot of resisting with; philosophy I do too, but I think if I had a sense of direction about it I could read it. [NB 11F.251; RT, 130]

All reading begins in the revolt against narcissism: when a book stops reflecting your own prejudices, whether for or against what you think you "see in it," & begins to say something closer to what it does say, the core of the reality in the "objective" aspect of it takes shape & you start wrestling with an angel. [NB 44.379; LN, 1:184]

I can't seem to read until I know what direction I'm reading in. That's not the same as knowing what to look for, which in itself is a closed deductive circle. [NB 19.209; TBN, 48]

Reality and Illusion. The profoundest form of drama is the romance form found in late Shakespeare or Japanese No or Bunraku: illusions etched on the ether. Reality & illusion are reversed in *The Tempest,* yet reality is only an illusion that lasts a little longer. For God all we do and are is utterly unreal: what does God regard as real? I suppose whatever of divine nature clarity or creativity produces: himself in a mirror.
[NB 11E.33; RT, 325]

The Real King. The real king is not that man there with a unique authority; the real king is the invisible presence which is the real individuality within a community. The real king in short is the one who is symbolically killed, eaten & drunk in pieces, & then rises again as what's really individual in each of us. [NB 11C.19; RT, 346]

Reason. When a man of eighty says he never felt better in his life everyone knows he has never been so near his death, but the statement may be true for all that. I used to think of people who never believed anything except on evidence or reasonable deduction therefrom as materialistically minded. Now I just think of them as stupid. That looks from outside as though I were getting bigoted & provincial, but I know I'm not, or if I am it doesn't matter. Peace, it's wonderful. [NB 3.95; RT, 40]

Rebirth. Reincarnation & Christianity: they say that in a bullfight the bull learns so fast that he must be killed in the end, because no toreador would have a chance against a bull in his second fight. This seems to me a parable of human life. The horror of the wheel of existence is in the discontinuity of memory it postulates. There is a place for higher kinds of rebirth (e.g. the Bodhisattva) but even that must be qualified. The gospel says man must be reborn, metaphysically, psychologically, or whatever (water & the spirit is cryptic enough). If Jesus knew this to be essential he must have been reborn himself. The Eastern doctrine of karma says "man is born into the world he has made." In traditional Christianity that is true only of Jesus, who made the world & was reborn into it. So we can achieve only through him a process in which rebirth & resurrection are the same thing. [NB 18.139]

À la recherche du temps perdu. In the waste land or hollow-man world, time is always time *after:* the tick of its clock is an ostinato bass against an inaudible mighty melody (the real music of the spheres) of moments that were heard only as "might have been." The recovering of time begins in the recollection in tranquility: the use of the moment after to start rolling back the Red Sea of habit and inertia. The stupid giants that are so often even in the lower world are the giants of habit, and they are both Blake's kings who formed this world and Proust's kings immersed in time. [NOTES 58-2.8]

Recognition. Note that recognition (which *is also* repetition) emphasizes the reality of the past. It's the opposite of the *Maya* theme of the unreal present. [NB 10.21]

Recognition means both discovery of the new & *recognition* of the old. The latter is the total comprehension of the work or spectacular apocalypse; the former is the absorption into the personality. But this identifies recognition with imagery, not with narrative. Perhaps there's a stage of identification that bridges the gap between reversal (of *movement*) and recognition. I'm looking for a Mosaic or Pisgah view, the first or preliminary apocalypse. [NB 11B.37; RT, 354]

As a technique of focussing the mind, literature is a medium of meditation. We haven't got as far as the mystics, who speak of becoming what they behold.... This starts with recognition: that we have probably lived through what Lear and Gloucester have lived through, though no doubt on a smaller scale and certainly unconsciously, for the most part. [NOTES 52.641; LN, 548]

Recognition Scene. It would be nice if I could bring off a recognition scene of the impasse of the culture of the sixties, after wearily plodding down through Rimbaud & Beckett & Celine & Mailer & Genet to a point at which—possibly in Genet's perversion of a perversion—some upturn begins to look possible. [NB 12.30; TBN, 135]

Recreation. It's the function of poetry to recreate the hieroglyphic or mythical form of knowledge in each generation, and the function of metaphysics to recreate the hieratic form in our generation. Perhaps metaphysics is too narrow a term, but the Kierkegaard-Heidegger tradition recreates hieratic in the post-Hegel era. Dante and Milton are the great recreators of substance and principle respectively, and Goethe along with Hegel marks the transition to the third stage. A lot of this is bullshit, naturally; but there's a genuine intuition here, and given time (tick, tick) I think I can work it out. [NOTES 54-5.28; RT, 276-7]

I'd like to get rid of the blocking metaphors about the burden of the past, maintaining standards, keeping up traditions, & other euphemisms for staggering under guilt feelings. This again connects with my use of the Bible. In its historical & ideological context the Bible is male-centered, white-centered, Christian-centered, theist-centered. In its mythical & metaphorical contexts these limitations become metaphors for something that includes what they exclude. Perhaps these centers carry the predominant emphasis in the culture of the past: as Newman said of English literature, the bulk of it will always have been Protestant. One has to recreate. That's why, of course, there's so much yapping about deconstruction and, more especially, "supplements." The real supplements are implied in the text, not in the psychology of the writer. [NB 44.545; LN, 1:217]

Marxism, Thomism, feminism, and all religions in their "fundamentalist" aspect are imperialisms. They want their power to extend throughout the whole world, and the conception of reconciliation or total agreement in propositions rationalizes some such impulse. The fallacy as always is that they use the wrong language. Culture decentralizes, and the more it does so the more readily it can communicate over vast distances of time and place and culture. Creative culture individualizes, being related to the spiritual body, where alone the world as "global village" resides. The mob-man assimilates to what's around him; the individual is equally an out-growth of his society, but he recreates. The work of art is a symbol of that recreation, and the totality of art is the new creation.
[NOTES 53.157; LN, 2:643]

Redemption. Man redeemed is woman, and there can be no redemption apart from the transformation of nature. The white goddess and black bride interchange colors, and the red harlot splits into the unredeemed Whore and the forgiven Magdalen figure. Adonis and Adam are both red. The wind in the garden is the father/soul and mother/body alchemic union: they both die and the Spirit is born.
[NOTES 52.842; LN, 2:585]

Reincarnation. If I believed in reincarnation I should want to be reborn as a perfectly educated man, i.e. able to distribute rhythms properly, social, intellectual, spiritual, physical. I suppose that's why music is the ideal art. [NB 21.14; RT, 142]

Reincarnation is the compromise between rebirth & resurrection. It goes with, & confirms, the manic-depressive cycle running from cosmic to pharmakos [scapegoat] consciousness. Resurrection however is also a second "birth," because the power that raises is not voluntary. [NB 21.542; RT, 241]

Reincarnation is not a doctrine, whether true or false: it's experience, a kind of self-guided fantasy. The conception of interpenetration makes it easy to see how one can enter various personalities. [NB 50.143; LN, 1:284]

Religion. I feel dissatisfied with, even contemptuous of, the religions I know. It isn't the religion itself that bothers me but what it does to people. It doesn't seem to be anything more than an intellectual, even a moral handicap: how intellectually honest or genuinely charitable is it possible to be…in spite of having it?… Yet a definite repudiating of religion doesn't suit me either: the orthodox Marxist & Freudian teachings are quite obviously horseshit. Do I want a new religion? No, not in doctrine, anyway: I don't find at any level of my mind an ideal of belief. One dead, one powerless to be born: there must be some other way of formulating the whole problem. Seeing is believing, must be the answer: if I want to believe more than I see I'd better improve my seeing apparatus. [NB 3.179; RT, 70]

The church & the world both educate, but the world does a far better job, & in modern society the relevance & value of a religion is gauged by the quality of its worldliness (i.e. its urbanity). Matthew Arnold's argument, put on a historical basis, would be something like this: originally all cultural activities were in a sense religious. To the extent that *a* religion separated itself from the rest of culture, it started heading for sectarianism. To the extent that it rejoins the total body of culture, it improves itself as well as the culture. [NB 27.401; LN, 1:73]

I'm no evangelist or revivalist preacher, but I'd like to help out in a trend to make religion interesting and attractive to many people of good will who will have nothing to do with it now. The literalist view of meaning makes those who take it seriously hysterical. Before long they're saying that serious writers are wallowing in filth, that children should be spanked as often as possible, that not going to church/mass on Sunday is a mortal sin, that it offends God to call one's bum an arse, & the rest of the dreary rigmarole. I suppose the root of the hysteria is the threat of hell: I note that these people are always hailing with delight something like herpes or AIDS or, of course, any uncertainty connected with evolution or the pill. Under the law, the more religiosity, the less charity.
[NB 27.408; LN, 1:74]

Oh, God, I'd like to say something new about religion & nobody really succeeds in doing so. [NB 11F.20; RT, 76]

I have long had the ambition to write something in religion that would gain some new perspective on the subject. My particular interest has always been in mythology & in the imaginative aspect of religion. I have at least not addled my wits with any nonsense about "evolution" in religion. I do not mean that evolution is nonsense in its own sphere, which is biology, but when human institutions are assumed to develop from the ape-like to something like what the writer approves of, we do get nonsense. Briefly, my thesis is this: imagination has been a constant since paleolithic times, as the cave drawings prove. The whole imaginative picture of the world which underlies both religion and the arts has been constant from the beginning. What has "developed," "advanced," etc. has been certain social & political forces, mostly of centralization. That has shifted emphasis away from local cult, epiphany, vegetation gods, & so on, towards the sky-father.
[NB 21.96; RT, 157-8]

Religion and Art. One thing I didn't have too clearly in mind when I wrote the Blake book is that the total imaginative power we feel in a language or a religion is, like the Bible, sifted by tradition so that it is a cultural product, & a cultural product suggests imaginative totality as no one man can ever do. The individual's powers are limited & predictable, or if they aren't he soon passes out of our range. But a big library really has the gift of tongues & vast potencies of telepathic communication. You can't "substitute art for religion" without making art include religion, & so recovering it from the individual or ego-centric sphere. That's really what I'm trying to do.
[NB 3.128; RT, 52]

Religious-Secular Antithesis. In a more sensible Christian world people would move in and out of Catholic and Protestant lifestyles, instead of all this ideological crap about once-for-all baptism or conversion, always having to be either in or out of the church. Maybe that will happen when we get rid of the religious-secular antithesis, stop thinking that "Why does a God permit so much evil and suffering?" is a serious question, and start asking the question in its genuine form: "Why do *we* permit so much evil and suffering?"
[NB 44.193; LN, 1:143]

Representation. Representation implies picture-making, still central in Wittgenstein, and painting, being always a representation even when it doesn't represent anything (it represents intransitively), is, once again, a vision of an unborn world. When it's born, it becomes three-dimensional but not objective.
[NOTES 54-1.75; LN, 2:679-80]

Resemblances. It's no use saying I like resemblances more than discriminations: literature is an art of analogy & identity, and resemblances are positive. Again, it's no use saying my genres are a false analogy to biology just because it's impossible to work out an *a priori* theory that things must be so. Even if you start with a completely chaotic view of art, like

243

McLuhan's view that art is anything that A can put over on B, the next step will tell you that putting over involves the conventionalizing of what you say, & so genres arise. [NB 19.414; TBN, 95]

Resisting Deductive Systems. All my life I have been resisting the demands of deductive verbal systems. First there was mother's Protestant Bibliolatry, demanding that I deduce everything from the Bible, as Canadian Methodism understood the Bible. Then there was Catholicism, demanding that everything should be deduced from that Wonderful Synthesis of everything the Church taught & was ever going to teach, even if it taught some damn fool thing like Papal Infallibility. Then there was Marxism, proving conclusively that nothing could be done about what was wrong with the world except what followed deductively from the principles of Marx. Freud was much less a bother, but he did bother, and now there are close to a billion Chinese screaming their guts loose about the thoughts of Chairman Mao. In resisting these I don't feel that I'm necessarily defending or rationalizing bourgeois, capitalist or liberal-humanist values. I know that Marxists say that I can't have any ideas that don't ultimately rationalize my social context, but I know better. I want of course to be an important thinker in my own right, but that isn't all of it. Briefly, I do best by standing outside all these systems, including Protestantism, because by doing so I can chop a few holes in verbal systemization that I can see through & breathe through. I do want to try to understand the hold that such systems have on people, & the extent to which it's demanded of all thinkers that they keep their thoughts in verbal conformity with the Declaration of Independence or the Koran or whatever the hell it is. I have two leads. One is my structure of mythology point, and the distinction of closed-deductive & open-heuristic myth. The other is the point that came at the end of the Keats paper: the community is based on (verbal) communication, which in turn is based on communion, with God or the Ter-ewth or, more frequently, the communion of saints. (Notice how often the Master is the third of a line: Moses-Elijah-Jesus; Moses-Jesus-Mohammed; Marx-Lenin-Stalin or Mao, and, for me, I suppose, Shakespeare-Milton-Blake.) What

I want is the right to attempt a direct communion of my own, and the bourgeois liberal set-up I'm in, especially being in Canada & not in the U. S., is loose enough to let me do that.
[NB 19.334-5; TBN, 75-6]

Resurrection. The resurrection is revealed in the risen *event* or experience. It may be a work of art or a moment of charitable illumination, but it's the microcosm of the total vision of life that perhaps the mythical framework presents macrocosmically. What rises, as *The Winter's Tale* shows, is nature herself, or body only. Church my ass: it's Nature that's the bride of the risen Christ, the "Earth" of Blake's Introduction [to *Songs of Experience*], & I suppose Jerusalem too, if that's expanded to include Beulah, the married land. [NB 21.483; RT, 229]

When Jesus says "I am the way" time stops. There is no journey through unknown country: all the disciples have to do is walk through the open door (another "I am" metaphor) of the body in front of them. That is, I think, impossible before the Resurrection. Perhaps everything that happens in the gospels is not an event but a ticket to a post-Resurrection perform-ance. Except that the spiritual reality is not so much future as an expansion of the imaginative possibilities of the present. The myth confronts: it doesn't prophesy in the sense of foretelling.
[NB 44.260; LN, 1:159]

As far as I can read it, the center of Christianity is not the salvation of the soul, but the resurrection of the body.
["SYMBOLISM IN THE BIBLE," LECTURE 11; RT, 501]

The full spiritual vision of the Resurrection cannot be conveyed in words unless there's some sense of the miraculous: hence the miracles in the Gospels, and the impossibility in nature of realizing Isaiah's peaceable kingdom. It's a world in which the dead from the past are redeemed and the future has lost its remoteness, apocalyptic but not millennial. God is all in all there, not a sovereign whom everyone wants to dethrone. Yoga, Zen, Tao, are Oriental ways of reaching this world: Resurrection is the Biblical one. Without that, as Paul says, we may as well give up the whole Christian enterprise. And we should not think of resurrection as a survival after death, but as an awakening from death, which includes ordinary life. Whether this takes one life or many, or whether some such notion as Purgatory makes sense of it I don't know. [NOTES 53.235; LN, 2:657]

Revelation. So far as *The Critical Path* was about religion, I put its theme to myself as: "mythology being a human language, it is not revelation." This turned into: "this book raises no specifically religious issues, only issues concerned with the human understanding of religion." These two formulations were based on Barth's principle that God is never identical with what we call God. Now it's turned into something like this: "The use of revelation to bind societies together in a myth of concern is perhaps ultimately illegitimate. If so, a myth of concern is a perversion of revelation." I suppose the moral is that all religions are one and that revelation can only come through an individual. For Blake the sin against the Spirit was natural religion, but a society with a closed myth of concern perhaps defines it more accurately: "Synagogue of Satan." [NB 12.499; TBN, 252]

Knowing what creation is, however superficially, gives one an insight into what revelation is. Revelation is not any kind of special knowledge: later, in the wisdom books, wisdom is explicitly separated from any type of knowledge. Revelation is the power of expanding one's consciousness. As pure myth, creation is a story about something that happened long, long ago: it's natural for stories to begin with "once upon a time." As a phase of revelation, creation is the presenting to consciousness of a world with things in it, an ambivalent world which both is and is not related to our consciousness. We didn't "make" it: but if that were the only point the creation story is making the world would be a place of pure alienation. We do see it and hear it: the creation begins with light and air, the means of seeing and hearing. [NOTES 52.292; LN, 2:485]

Reversal. In narrative one principle of great importance is the reversal. This has two aspects, turning away from the beginning, & turning forward to the end. This is the pre-*anagnorisis* part of the narrative, & while there is often a point of reversal or peripety clearly marked, there often isn't. Perhaps reversal in this sense is really the whole narrative *qua* narrative.... The reversal provides the two movements of highway & labyrinth, direct & confused movement. There's a higher labyrinth of the dance or disinterested movement above. [NB 11B.36, 38; RT, 354, 355]

Revolution. On the principle that every failed spiral is a cycle, Spengler's account of history is a more cyclical one than he intended it to be. The other side of Spengler is of course the Marxist theory of revolution, which fastens on two specific examples, the English 17th-century one and the French 1789 one, as models for a world-wide revolution, of which the Russian was the first. But this model is the antithesis of the capitalist revolution, and historically the Soviet revolution ended the antithetical phase: China tried to ignore this and assume that the same conditions held, but they no longer did. The Marxist model is closely related to my post-Romantic world-view, and we're in the age of an interpenetrating model now. Incidentally, the age of Augustus-Jesus was the trough of a Spenglerian transition—I'm not sure if his "Magian" theory accounts for it or not. I've always felt that Toynbee was one up on Spengler there. [NOTES 52.725; LN, 2:565]

The few occasions in history when there seems to be a revolutionary movement towards something sensible occur when people are utterly fed up with what they've got. Revolts against Communism are easily explained on such a basis now: the enthusiasm for the New Learning of humanism in the sixteenth century indicated that intellectuals were utterly fed up with scholasticism. Always malignant clunkheads then crash down and pound it to rubble again, just as the Catholic and to a lesser extent the Protestant authorities in Europe extinguished all enthusiasm for genuine learning. [NOTES 53.154; LN, 2:642]

Rhetorical Craft. I'm not wise enough to write a wise book (wisdom soon gets beyond words anyway) nor learned enough for an erudite book. What I might have is the rhetorical craftsmanship that's more relevant to such a job than either. Of course, it would mean living longer. If Kundalini woke up in my balls and shot all the way to the thousand-petalled lotus or whatever the hell in my noodle, I'd doubtless be a far better visionary, but I wouldn't necessarily be a better writer, any more than I'd be a better pianist. Those things are separate crafts. The distinction may not work with sacred books, which makes things tougher for theory.
[NB 44.327, 330; LN, 1:173-4]

Rhetoric of Personal Assertion. I am always being asked: can a man write a poem outside your system? The motivation behind this question is often a view that thinks of poetry as the rhetoric of personal assertion, & many, especially the young & aggressive, like to feel that there are no limits to that.
[NB 21.137; RT, 164]

Rhythm of Nature. Reading Sun Tzu Wu on *The Art of War,* I note that for him an infantry campaign is a branch of hydrostatics, spreading over the terrain like a flood & following its curves. Nowhere is there resistance to nature, but always an attempt to integrate the army with the rhythm of nature: feel its beat, as T.E. Lawrence says. This is the basis of Spengler's "garden" or wandering-free-in-nature rhythm: because of the completeness with which the Chinese seized the idea of war, they were able to evolve from it. The attempt to seize & control the rhythm of nature is very dangerous, & usually fails, driving the Phaethon who fails mad. In this conception nature is a wild horse, as in Jung & perhaps Yeats' "centaur" image. The mania of the Bacchae is the inevitable result, perhaps: certainly a frequent one. But Plato, especially in the *Phaedrus,* gives some hints about how to control it. Anyway, this beat of nature, the dynamic formulation of the Renaissance static nature on which art is founded, is the *Wille zur Macht.* [NB 32.43]

248

Rich and Poor. Samuel Butler's *Notebooks* are very uneven, and there's a lot of tripe in them, especially when he gets on his hobby-horse of future fame being the genuine form of immortality—God, what shit that is!—but sometimes he speaks with the most paralyzing common sense. "The principal varieties and sub-varieties of the human race are not now to be looked for among the negroes, the Circassians, the Malays, or the American aborigines, but among the rich and the poor." [NOTES 58-3.25]

Role Models. Regarding the Paul de Man scandal, why should we expect public figures to be role models, exuding all the approved sentiments? His record could hardly be worse than Heidegger's, but who denies Heidegger's importance? Heidegger, Frege, Spengler, George, even Wagner: all people of great importance: every one a kraut clunkhead as dumb as the beer barrels in Munich. Jung too, for all his dodging. Sartre: the incarnation of the *Trahison des clercs,* the juvenile delinquent of the intellect. Camus used to complain of being taken as a moral oracle, but that was just the public saying: "Sartre and Camus—well, at least Camus is a grown man." [NB 44.732; LN, 1:250]

Ronald Reagan. Television brings a theatricalizing of the social contract. Reagan may be a cipher as President, but as an actor acting the role of a decisive President in a Grade B movie he's I suppose acceptable to people who think life is a Grade B movie. [NB 27.282; LN, 1:50]

American civilization has to *de-theatricalize* itself, I think, from the prison of television. They can't understand themselves why they admire Reagan and would vote for him again, and yet *know* that he's a silly old man with no understanding even of his own policies. They're really in that Platonic position of staring at the shadows on the wall of a cave. The Pope, again, is another old fool greatly admired because he's an ex-actor who *looks* like a holy old man. [NB 44.492; LN, 1:208]

Why do Americans continue to cherish Reagan, including millions of Americans who know he's an ass? I think they're bored by their own indifference to the world, but can only focus their minds on a boob-tube leader. [NB 50.85; LN, 1:273]

The Soviet Union is trying to outgrow the Leninist dialectical rigidity, and some elements in the U.S.A. are trying to outgrow its counterpart. But it's hard: Reagan is the great symbol of clinging to the great-power syndrome, which is why he sounds charismatic even when he's talking the most obvious nonsense. The Pope is in an even tougher spot, trying to maintain the Catholic dialectic even when it's disintegrating all around him, even among Catholics. I must feel insecure about a sentence when I put three "evens" in it. [NB 50.708-9; LN, 1:397-8]

Rossini. Well, well. Rossini had always been to me the type of the detached artist, who simply quit when he'd made enough to retire, instead of flogging his genius every inch of the way, like a true artist. Now I discover a humorous but oddly touching piano piece called "Marche et reminiscences pour mon dernier voyage." It's a funeral march, with a very curious second theme marked "frappons." Then follows snatches of all his operas, from *Tancred* to *William Tell,* with the funeral march interpenetrating them. At the end the "knocking" theme returns, & as the piece resolves on its tonic there are the notes "on ouvre," and finally "j'y suis," then "Requiem." Maybe Shakespeare, too, cared more than I've been assuming. [NB 18.43]

S

Sacred Books. All sacred books are neurotic in proportion to the amount of yelling they do about the punishments of unbelievers, and the proportion in the Koran is high. The neurotic impression is increased a hundredfold by the oral pre-literate style, which depends on & demands endless repetition. The definitive, or once-for-all, statement is either existential—an oracle applying to a certain person at a certain time—or written down. Written unique statements become Promethean, & afford a clue leading out of the labyrinth, when they're chained together by a dialectic, whether conceptual or poetic. [NB 11F.71; RT, 85]

Samuel Butler. Samuel Butler is a man who, like William Morris, has gone out of fashion, and the popular impressions of him are all wrong. He's generally thought of as an amateur who blundered into the Darwin-Lamarck controversy on the Lamarck side without knowing what he was talking about. But in this era of DNA molecules and genetic codes Butler's identification of heredity and memory is in so different a context from the old inheritance-of-acquired-characteristics dispute that the latter is hardly worth considering anymore. Besides, at the very beginning of the best of his biological books, *Life and Habit,* he says he's not trying to write as a scientist, however untrained a one: in Arnold's phrase, he just wants to let the mind play freely and speculatively around certain subjects connected with habit, unconscious memory, and the like. Civilization owes an immense amount to these play-thinkers, even when they lost their vogue and are "forgotten." Bernard Shaw did what he could to keep Butler in fashion, but Shaw's out of fashion too, and, of course, there's a lot less to be said for his "creative evolution" notions than for Butler's views of unconscious memory. [NOTES 58-3.13-14]

Samuel Butler has fascinated me ever since he was introduced to me by Bernard Shaw in my teens. When I later came to teach him in university, he had the reputation of being a minor Victorian satirist who waded into the evolution controversy without knowing what he was talking about and aligned himself obstinately on the wrong side. I was never satisfied with this: as a critic I know that no really brilliant writer can ever be wholly wrong about anything he writes about—he may often be wrong-headed, as Butler himself was on many other subjects than biology. But there's always a core of something genuine, even if it's about something other than the alleged subject. [NOTES 58-3.1-2]

Saving Remnants. The spiritual community is small: this survives in the traditional sense that only a few get saved, on the analogy that only a few of nature's sperms and germs become fertile. History turns on saving remnants. [NOTES 54-1.68; LN, 2:679]

Schematology. All my critical career has been haunted by the possibility of working out a schematology, i.e., a grammar of poetic language. I don't mean here just the stuff in *Fearful Symmetry* & *Anatomy of Criticism* & elsewhere, but the kind of diagrammatic basis of poetry that haunts the occultists & others. Whenever I finish a big job I seem to return to this. Right now, Poe's *Eureka* is turning up on my agenda again, and I'm beginning to think that it's the time for reading Boehme. In other words, once again I have a hope of reviving of making precise & detailed suggestions about—let's say the diagrammatic basis of schematology.
[NB 12.333; TBN, 212]

I have always wanted to write a book that will be schematic in form as well as in content. The original version of *Fearful Symmetry* had a hundred sections. Eros: twenty-eight sections, the lunar number of the cycle.

Logos: twenty-two sections, the last one, corresponding to the Fool in the Tarot pack, dealing with the theme of redemptive descent. Adonis: twenty-eight sections again, and then Thanatos, twenty-two sections, with the escape theme the last one. [NB 12.12; TBN, 130]

I don't like over-symmetrical schemes, & the only reason I feel I may be able to trust this one is that it does seem a real consolidation of ideas and plans I have had for at least ten years—ever since, in fact, I first realized that I had the germ of a book on Blake in me. Further, perhaps writing out of the scheme will enable me to relax: the trouble with grandiose cyclic-epic schemes is that they make their conceivers sound very solemn & pompous, & also make them frantic cultural go-getters. If each book I write represents in itself a good life's work—and I think the Blake does—I can take my time & not give a damn if I don't finish a huge table of contents drawn up in my younger days when life stretched off to vast infinity. [NB 42.25]

Scholarly Handicap. One real handicap in my scholarship is the immense difficulty I find in finishing long works of fiction. I seem to get the point after about 100 pages. Right now it's Svevo's *Confessions of Zeno*. [NB 12.314; TBN, 208]

School of Piranhas. Whenever a subject begins to look exhausted it moves to another level of comprehension. The great example here is physics after 1900. Criticism is not going to be exhausted, but most academic critics have a lurking fear that it is: look at the way they fall on every new poet or novelist like a school of piranhas. [NB 50.616; LN, 1:382]

Science. Science cannot destroy mythology: science cannot destroy anything except an earlier version of the same science. [NB 21.137; RT, 164]

Science of Criticism. In some ways I regret having raised the word "science" in *Anatomy of Criticism:* people think I was starting a critical-establishment move. But I wasn't thinking of academic bureaucrats: I was thinking of confused undergraduates. [NB 27.115; LN, 1:21]

Sci-Fi. I've been reading, more or less at random, in science fiction for varieties of the parallel-world conception which seems to me a possible exit from the present up-down mythical universe dilemma. Reincarnation is now being trumpeted as practically established scientifically: it isn't, and I still think there's a fallacy buried in it somewhere, but there's probably a pattern it fits. I read the four volumes of Philip Jose Farmer's "Riverrun" series, but they were a bust. Now I'm reading Zelazny's two-volume "Amber" series, which at least has better patter. They seem to me a development of the Eddison series, where the ideal world is conceived as an archaic one, reminding me of Lawrence's proposal that if men wanted to fight they should repudiate modern hardware, get into armor and have a good old heroic hack. Eddison isn't quite as silly as that sounds, but his fantasy world is simply the old chivalric-romance one back again. We seem to be in an age of neo-Ariosto. [NOTES 52.983; LN, 2:606-7]

Secrecy. Secrecy: the narrative or sequential kind, where you're teaching chapter one, and conceal chapter two, which depends on it, until tomorrow. The ironic kind, where the *teacher* asks the questions to create a space for the student's mind to grow. The esoteric kind which is academic freedom, protection against the malice of fools. The apocalyptic kind, where you explain something with complete lucidity to someone who says: "I don't find this convincing." *Nothing* can be done about such people: that's one of my auguries of experience. They're self-censored, and while all censors are irrational bigots, the self-censored are the worst.
[NB 50.395; LN, 1:334-5]

Secret Books. This lower world, the world of signs, of secrecy, & of oracles, is also the world of writing—proclaimers have to depend on a writing *secretary* or keeper of the secrets. Christianity, Islam, & probably Judaism, have the conception of the secret books of life in which some angel writes down our largely forgotten acts, & confronts us with them at the Last Judgement. The dark world is the world of signs, of which the archetype is the sign of Jonah, the prophet who descended to that world. It stretches from the paleolithic cave of magic animal pictures to the descent to the cipher or oracle which we have in Arthur Gordon Pym, in *Endymion*, in Rabelais' bottle oracle. This all contrasts with the claim of Jesus & Mohammed to have said nothing in secret — secret traditions always have a gnostic, sufi, mahayana sense of heresy about them: the exoteric tradition is what is primary & holds society together: the gospel, not the mystery cult. [NB 11F.73; RT, 86]

Seeing. Michael Foucault has written about the control of a space of visibility as the central idea of 19th-century hospitals and the like, and cites in particular Bentham's invention of a Panopticon. Ramifications include *1984* and its "telescreen." The idea of a watching God, developed partly to inspire children with guilt feelings about masturbation, is closely bound up with the sense of *shame* about sex, the need for covering the body which Adam felt when he realized that God was looking for him and wanted to see him. The etymology of dragon means the all-seer. The God who watches is a demonic God; as I've said, the true God is invisible because he does the seeing. But what does he see? Something to do with seeing to recreate and not to judge, much less punish. The taboo about seeing God is of course the reverse side of this.
[NOTES 52.701; LN, 2:559]

Self-Acclaim. Note to cheer myself up with: I'm not a great 17th-century poet like Milton, or a great 18th-19th-century visionary like Blake, but I am a great 20th-century reader, and this is the age of the reader.
[NB 44.461; LN, 1:203]

Self and Persona. I don't ordinarily think much of myself as a public figure, but when I do see myself on television and realize what other people see, which is no more what I feel myself to be than a cigar-store Indian, I realize

the kind of contrast involved in my own separation of the Jesus within each potential resurrection and the Jesus of the gospels.
[NOTES 52.173; LN, 2:457]

Self as Eiron. The eiron role, or making oneself small, is the foundation of all existence, not merely social courtesy. I am a much better person to others than I am to myself: to myself I am a rather poor creature. What I am to myself tends in the direction of what in an omniscient mind would be the vision of justice. Ultimately I am nothing at all, which is what Buddhists mean by saying things have no ego-substance. Immediately, I am a certain capacity for being remade, which is what I really want as distinct from what I think I want. As the latter, self-knowledge soaked in illusion, I would survive death only as a neurotic, whimpering, craving ghost, wanting to be "understood." The vision of others is also of course full of illusion, but it tends in the direction of what an omniscient mind would be a vision of mercy. One remakes oneself, or tries to, for God's eyes alone: my social reputation is pure accident, like birth in the aristocracy. Still, here as elsewhere reality & illusion are turned inside out: the soul I am trying to save is more clearly revealed by what I seem to be to others than by what I wake up with in the morning. The instinct to make an obituary eulogistic is a sound one. [NB 19.260; TBN, 59]

Self-Remembering. When I was younger I could throw myself into something like a trance by simply thinking of myself as an ego, a perceiving subject *here, this* consciousness. I suppose this is what that second-rate master Gurdjieff (maybe he's better as a teacher than as a writer, at first or second hand) means by self-remembering. Increasingly, as I go on, this self-remembering becomes projected as a nostalgia in time—Proust's lost paradise. My happiest & most intense moments are *remembered* moments associated with specific places like the streets of Toronto. The tearing down of houses & other familiar landmarks I find emotionally disturbing, yet of course at the same time I understand how phony that feeling is. In remembering, the moments of the past are suffused with an intensity of pleasure, plus an intensity of nostalgia. At the time, I was living in my usual mixture of dither & apprehension, but in the past it becomes purified. We are constantly dying, and our past lives enter heaven to be lived over again with pleasure, or into hell to be forgotten or remembered only for purgation—in fact purgatory would be better, as there's no hell in that sense. (It's not that hell is other people, but hell is certainly what other people do to you.) [NB 21.26-7; RT, 144-5]

Self-Transformation. I wonder now if I shouldn't set myself a psychological goal, one involving myself as a person. I'm trying to get out from under what I call the body of this death; and to escape from that will require a long and arduous discipline, which so far as I can see I shall have to do without a teacher. Consequently I don't know how far I shall get; but suggestions have been cropping up in two of my most recent articles that the study of literature is one of the paths to self-transformation. That would suggest the possibility of a book on that subject in which Blake himself would obviously have to be a central figure. Rimbaud certainly; de Nerval and Rilke probably, Yeats almost certainly, would bulk very large in a study of the poetic imagination as doing the kind of things that the drug people say drugs do. [NOTES 55:1.10; LN, 2:722]

Selfish vs. Egocentric. The difference between being selfish & being egocentric is that the selfish person is aware of his ego; he's aggressive & defiant about it, & feels the need of protecting it. The egocentric person is like the child who refers to himself in the third person; he's a kind of parody of a mystic, & feels toward other people a kind of perverted love: they are his creatures, things he has allowed to find their shadowy being in his dream. He appears selfish only when disturbed, when some incongruity between dream & reality forces its way in. But conscious selfishness is an imaginative advance. [D 49.130; DNF, 104]

Senility. I wonder why we don't find the antics of senility as delightfully charming as those of infancy? It seems illogical both to feel exasperated with the senile & to disregard the claims of wisdom & consolidating of Being in Becoming. [NB 34.28]

Senser of Occasions. Back to this silly creative-critical dichotomy: what's "creative" in me is the professional rhetorician, the saviour of occasions, the person in constant demand for convocation addresses, after-dinner speeches (which I almost never give) and church services. This stuff being mainly oral, the bulk of it has disappeared. (Into Los's Halls, I trust.) But it's what I really do best: I'm one of Jung's feeling types, a senser of occasions. I'm usually first-rate at impromptu. I forget what point I was going to make of this. In prefaces & the like, that I'd greatly prefer to see the occasion preserved…. Naturally, I've had some resounding flops. I'm also particularly good, or used to be, at answering questions: my ability to translate a dumb question into a searching one has often been commented on. This should be leading to something useful, but it hasn't yet. The central thing is that my "creative" faculty is the power of *personalizing* occasions. My written texts are, whatever Derrida says, incarnational or prophetic, and reading them ought to lead to reincarnating them.
[NB 44.718-19; LN, 1:247-8]

Serenity / Wrath. Serenity is the opposite of the sentimental cheerfulness advocated by professional optimists. Wrath is the opposite of irritation, being an expression of strength & clear-sightedness as the latter expresses weakness & panic. [NB 3.8; RT, 6]

Serpent and Breast. Cleopatra has (in Shakespeare) only one maternal image, the serpent at her breast, where images of birth, sexual contact & death are all the same point. [NB 23.81; RT, 379]

Servant-God. Schelling says (perhaps an overstatement) that every mythology has a supreme god who is known to be the successor of a previous god. That's what has always bothered me about the "sovereignty" metaphors applied to God: they mean he's a supreme God, therefore belongs

to a historical ideology, history being a category superior to Him. The only supreme God is a servant-God. Christ is certainly Kyrios, but within us he's a servant: he ought to be master but he practically never is.
[NOTES 53.126; LN, 2:636]

The Seven Ages of Life. In this world life has, as Shakespeare says, seven ages, of approximately a decade in length. The first years, up to ten, are the age of gluttony. Of the acquisitive appetite in its simplest & most directly demanding form. The teens are the age of wrath, of the resentments of parent-rebellion and violent aggressiveness. The next decade is the age of lechery, when the coming of sexual experience brings with it idealisms, ambitions, & similar emotions. These focus into more practical & limited objectives as the 30-40 age of envy begins & one struggles for a career. The forty-year mark is the menopause era for women or something similar for me, & brings the seed of avarice or anxious inventories of resources. Then full maturity, or the age of pride, sets in & lasts until the end of life when it modulates into the age of sloth. [NB 20.3]

Sex Books. Sex books in a bookshop are not there to tell you anything you don't know; they're there to keep your mind on the subject. Similarly with devotional literature, Christian & Marxist.
[NB 21.310; RT, 198]

Shadow of Desire. Is it possible that my "real" desire, or ritual one, is to write musical comedies or funny stories & make a lot of money & live the life of Riley, & that my books are the shadow that desire has thrown into reflective laughter in its turn? [NB 3.121; RT, 50]

Shaking off Infinity. There is no end to numbers, but one can get tired of counting. There is no end to the universe, but one can die and annihilate it. Perhaps that's the reason for death: to shake off infinity. Beckett's Murphy thought that the Resurrection was God overdoing things again.
[NB 50.700; LN, 1:396]

Shallow and Deep Consistency. I've said that the original writer continues convention at a deeper level: this is an application of the general principle of shallow & deep consistency. Shallow consistency is continuity, habit, doing what one has always done. At certain points a deeper consistency emerges which is discontinuous with the shallow repetitions of habit. Proust remarks that the actions which most deeply reveal people's character are often overlooked by others as though they were hallucinations. [NB 12.507; TBN, 254]

Shaman Sex War. A priest personifies spiritual fatherhood, but as insofar as he is male he is still involved in a sex war, his body, like that of all shamans, tends to become hermaphroditic. The number of priests with a fat, wide, spectacled, intelligent & yet somehow simplified face in which it is hardly possible to distinguish the male & female elements is startling. Therefore when one seriously tries to think of Ishvara as a Father, he similarly becomes hermaphroditic & demands hermaphroditism from his followers, as in Swedenborg & Balzac's *Séraphita.* [NB 34.50]

Sheep and Goats. I can't believe the sheep & goats of Jesus' parable as people. People aren't sheep & goats: inconsistent mixtures of charity & pride. Individual life may be a vale of soul-making, as Keats says, but if so the soul that's made isn't an individual soul. Man's building up a heaven & a hell, and can't live wholly within either, though the focus of will & consciousness may, perhaps, find its center of gravity in one or the other. Once the separation is achieved, of course, hell, the narcist mirror of heaven, is lost, & only the reality is left. [NB 11F.103; RT, 93]

I've always said that the sheep and goats of Jesus' parable can't be people: they're states of mind, but if they're people we get that frightful bastard that chases everybody to hell, and he won't do. Once again, I should remind myself that everybody has a lost soul, and should make sure it gets damn well good and lost. At the same time the Judge of that god-awful parable can't be wholly inside, because that's reducing it to psychologism and saying that he's "not outside," which is precisely what I can't say. [NOTES 52.174; LN, 2:457]

Shinto Shrine. When I was in Japan I visited a Buddhist temple, several buildings all dignified, rather sombre, and in exquisite taste. At the top of the hill it was on was a Shinto shrine, incredibly gaudy, as though it were made of Christmas candy, the bushes around having rolled-up prayers tied to every twig, like women with their hair in curlers. My immediate feeling was that it was good-humored and disarming: I had no hostile or superior feelings about it at all. So why did hostile and superior words, like "superstitious" and "vulgar" start crowding into my mind? Did *God* tell me he thought it was superstitious and vulgar? [NB 44.436; LN, 1:197-8]

Short Story (with commentary). I heard of a married couple of Polish Jews picked up by the Nazis, the man sent to Dachau & the woman to Auschwitz. Miraculously they both survived & both remarried, assuming the other was dead, & both had children. The woman discovered the existence of the first husband & consulted a rabbi. He said there must be *no* direct connection of any kind with him, otherwise she'd be adulterous & her second-marriage children bastards. Nothing to me what Jews do or think: I simply note how frenziedly anxious humans are to catch themselves in rat-traps, and how eagerly they interpret the will of a God who could *only* be a shit and a stinker. [NB 44.460; LN, 1:203]

Showing Forth. All the arts are speechless: they say nothing, but merely show it forth. This is obvious in painting & music, & will need a little reassuring blather to demonstrate in literature. Poem *qua* poem says nothing. The author may be nervous about this & insist on saying something, but this is always an impurity in the art, & can be disregarded or overruled by the critic, whose axiom must be, not that the poet doesn't know what he's saying, but that he can't say what he knows. [NB 7.119]

Silence. Zen is the gabbiest encourager of silence I know. [NB 11E.19; RT, 322]

Whether I have any more books to write or not, I still want to consider the points of silence in religion: the silence of before being, expressed by the word creation; the silence of after being, expressed by the word apocalypse; the incarnating of those silences in human birth and death.
[NOTES 55:1.11; LN, 2:722]

Simplicity. The King James translation has been a great deal praised for its simplicity, and that simplicity certainly exists. But there are two kinds of simplicity. One is the democratic simplicity of one person writing for other people in as lucid a way as he can, so that he is not putting any barriers into his reader's path. But there is another kind of simplicity, a simplicity of authority that is most clearly present in such things as military commands. The officer's orders in an army have to be as straightforward in their syntax as possible—what literary critics call paratactical—and they have to be given in the fewest possible words, because soldiers will not hang themselves on barbed wire in response to a subjunctive mood or a subordinate clause. If there is adjustment or explanation to be done, it is for subordinates to do it. The simplicity of the Bible throughout is the simplicity of the kind of authority that comes from being unquestionably the boss of the operation.
["SYMBOLISM IN THE BIBLE," LECTURE 21; RT, 577]

Simplifications. Steppenwolf is told that his werewolf myth about himself is a "mythological simplification," because everybody is hundreds of personalities. But he goes on with his werewolf myth all the same. It seems that there is something numinous about all simplifications, even the early speculations that oversimplify. One would not attempt a NASA program on a basis of Heraclitus, but his oracles can be seminal just the same. Similarly of course with the gospel. [NB 50.347; LN, 1:325]

Sin. I regret very much that the gospel reports Christ as saying that the sin against the Holy Spirit *is* unforgivable. The sin against the Holy Spirit *is* original sin itself. Perhaps it can't be "forgiven," but it must be annihilated, or the whole Christian structure, which depends on a love that forgives *everything*, is a lot of balls. That's what I think now, anyway. An unpardonable sin means a stinker God, and I will never accept such a creature in the Christian set-up. [NB 44.441; LN, 1:198]

Slag-Heap of Eternal Verities. Freud's pleasure-principle is supposed to collide with a reality-principle: what it practically always collides with is an ideology-principle, something already headed for the slag-heap of eternal verities. [NB 50.330; LN, 1:321]

Sleeping God. One of the evangelical hymns I was exposed to in my childhood was "Coming By and By," which said in effect it certainly looks as though our God was asleep or on a journey, but you just wait: he'll wake up one of these days and then you'll see. I sometimes wonder whether Baal on Mount Carmel, saying "to hell with this crap," didn't prove himself thereby to be the true God, or at least closer to his nature. [NB 23.70; RT, 377]

Small Audience. If someone were being hanged outside this lecture hall I should have a very small audience. [NB 9.352]

Social Impermanence. Romance and fantasy are inevitable for writers who don't believe in the permanence of their own society. [NOTES 54-8.49]

Socialism. At present we have capitalist and socialist societies, but the old notion of socialism as the fulfilment of capitalism, so sacrosanct in my youth, I don't believe in now. I think socialism as it got established was only the antithesis of capitalism, and the fulfilment is ahead of us. The core of the fulfilment is what we call democracy, which I see, at least at present, as a tension between politico-economic and cultural rhythms.
[NOTES 52.675; LN, 2:553]

Socrates. The transition from wisdom to prophecy is Job in the Bible, but it's also Socrates…. Socrates is a unique figure: Plato & Aristotle really continue the wisdom tradition, though not of course in its pre-Socratic guru form. Socrates is a curiously negative prophetic figure, a consulter of oracles but a breaker-up of the continuous anxiety-patterns. Nobody in the Biblical tradition is much like him, though his rational questioning line does come into the Talmudic & rabbinical (Haggadic) traditions. [NB 11E.55; RT, 330]

Sonata Form. It looks as though this book [on the Bible], like *Fearful Symmetry,* is in sonata form. Exposition: Word & World. Development: The Word in the World. Recapitulation: The World in the Word. [NB 21.619; RT, 256]

Soul vs. Spirit. Soul is the essence of the body and escapes from the body at death. The East says it can't go anywhere except into another body. Spirit is the substance or *hypostasis* of the body: it can transform the soul-body into itself. [NB 27.11; LN, 1:4-5]

Sources of Revelation. Curious how anxiety focusses on some "improvement" that men have made to their alleged sources of revelation. Methodists used to attach all their anxieties to dancing, playing cards & drinking alcoholic beverages, which are either ignored in the Bible or actively encouraged there. Catholics make a terrific howl about birth control, until the theory that there can't be too many Catholics became so obviously unworkable that they had to say it wasn't a dogma after all—oh, did you think it was? [NB 23.40; RT, 373]

Speaking in the Dark. Curious paradox in my own writing I should look into: I wrote the Masseys [*The Educated Imagination*] in a deliberately colloquial speaking style, to minimize the reading barrier. Yet this sets up much more of a *personal* barrier than any of my essays that are written in normal prose. What I aimed at, & what I got, was the sense of a disembodied oracular voice speaking very clearly in the dark, not of me conversing with a reader. It had the same effect that I've noted in the discontinuous aphoristic form. In *epos* the personality disappears as it doesn't in the most objective fiction. [NB 19.164; TBN, 37]

Speculation. A certain amount of free, in the sense of irresponsible, speculation is a good thing, because it's part of the wise process of letting things come & not forcing or cramping or repressing them. That's what Goethe told Schiller, anyway. At present I have "unity of being is the analogy of the non-rising of discrimination" as a governor twirling around on top of my thoughts, until I realize that it neither makes sense nor does not make sense. But this is speculation, relaxing the eyes by focussing them on distance. In all forms of communication everything depends on a passionate desire to tell the truth, not as a moral principle, where it's subcivilized ("did you or did you not steal the jam?" is the level of moral truth), but as the normalizing or balancing principle of all articulate speech; as, in short, our only guarantee of sanity. [NB 3.120; RT, 49-50]

Spengler. What fascinated me about Spengler when I read him was the vision of every historical phenomenon being a symbol of all the other phenomena contemporary with it. Every age presents a symbolically interlocking group of phenomena: I suppose that's what the word "culture" means. I reacted against that, because of the over-dominance of that dimension of history, but it really means that the narrative of history can be halted at any moment and looked at as a thematic stasis. [NB 50.728; LN, 1:401]

I've realized that my attraction to Spengler, which puzzled me so at first, was the result of divining in him the principle of historical interpenetration: everything that happens is a symbol of everything else that's contemporary with it. Such a perspective helps one to escape from the abstracting of culture, including the arts and sciences, from what I've called the dissolving phantasmagoria of political events. [NOTES 53.22; LN, 2:617]

Spirit. Spirit is subjectively air because that's the most primary of primary concerns (I mean of course breathing is): it's objectively air because the invisible air makes the rest of the world visible. Spirit, then, is the unity, expressible only by metaphor, of subject and object in which the essential reality of the two are one. The difference between soul & spirit is that soul is *anima,* receptive & creaturely, and above all individual: a group of souls are still aggregates. We use "body" to mean a plurality as a higher individual: that's why it's only "body" that enters the resurrection by becoming spirit. That's where the part-whole paradox begins.
[NB 44.382; LN, 1:185]

God is a spirit: man is a mixture of spirit and shit. Whatever isn't spirit gets shat, including I think his soul—I still feel that soul is something to get lost, not saved. [NB 50.268; LN, 1:309]

The spirit being attached to the soul, it can't be independent of space as long as the soul is alive. Does it just junk the soul or does it go on caring for it? St. Thomas links the spirit both with death (change of state) and with omnipresence, but of course he's primarily talking about the Holy Spirit. The Holy Spirit is one, but it exists individually in each man, until the body returns to dust and the spirit to the God who gave it. One thing is sure: the body dissolves into nothing and there are no reliable accounts of souls returning. [NOTES 53.124; LN, 2:635-6]

I seem to be working out a Bergsonian pattern: what's below consciousness, traditionally called the body, may suddenly fuse with what's above consciousness, or spirit. These are the moments of inspiration, insight, intuition, enlightenment, whatever: no matter what they're called or what their context is, they invariably by-pass ordinary consciousness.
[NOTES 53.260; LN, 2:661]

Spirit Principle. The search for the powers of man takes one through some very anti-Christian areas, such as Rilke and more particularly Rimbaud;

but if one keeps the "spirit" principle in mind they do fit together. Emily Dickinson…knew the name of what poets are searching for, and didn't assume that it was captured by a church of any kind.
[NOTES 52.670; LN, 2:552]

Spiritual Alchemy. Forms of spiritual growth: the father-soul and the mother-body (dying to) bring forth the spirit-child. I think this is alchemic. Odyssey pattern: the old beggar, least likely to succeed, growing in reverse of ordinary aging until he becomes not just master of the house but the body of the house. Hegel's *Begriff*, the infant exposed and abandoned by the common-sense world, turning out to be the Prospero of the whole show. [NB 27.98; LN, 1:18]

Spiritual Authority. They talk about liberation theology. We've spent centuries realizing that order and authority are not as necessary as panic and selfishness thought they were: spiritual authority, which is order without authority, is all we need. I wonder how the same principle applies to what's called liberation theology: only spiritual liberation will be any good, even though it has to be built on physical concern. [NOTES 53.40; LN, 2:620]

Spiritual Enemies. One negative evidence of the substantiality of spirit is that spiritual enemies don't die: they always return like flies to horseshit. The power that can send them into the "deep" is a greater one than we can imagine: that's the polarizing operation at the end of the world.
[NB 27.46; LN, 1:10]

Spiritual Evolution. I have four primary concerns: Hegel has just one, namely freedom. I think all history is evolving spiritually towards fucking and a bottle, like Rabelais. Nobody knows what to do with freedom: they do know what to do with a bottle and a cunt. [NOTES 53.37; LN, 2:620]

Spiritual History. I keep telling my students that in the 20th century nothing has improved except science and nothing remained stable except the arts. The former is real history, following the continuum of time and giving it shape; the latter is spiritual history, omni-centered and continuously present. [NOTES 53.46; LN, 2:621]

Spiritual Values. A lot of what I'm saying seems to lead toward the view that the arts should express or illustrate spiritual values. Many artists (e.g. Canadian painters of the Lawren Harris-Emily Carr period) would endorse this, but for academic critics it's a boob notion, perhaps less contemptible than trying to get Margaret Laurence or Alice Munro out of school libraries, but not much more enlightened. The point is that expressing or illustrating means allegory. I think the arts should be spiritual values, not express verbal platitudes only vaguely connected with them. But of course they would express or illustrate something, which leads to the principle that the only critical criterion worth a damn is the apocalyptic one. The only real forms of life are heaven and hell, and bad art is simply art that expresses a delight in living in hell, endorsing hatreds and the like. I think it would be found that art that does this is invariably ephemeral and trashy. Again, of course I'm overlooking the vast amount of bad art that's well meaning. I'd better get going on something else.
[NOTES 54-1.53-4; LN, 2:675-6]

Spiritual Vision. The two components of the double vision are, of course, the vision of the *soma psychikon,* the conscious soul-body unit, and the vision of the *soma pneumatikon,* the spiritual vision. The latter is usually regarded as "superior," but I distrust hierarchical metaphors even when I use them. The spiritual vision is traditionally thought of as "inner," and hence esoteric, concealed from the multitude—even Jesus talks this way in the Gospels. But after the Resurrection the spiritual vision became openly manifested and displayed. The only thing that's superior about the spiritual vision is that it isn't bounded by the Heideggerian categories of birth, thrownness, and above all death. Otherwise, it's as silly to argue about superiority as to argue about whether the bones or the flesh are more important in the body. [NOTES 53.25; LN, 2:617-18]

Spiritual World. The spiritual world is the order of being in which what is in this world expressible only by metaphor becomes existential. To reach this we have to go beyond the unities of myth and metaphor to a completely decentered and interpenetrating universe: the stage represented by the decentered Bible. [NB 44.396; LN, 1:188]

The spiritual world is a *bodily* world, not a metaphysical one. It's most easily seen in the arts, which em*body* the spiritual vision of a people. And here, by way of Yeats' *Byzantium* is a link between imagination & life that would, if I could grasp it, clear up the whole "after-life" business. [NB 24.232; TBN, 330]

If the word "spiritual" has any function for you—and even Marx uses it —your God is alive, & you don't have to think in such stupid terms as "*a* God." [NB 50.365; LN, 1:329]

For a long time I've been preoccupied by the theme of the reality of the spiritual world, including its substantial reality. The glimmer of another series of lectures rises in my mind. Four, perhaps: the New Testament; Dante's *Paradiso;* Hegel's *Phenomenology;* Blake's *Jerusalem.* [NOTES 55:1.1; LN, 2:720]

Spirituality. A lot of modern writers want spirituality rather than religion. They are usually more attracted by Oriental cults (mainly kundalini and za-zen) but in of course a very cleaned-up version. This makes me impatient, and one of my motives in writing is to show that everything is in *this* tradition too. But of course the psychological *use* of religion is more Oriental. [NB 11H.11; LN, 2:713]

Stars and Stripes. Curious, & very Blakean, how the stars recur in America: of the Stars & Stripes, the former alone have any profound significance to the Americans themselves: cf. The Star-Spangled Banner, the biggest state as a Lone Star state, the insignia of generals & aeroplanes. Russia isn't any different with its red star. There must be some reason why, for instance, newspapers could be called suns or stars, but not even a monthly magazine a moon, though the number of those sold to women might suggest it, considering what sort of things they exist to advertise. As for the stripes, the red & white reappears. I expect the barber's pole, the same thing in spiral form, has nothing at all to do with surgery. Thirteen is an obvious number; forty-eight the Levite-city number [Joshua 21] marking the crisis of American imperialism. [NB 34.25]

Story. Well, that's the story: what do you make of it? Life is a slow & laborious process of discovering that reality inheres in what we make and not in what's presented to us. To die is to be faced with the same question again. Worshippers of Satan the accuser put this in the form: well, that's what you did, now take the consequences, which usually means hell, or occasionally a heaven boring enough to be hell. I'd rather have it (because it's what I want it to be that will be decisive) in the form: well, that's it: now what? That is, the equation reality = what I make will become an absolute. If limits do not disappear, they certainly must recede greatly.
[NB 27.191; LN, 1:34]

Stories distort events, but every story tells the truth about itself as a story, & some truth about its teller.
[NB 10.109]

Strindberg's Goofiness. There is nothing subjective in literature, no, repeat no, private associations or images or symbols. Strindberg's fear of being poisoned by his cooks started as a private neurosis, but as soon as it got mentioned in his plays we're into (a) contaminated and polluted food, a social problem (b) the great theme of nausea (c) a literary tradition going back to the Harpies in Virgil. We speak loosely of its being "essential" to know about Strindberg's goofiness, but it's not essential: it's interesting and valuable information, documenting what we could guess anyway, but there's a lot of such "essential" information about, say, Shakespeare that

270

we don't have in spite of Caroline Spurgeon. And we get along all right without it. [NB 50.726; LN, 1:401]

Structural Poetics. I've often said that criticism has to go beyond commentary, which is, if essential, also facile and doesn't build a structure. But I haven't said clearly that commentary is concerned primarily with what is displaced: vivid characterization & the like. Only structural poetics moves toward a *telos*.
[NB 19.232; TBN, 54]

Structure. Iconic meditation or concentration on an object assimilates poetry to the visual arts (concrete, etc.), as in the Elizabethan *ut pictura poesis*. That's the basis of the "structure" metaphor. Post-structuralists say that it's illusory to use the spatializing metaphor of structure, but that's just the idling machinery of negativism running on its own: to gain a simultaneous understanding of a poem as a unit is both possible and highly desirable. The only thing is that it isn't an ultimate goal: as soon as you've reached it you discard it like a snake's skin or a nautilus's shell.
[NOTES 52.416; LN, 2:507]

Student Conservatism. We're still not out of the silly antithesis of either individual or society, and don't seem to realize how preposterous the *Atlas Shrugged* and *Looking Backward* versions of it are. It's no good complaining that our students are conservative: where are they to go? The gang-of-four dynamic in the sixties couldn't have been sillier. Yet I hear people saying in effect: it doesn't matter what students say & do as long as they're not conservative. Why the hell shouldn't they be conservative? Do we fill up our day-care playgrounds with dangerous obstacle courses so they'll be sure to break their necks?
[NB 50.747; LN, 1:404-5]

Student Protest. The Children's Crusade [the student protest movement], however profoundly significant as a symptom of social malaise, was not in itself a social development of major importance, & its intellectual contentions negligible: it fact it often prided itself on not having any. [NB 11F.196; RT, 119]

Students. I was lecturing on Biblical wisdom and Ecclesiastes today, saying that "there is nothing new under the sun" is a statement about knowledge, while "there is a time for all things" is a statement about experience, and means that in that realm everything is new. A very bright girl asked me about this, realizing that the vision of the natural cycle with which the book opens coincided with my creation myth of the revolving mother. In answering her I had to say something I had not thought of before: that as soon as you say "there's a time for all things" you've invoked the creating father and his appearance in time. A second student asked me about the difference between analogy and metaphor. I said that such a statement as "God is love" could mean that love, a mere finite word, was being used as an analogy to something infinite, or that the two were being metaphorically identified. It then occurred to me that the metaphorical meaning was only possible in an incarnational context. Useful people, students. [NOTES 52.257-8; LN, 2:478]

Stunned Paralysis. All minds are passive to impressions 90% of the time, and probably people are more affected by oracles than they admit. When I'm sleeping peacefully & Helen [Frye's wife] flashes a light suddenly in my eyes, my sense of confidence gives way in a curiously disturbing fashion and I lie awake for the next half-hour. The same thing happens when I give a confident tug on my shoelace and it breaks with a sickening jerk. On a larger scale, it must be the breakdown of the tentative pragmatic synthesis of experience which is the basis of confidence that accounts for the stunned paralysis following a catastrophe. [D 42.7; DNF, 6]

Stunts on Cue. In the Book of Kings Elijah calls on Jehovah, who sends down fire from heaven, burns up an offering soaked with water, which impels the people to endorse a total massacre of Baal's priests, then brings a thunderstorm out of a clear sky and breaks a drought. The priests of Baal shout and invoke and pray and cut themselves with knives; Baal opens one eye, says "the hell with all *that* crap," and goes back to sleep. Which is closer to being the true God? Why, Baal, of course. Whoever heard of a real god jumping around on cue to do stunts, like a sorcerer's apprentice (which is really all he could be)? I remember an evangelical hymn of my infancy:

> *A better day is coming,*
> *The morning draweth nigh...*
> *When God the Lord shall listen*
> *To every plaintive sigh,*
> *And stretch his hand o'er every land*
> *With justice by and by.*

Translation: it's true that our God seems to be asleep or on a journey, but just you wait: sooner or later he'll wake up and really show you. O.K., but the point is that whatever gets projected into the future, the God they're worshipping right now is sleepy Baal, not jumpy Jehovah.
[NOTES 52.526; LN, 2:528-9]

Stupid Categories. Time, space, and matter are *stupid* categories. The residual theism that's in all of us instantly says "Well, we're stuck with them," and gets an orgy of masochistic satisfaction out of feeling realistic.... They're stupid. Any God who created them was an ass; no God did: we did, and we damn well should have done better. No point in that: I don't even feel better. [NB 12.96]

Style. My style, after *The Critical Path*, is getting more lapidary, each sentence an epigram, though I still struggle for the sequential & causal. In short, a style corresponding to what I postulate...for the Bible itself. [NB 21.568; RT, 246]

Subject-Object Duality. The Buddhists keep saying, with tremendous and unending prolixity, that the subject-object duality is horseshit. Okay, it's horseshit: what's so infernally difficult about it? The fact that it's so difficult to overcome derives from the fact that the metaphorical kernel of subject & object is the contrast of life & death. The person for whom *that's* disappeared really is a sage. [NB 44.109; LN, 1:123]

Subtext. It doesn't matter how often I'm mentioned by other critics: I form part of the subtext of every critic worth reading. [NB 44.472; LN, 1:205]

Sundays. I haven't yet figured out what to do with Sunday, and my anxiety to have it all to myself gives me Kierkegaard's "dread" or *angst,* about which he talks very well, except that he doesn't see that *angst* is the state of Blake's Spectre of Urthona: the egocentric or proud desire to *possess time,* the revolt against the consciousness of death. My possessive attitude, not only to Sundays, but to time generally, is bothering me a good deal, but hanging on to time is the last infirmity of noble mind. The Jewish Sabbath was a day of rest at the end of the week: the Christian Sunday is a day of leisure at the beginning of the week. Leisure is the opposite of laziness, & hasn't really any more to do with rest than with work. It's the essential condition of creative life, the relaxation from ritual, the removal of the censorious urgency of routine, in which that free association of ideas which begins the creative process is allowed to function. In short, it's listening to the Word. Surely that's what a member of the leisure class should do with Sunday. A day spent in a synthetic waste of time—sports & the like—seems to me an inevitable but hysterical reaction from drudgery. [D 50.25; DNF, 222]

Swallowing the Father. It occurs to me that what I did in writing *Fearful Symmetry* was perform the act described in much the same way by Freud & Jung. This is the act of swallowing the father, integrating oneself with the old wise man. Presumably I shall never find another father, not even in Shakespeare, & should realize that I am essentially *on my own.* I've really reached an individuated stage of thinking, if not of personal life. There's more to it than that—Blake is right in a way no one else is—but that's the psychological aspect of the book. What I should do now, or one of the

274

things I should do now, is explore mandalas. This is linked with the ideas I've had about the geometry of thinking—I could, perhaps, work them out from the 19th-century people. Perhaps, too, if every poem is necessarily a perfect unity, every thinker is necessarily perfectly right. That is doubtless just another way of saying that one seeks understanding rather than a judgment of value. Yes, it was certainly a father-swallowing—necessarily a perfect unity, every thinker is necessarily perfectly right. That is doubtless just another way of saying that one seeks understanding rather than a judgment of value. Yes, it was certainly a father-swallowing"—look at the people I sent my free copies to—Dad, Pelham Edgar, the dedicatee, Herbert J. Davis, Keynes, Wilmot B. Lane, Currelly: every one a father-figure, with the possible exception of Keynes. That may have been partly the reason it was so personal a book. [D 49.110; DNF, 94]

Swearing. I was thinking recently of Jesus' command not to swear, of how right he was, & of how miserably hypocritical the 39 Articles are when they revoke his order. Then I thought that if obliged to take an oath in a court of law I should have to hold out for affirming, realized I just wouldn't bother, & finally said in exasperation that I simply am not a religious Houdini, & don't know how to fight my way out of these moral traps. I felt profoundly consoled by that, though intellectually unsatisfied. [NB 31.27]

Sweeping Generalizations. It is true that I attempt overviews, and my style in consequence features what are called, in the sweeping cliché of tunnel vision, "sweeping generalizations." [NB 44.697; LN, 1:242-3]

Swift. Swift is another one of that Irish group overshadowing Yeats, of course, but I've only just realized why. Swift is an extrovert, so you have to figure out what he believes in by implication, more or less, but I think he has a vision of simplicity at the center of society. Simple writing, simple living (hence cleanliness) simple thinking. Human beings can't make this kind of society, the natural man favoring affectation, private enterprise (Whiggish laissez-faire) and esoteric professional techniques, especially in religion, law and science. Hence the Yahoo-Houyhnhnm deadlock, the inability of achieving Houyhnhnm ideals with Yahoo material. Hence Swift is thrown back on the church, which has got its standards of simplicity (which includes also all the liberty, equality & fraternity possible to man) from God. Sure it can get corrupt, but still it's responsible to God for those standards, & so isn't quite the world. So Swift also has that governor-principle I found all through the 4k course ["Nineteenth-Century Thought"], and with him it's the Church, as, in different contexts, it is too for Milton & Coleridge. Perhaps it is the Church. [D 50.426; DNF, 383]

Symbol. The symbol is the minute particular, the spiritual atom, the monad full of mirrors (perhaps after all *not* windows), the grain of sand reflecting the (spiritual) world, the primitive like an orb. Its context can be present or absent. In the former case it's the center of the world: in the latter the world is decentered. Or the metaphors could be liquid instead of solid: when present (the context, I mean) we have "oceanic" submergence; when absent, the whole is the part of the part.
[NB 50.20; LN, 1:259]

Symbolism. Every once in a while in studying symbolism I feel a surge forward as though my unconscious has handed me another cabbalistic symbol from a kind of universal Tarot. Freemasonry I understand systematizes this into a technique. I think a similar process is the central part of the New Testament conception of the gift of tongues: whether actual languages in the literal sense were produced by collective excitement I don't know: doubtless it's possible, but would it be anything more spiritually valuable than a curiosity if it did happen? Surely the feeling of a pattern of universal meaning coming clear piece by piece, so that those who understand it could talk to each other in shorthand, would be predominant, & would be part of the so-called gift of prophesying. [NB 3.90; RT, 38]

Synchronicity. I arrive at the last page of this notebook on August 30, 1970. My mother & father who were exactly the same age to a day were born on August 30, 1870. My mother died in November of 1940, when Western culture entered the point of demonic epiphany. [NB 12.572]

Syncretism. I have always distrusted what I call Reuben the Reconciler in thought: the syncretism that "reconciles" Plato & Aristotle or St. Thomas & Marx. I think every great structure of thought or imagination is a universe in itself, identical with & interpenetrating every other, but not similar or harmonizable with any other. Syncretism is Coleridge's fancy playing with fixities & definites, & it leads to the net of relations, not to the archetypal universal unique. My earlier notebooks, where I wanted to move all the big names in modern literature and thought around like chess pieces, were fanciful in this sense. What I now want to do is pick epiphanies out of them for my own purposes. [NB 19.172; TBN, 39]

T

Talk. I talk very well; it would be nice to know what I was talking about, but if I did I might stop writing, as St. Thomas Aquinas did when he died. If it's necessary for me to know I'll be given the knowledge.
[NB 50.66; LN, 1:270]

Talking Teachers. Of the great religious teachers, Jesus, Buddha, Socrates, it seems for some reason significant to say that they do not write. They talk, though, and their words are recorded. Philosophers who seem close to an "existential" position seem to give up the continuous prose form in favor of an aphoristic sequence. [NB 33.45]

The Tarot. The reason I'm hung up on the Tarots at the moment is that a pack of cards has a close *technological* resemblance to a series of pericopes & kernels of concern. A new *sequence* appears every time they're shuffled. They're also a kind of original or hieroglyphic alphabet, & while the sequence is infinitely variable, the total simultaneous pattern always extends from alpha to omega. [NB 21.190; RT, 174]

Teaching. In the first stage of university teaching one is an embarrassed medium, of limited personality, reading carefully from notes and trying to let the subject reveal itself in the clarity & patience of the exposition. The second stage is less bashful; one wants to hold attention; one looks up more frequently from the now mastered notes, to teach this point to this boy, the next point to that girl over there. In the third stage...one takes the whole class in at once in a friendly personal address. Now at each step

there is the danger of realizing how one looms before them, & consequently of becoming a Covering Cherub, an opaque black priest, or rather preacher, putting on a personal show for the benefit of one's own pride. The danger increases proportionately with the increase in confidence. I am more subject to it than Robins, & when I fall into it I command an admiration that falls short of affection, as he, being diffident & afraid to loosen his personal hold, commands an affection that falls short—just short—of admiration. I think there is a fourth stage in which one looks beyond the students to something they have to turn around to see (& hence away from the lecturer) & a fifth stage with which the lecturer has nothing to do, in which they realize that what they have turned around to see really is what is behind the lecturer, & accounts for his being there, so that the whole room from the professor's bum to theirs is full of the spirit of Marvell or Donne or Keats or whoever it is. The lecture is not an act of love, for the act of love is a synchronizing orgasm, and the lover of students uses sexual language: he worries because he had all his material ready, & yet it didn't "come off" & he blames their frigidity or his impatience. Doubtless some lectures do or don't come off, but in the act of vision the response is unpredictable. Some see; some don't see; some see something else, very intensely; some see nothing for hours & then suddenly come to.
[NB 3.76; RT, 31-2]

The scholar is a mental explorer: he finds out & communicates what the rest of the world does not know. The teacher is often, even normally, in the position of one who knows, instructing those who do not know. But it has been understood ever since Plato's *Meno* that the real function of the teacher is to remind the pupil of what he potentially knows already. That is why it is the teacher, Socrates, who asks the questions, not the student. The teacher aims at lucidity for himself and recognition from his reader.
[NB 11B.82; RT, 359]

The St. John's College scheme: Parts of it appeal to me very much, but it seems more like a professor's program of self-culture than something to teach to students—also, the requirement on the teacher to be able to teach everything including mathematics & science seems to me to confuse an amateur ideal of culture with a professional technique of instruction. I could do it—at least there was a time when I could have done it, & I imagine I still could—but it would be, not real teaching, but a deliberate *tour de force.* No one can be a great lecturer—I think I have the adjective coming to me—without sublimating a considerable amount of exhibitionism, but a teaching job that was a deliberate exhibition of versatility would focus on that, & turn me into a hopeless show-off. [D 49.86; DNF, 83-4]

University lecturing is not teaching but a form of intellectualized preaching. You can go into all the world & preach the gospel, but if you try to teach any more than about twelve disciples you've had it. Teaching relates two individuals through Socratic love, which has to be homosexual. I can't really teach a woman, because, being a woman, the things organic to her learning process are female, & shut me out. All I could do would be to identify myself with her animus, which puts me, as I've discovered & elsewhere remarked, in a hell of a spot. To teach a boy is to form his character, which means partly to unite him to the males of the tribe. It also involves the sort of love which sees with complete clarity what the boy's character is: you can't, that is, teach a frivolous person in the way you would teach a preternaturally solemn one. I'm not a teacher according to this line of thought; and I wonder if it's possible without some physical interest in men, or sublimation of it. Even Jesus had a beloved disciple, as Marlowe pointed out. I can trace no such interest in myself. [D 49.101; DNF, 90]

Television. The relation of communication, community, & communion. We think of communication as a message from an active A to a receptive B. On this basis we make a distinction between popular & educational programming, just as the BBC has a "Light" & a "Third" program, Third being a euphemism for Heavy. One says "this is what you really want," & provides a narcist mirror of escape based on simple-minded inference from the work ethic: you're tired & want to take your mind off your work.

The other says "this is what you really ought to want," & assumes an informed & responsible elite in the more sedentary middle class. In this setup the entertaining is by definition the opposite of the boring.
[NB 11F.107; RT, 94]

Television is like a telescope, a new method of perception which tells us more, but also makes what it sees look cold, dead, and inconceivably remote. Global village my ass. (Every idea contains its own opposite or antithesis.) [NB 11F.115; RT, 97]

Telos. Teleology: Socrates following a line (the inevitable metaphor) of thought in the *Republic,* with Glaucon supplying the punctuation. Mozart's symphonies, with the feeling that you could have written it yourself if you'd thought of the first two bars. My feeling that I had written *Fearful Symmetry* in sonata form. Stretto in fugues & *anagnorisis* in drama.
[NB 19.98; TBN, 22]

Nation means something socially born; nature means that which is born; principle means that which begins. The Aristotelian conception of nature is focussed on *telos:* I wonder if this is the real point in the Greek revolution? For without *telos* we're still in the Oriental world of *maya,* where things appear (get born) and therefore disappear (die), and where all reality has to be separated from appearance. The fact that birth implies death suggests an endlessly turning wheel. Telos is incarnation or embodiment in reverse, the wheel of chronos reaching a point of kairos. With Vico the *maya* wheel reappears in the West, & since then we have developed mayan process-philosophies, which tend to deprive the intellect of a focus. This focus or *telos,* the completed form, is the objective counterpart of individuality.
[NB 19.150; TBN, 34]

The Temenos of Art. It seems to me that there's always something of the *temenos,* the place marked off from experience, in the work of art, & that the cult of "happenings," which tries to dissolve art back into experience, is mob art, the *dérèglement* which Rimbaud fled from & later condemned as "bad," the kind of thing going on in *The Plumed Serpent*. It has something, I don't know yet what, to do with reversing the dream in the direction of medium & séance. The question "can you tell the truth without lying?" has two answers: one at the top connected with myth, one at the bottom connected with "tactics" and propaganda. At the top the "lie" may be partly the nothingness concealed in being. Perhaps truth cannot render being, & only myth can render the mixture of being & nothingness.

[NB 12.171]

Tension of Opposites. The 30s of this century were frightened by the power of the masses led by a mass-man, and religious people turned to the Incarnation, the Word made flesh, as the source of verbal as opposed to brutal power. But the Incarnation is only the Apollonian or order side of the Word; the Resurrection, the Dionysian expression of the power, completes it. Well, who denies that? I'm trying to get at the tension of opposites.

[LN 44.707; LN, 1:245]

Teufelsdröckh. I have a hunch that at a certain point we re-enter a world where the stars are again visible. The greatest Thanatos works of literature are the *Iliad* (ultimately that, I think, rather than Adonis tragedy) and the *Inferno*. In the latter the undisplaced journey begins with Dante entering Satan's mouth & being shot out of his arse at the bottom of everything, so that Dante is literally a Diogenes Teufelsdröckh, a God-born devil's dung, the interval being the point of mysterious return frequent in epics, corresponding to the cave of the nymphs in the *Odyssey*.

[NB 6.55; TBN, 119]

Text as Raindrops. To those accustomed to written books, a synchronic orally composed book like the Koran is intolerable. But Moslems wouldn't think of it diachronically, with unrepeated statements gaining the emphasis of repetition by being in dialectical sequence. They think of the Koran as words descending from heaven as rain descends from the sky, all over the

place at once, and if you're looking for rain to break a drought, you don't complain that one raindrop is much like another.
[NB 11F.80; RT, 88]

Text in the Class. The "publish or perish" syndrome created a variety of prefabricated formulas for enabling sterile scholars to become productive: they were aided by a recrudescence of the old myth-as-lie syndrome. I don't want to attack or dismiss any genuine development, but there is certainly going to be a text in my class, however enormously flexible and approximate the "establishing" of that text is to be. Texts, starting with the Bible, expand in meaning because they mean first of all what they say, & because they mean that they can mean infinitely more. We've never believed that poets really do mean (start with meaning) what they say.
[NB 50.621; LN, 1:383]

Theism. I'm a theist because I think the human is divisible, part of it being "all too human" & only a part divine. [NB 11F.102; RT, 93]

Theme with Variations. It would be interesting to try writing a theme with variations, as an application of archetypal criticism. The theme might be something like Beaumarchais' Figaro play. This is the situation comedy of a girl held prisoner by a displaced father who wants to marry her, but is baffled by the hero. Var. 1, *Allegro Moderato,* could deal with the structure of New Comedy from Plautus on, so far as it deals with this theme. Var. 2, *Andante con Moto,* would analyze Hoffmann's Salvator Rosa story in relation to Hoffmann's other work. Here the girl is an inner anima tyrannized over by a superego: sadism, or abusing the anima, being a suppressed theme, though important enough to account for the counter-sadism in baiting the pantaloon. Var. 3, *Allegretto Scherzando,* could deal with the commedia dell'arte patterns; Var. 4 with their development in Shakespearean comedy & romance; Var. 5 with Jungian and the traditional alchemical applications; Var. 6 with Mozart, linking the Figaro theme & the Don Juan one; Var. 7 with a philosophical development I haven't located yet; Var. 8 with cosmological & mythological overtones, as in the St. George story & Blake's *Earth's Answer;* Var. 9 could be a *Presto Fugato,* summing up all these themes. [NB 15.16; RT, 315]

Theology. The story of the fall of Adam is a story of a breach of contract, which has always made it dear to the heart of theological lawyers, because it provides them with what passes for an explanation of the human situation. Why do we live in a world where we all die, and where we suffer various inconveniences ranging from earthquakes to mosquito bites? The answer in the Book of Genesis is: well, it was like this: many years ago, a hungry girl long past her lunch time reached for an apple on the wrong tree, and as a result, all this has taken place. The answer is insane, it's psychotic, but then, so is most theology; and at any rate, it is a kind of answer. The advantage of studying the Book of Job is that it deals with the same question: how has man come to be in this alienating situation? But there is no contract; there is no alleged explanation. There is no quasi- or pseudo-historical element in it. It is given simply in purely imaginative terms.
["SYMBOLISM IN THE BIBLE," LECTURE 18; RT, 554-5]

Theory. But *a priori* objections to whether I have a right to do what I'm doing don't interest me. A theory that explains a lot of facts is a good theory, & theory & facts have to be in the same plane. A psychological theory can only explain psychological facts; literary facts can only be explained by a literary theory. This is so obvious & elementary that I simply can't communicate with anybody who questions it, or thinks he's questioning it.
[NB 11F.244; RT, 129]

There are two kinds of theory. There are the dialectically organized theories, which lead to interminable argument & create innumerable schools, schisms, sects & cliques. Then there are theories that lead to theories, to a synoptic view of the subject. Those who complain about being imprisoned in my "system" are looking at it as an argument. But if I go to the top of the Empire State building for a view of Manhattan and see the Chrysler building, what I say is "there's the Chrysler building." I do not say "that's where the Chrysler building fits in." [NB 50.396; LN, 1:395]

In the *Anatomy* I passed beyond "new" or rhetorical criticism (without knowing much about it) because I was dissatisfied with its lack of any sense of context as a part of literary meaning. Right now I'm passing beyond post-structural criticism (without knowing much about that either) as a mode with no context either, but simply a reinforcing of an "anything goes" in literature itself with an "anything goes" in the critical approach to it. I don't think I want an explicit reference to this (there wasn't one in the *Anatomy*) much less any hostile comment (if I did that I'd have to read more than I want to of the stuff). But in my view of the Bible as a model of kerygmatic criticism, which I think of as getting past the imaginative creation for its own sake without going back to the old ideological dialectics, I think I'm passing beyond "deconstruction" into a reconstruction no longer structural. [NB 50.407; LN, 1:337-8]

I am not (directly) concerned with the familiar complaint that the elaboration of critical theory makes literature less accessible to the student instead of more so, but I am concerned with a direct & inductive response to literary experience. [NB 50.477; LN, 1:352]

Thinking. There is an organic as well as a logical (mechanistic) unity in thinking, & everyone has big thoughts & little ones. The size has no relation to the subject matter—that's the mistake everyone makes—but to the thinker. A man may have little thoughts about God & big thoughts about bicycle lamps, & his whole life may turn on a discovery about the latter, while God remains a vague haze of random mental illusions.
[NB 3.101; RT, 41-2]

Thomism. I suppose what my bourgeois liberalism really amounts to is the sense of the ultimately demonic nature of all ideological constructs. In the 30s & 40s the Thomist one had Gilson & Maritain in the front line: they were gentlemen, of course, but a mean-minded fascism lurked in the background. I knew that the Thomist setup was an illusion, and that Marxism (which didn't have any gentlemen) would eventually be exposed as another illusion. [NB 44.702; LN, 1:244]

The Three A's. Ecclesiastes deals squarely with the three A's: anxiety, alienation, absurdity. *Not* pessimistic or weary but a shrewd tough-minded attack on the bromides of popular proverbs, which he collects but tests with his touchstone of *hebel,* mist or vapors. "Vanity of vanities" really means something like "nuts" or "bullshit." The basis, as with all wisdom literature, is the contrast of wisdom, the tried & tested way, & folly, the new idea which is the old fallacy. The fool is the "one-dimensional man" in a sense opposite to Marcuse's: the man chasing the donkey's carrot of a definable future ideal, not realizing what's established by the cyclical vision at the beginning: that all future goals really come out of the past, a mixture of historical & childhood myth. [NB 12.207]

The Three Ages. The age of Rousseau ended around 1850, although the things it started—Bonapartism in France, Prussian imperialism and Romantic culture—kept going for over a century later. After 1830 came the age of Marx, which lasted up to the Russian Revolution, starting things which are still going on, and will for a long time yet. After 1920 came the age of Freud, which is now beginning to produce what I call the Freudian proletariat. [NB 19.428; TBN, 99]

The Three Bers. Coincidence is just unusable design.... Suppose I'm working out some idea about modern thought in which the names of Berkeley, Bergson & Berdyaev keep recurring. One part of me notes the fact that all three names begin with the same three letters. That has a certain mnemonic value (the memory grasps arbitrary associations much more quickly than real ones) & a certain quality that appeals to paronomasia & word-juggling, so that I could, if I were given to that form of facetiousness, talk about the "Three Bers." This is more or less where Joyce comes

in. But as far as my thesis goes, I say that the resemblance in names is "pure coincidence" or "purely arbitrary," or some other form of purity. Now I have no right to pronounce objectively on such a subject: I only know that it is a bit of relationship between them that I can't use. Perhaps an interpretation of experience is known to Yeats's instructors in which the similarity is profoundly significant. Perhaps I suggest my own ignorance of this by constructing a separate pattern of thought in the index, where Berkeley, Bergson & Berdyaev will be closely associated solely by virtue of their alphabetical similarity. I only know that I can't make the complete pattern if there is one, & refuse to feel impelled to investigate the music of Berlioz & the sculpture of Bernini for further enlightenment.
[NB 32.23]

The Three Stages. There are three stages of education in literature. First is the stage of literacy, the immediately practical learning to read and write, as fundamental a need as food & shelter, yet in itself only the ability to follow instructions. Next is the stage of liberality, participation in a *free* society, then participation in the myth of concern. And this, by God, is the first notebook I've ever filled completely in thirty years of keeping notebooks. [NB 19.445; TBN, 103]

Three Worlds. There are three worlds: the physical world, the psychic world & the pneumatic or verbal world. I prefer verbal (ultimately it will have to be "logical," although Ulro has usurped it) to pneumatic because it is wrong to say "in the beginning was the breath or spirit".... The physical world exists; the psychic world may or may not exist; the pneumatic or verbal or logical world neither exists nor does not exist. The point at which we begin to realize that mathematics is not a criticism of reality but an autonomous language is the point at which a teacher draws a chalk line on the blackboard & tells us, first, that that is a line, & secondly, that it is not a line. Or, even earlier, the point at which we understand that "three" is not three matches, & yet not *not* three matches.
[NB 7.97, 102]

Thrillers. I've just been reading a thriller of Ian Fleming's, and am astonished at the stockness of the material, combined as it is with a certain sophistication in handling concrete detail. Hero and heroine kidnapped by fiendish villains, who instead of killing them at once leave them alone & allow them to escape. Villain takes advantage of the situation to recount his life story as a cognitio; heroine threatened with torture, taking the form of displaced rape. For some strange reason the word "thighs" didn't appear, as it almost always does in that place in thrillers. Many years ago Edmund Wilson, in a *New Yorker* review, connected the Houdini situation with the dying & reviving god.
[NB 18.127]

Thurber. I drank several Manhattans & we moved on to the Thurbers. There I had a lot more drinks & dinner—well, supper—wasn't served until very late, so I got horribly sick and had two long agonizing sessions in the can puking my guts up. I forgot I had hay fever. Apart from that I enjoyed talking to James Thurber, who told me all about Harold Ross, who seems to be a strange and attractive mixture of toughness and innocence—possibly a much stronger character than Thurber himself, who seems to me to have the insecurity of someone from central Ohio who's still trying to adjust himself to the big bad city. Now how in God's name—I'm not drunk now—did I manage to compose a sentence like that, plopping one clause after another like horse turds and who-whoing like an owl?
[D 50.562; DNF, 441]

Tiananmen. June, 1989. The massacre of the students in Tiananmen Square and the utter complacency of the senility squad about it, their confidence that all they have to do is to keep repeating the big lie, has definitely established Marxism, from Lenin on, as what Blake calls the Synagogue of Satan. Nobody can support a Marxist political movement anywhere now without being, on the Burke principle, not just a mistaken man but a bad man. Gorbachev's *glasnost* looks better, but even it is imposed from the top down. [NB 50.756; LN, 1:406]

Time. The past is hell, the eternally fixed state where the ghosts of dead sins & errors are forever imprisoned. The future begins in childhood as a world of infinite potentiality. As life goes on, the future becomes steadily more predictable, & the life consequently less interesting. Children fascinate us; old men bore us because they conceal no surprises. At death the future finally merges with & joins the past—in Dante's hell the future but not the present is known. Life reaches its crisis *nel mezzo del cammino,* the sun at its highest in the sky, realizing with a shudder that it is bound to a cycle & must now descend. Hence the importance Jung attaches to the 35-40 period: its timing may depend partly on the length of the life, which of course the unconscious always knows. I think one has to be reborn now & start in fancy all over again in relation to a new kind of life, as though the sun at zenith were to think of itself as at the bottom of reality & start rising & straight up. That way, the imagination may grow stronger as the foolish body decays.... Each dimension of time breeds fear: the past, despair & hopelessness & the sense of an irrevocable too late: the present, panic & sense of a clock steadily ticking; the future, an unknown mystery gradually assuming the lineaments of the consequences of our own acts. [NB 3.146; RT, 59]

Time is specifically the enemy of sex: Marvell's *Coy Mistress,* the lemans & paramours of the Gardens of Adonis, and of course many poems of Donne. Thus the fall, which was primarily a fall of sex, brought the sense of time and the anxiety of continuity (with its past and future projections) into the world. Meditation (see the Fifth Walk of Rousseau's reveries) first turns off the sound, then the moving pictures, and when they're gone the kernel of play is left, energy without alienation. [NB 27.540; LN, 1:100]

In ordinary experience, time is a mixture of the irreversible and the cyclical. Demonic time, or life in hell, is Macbeth's "tomorrow": here time is simply one clock-tick after another, and everything that happens is irreversible. This means that everything tends, not towards death, but towards the kind of undying death expressed by the word entropy. The perception of the cycle, of the same thing coming around again, can be demonic too, but actually it introduces a principle of self-renewal into time. In the paradisal state, time would be pure cycle expressed in the images of the cosmic dance and the harmony of the spheres. Here again there is a mixture of two themes: the sense of the dance, or time as the servant and not the master or activity, and the sense of the present moment as staying. Above this, at least in theory, is pure present in the divine man. [NOTES 58-2.7]

Titus Andronicus. Stage direction in *Titus Andronicus:* Lavinia's hands cut off & tongue cut out, ravished—however they did that. Titus chops his hand off on the stage to prevent Aaron killing his two sons, but is too late & Aaron sends back the two heads along with the hand. Titus announces that he thinks this is a dirty trick, & plans revenge. Puzzle: how to get all the cold cuts off the stage? He takes the two heads in one hand: that being full of heads, he can't carry the other hand—*his* hand, which Aaron has returned. So he gives it to Lavinia, who hasn't any hands at all, has to take it with her mouth, and goes out like a retriever with the hand dangling from her puss. [D 49.176; DNF, 120-1]

Tolerance. I am what I am because of certain historical events: the Protestant Reformation, the Anglican settlement, the Methodist movement, the transfer of religious energies to the New World. Hence if I express a tolerance that grants to any position the capacity of moving nearer whatever truth is, I am also annihilating history, assuming that all religious theory and practice today begins in a kind of apocalypse in which past history has exhausted its significance as such. The nineteenth-century obsession with conversion, mainly from Protestant to Catholic positions, was a desperate effort to keep history continuous: I think it no longer works, if it ever did. [NOTES 52.209; LN, 2:467]

What I'm trying to work out is not "the truth" but what makes sense to me at the moment. What is much closer to "the truth" is the social tolerance that allows me to function. This tolerance is mostly indifference, but indifference is infinitely better than perverted concern. It assumes that the Reformation, like Communism in 1917, is a genuine revolution, but that the real revolution has still to come. That's the Second Coming that will convert the Jews, and the coming of the Messiah that will convert the Christians. [NB 11H.16; LN, 2:714]

Tons of Sewage. In a recent discussion an Old Testament scholar who's made a neo-fundamentalism out of what used to be a liberal position—i.e. we now know about the historical background, or will after we've sifted through fifty tons of sewage from Scoopadacrap, Turdistan. Milton & Blake didn't have the knowledge we now have, she said. As for St. John of the Cross, his ignorance of all the village fertility songs bit makes him ridiculous. I found myself so close to defending Bloom's "misreading" thesis that I wonder whether, like most post-Frye conceptions, it doesn't fit the Bible primarily. [NB 44.163; LN, 1:135]

Totem and Taboo. A child's world consists of the things he plays with, his toys, which are things in themselves & yet extensions of his own identity, & a world beyond of things he mustn't touch. He thus lives purely in a world of totem & taboo. [NB 34.30]

Tragic Immorality. One difference between belief & anxiety is whether one finds the tragic or the comic vision immoral. Comedy has sexuality & dirty words, both subjects of anxiety. But one reason why I have never come to terms with the tragic vision is its hideous immorality. The appalling creatures men worship, for one thing: Shakespeare's witches are great-souled compared to Hera & Athene, instantly bitching about any reverse to the Greeks because they're sore at losing a beauty contest, judged by a mortal at that. They're no better than Dante's God who creates hell out of divine love. And the immoral conception of the other world in the Christian hell and the Homeric Hades. And above all the immorality of the heroic skull-splitting code of great glory itself. I have to face this if I'm to write anything new. [NB 13.114]

Tragic Trinity. There are three primary tragic patterns: the murder of the Father, the basis of a rather desperate myth of Freud's; the sacrifice of the Son, & the isolation or pharmakosizing of the Spirit. [NB 9.408]

Trahison des clercs. Culture goes in the opposite direction. In spatial metaphors, it decentralizes, forming relatively small units while political and economic units get bigger and more centralized. In temporal ones, it moves in the opposite direction from revolution toward a pre-revolutionary stage of consciousness, where Jesus and Socrates are still alive and where their ideas can still be dangerous—that is, toward a society where the speculative is still wide open on all sides. The *trahison des clercs* occurs when intellectuals give way to their constant itch to be socially important, to help turn the wheel of history. [NOTES 52.677; LN, 2:553]

Translation. Translation is a key word now: the Bible attracted me because, poetic as it was, it seemed the essence of translatability. The critic translates literature into another linguistic structure (basically descriptive, but adapted to its figurative subject) that joins literature to other aspects of culture. [NB 44.550; LN, 1:218]

Travel. The traveller wants two contradictory things: he wants to see new things & he wants his immediate surroundings to be in continuity with his personal habits at home. The Hilton Hotel in Katmandu—in other words the movie-illusion of a foreign country within that country—is the answer. Tourist trade increasingly creates an illusion of a country which is presented to the traveller as the exotic aspect of that country, as what he came to see. Real life is hidden behind, some of it appalling in its poverty & tyranny, some of it assimilating itself to life elsewhere. And then of course there's the increasing possibility that the traveller from Spokane will meet somebody else from Spokane in the hotel lobby, & so help to recover his identity. [NB 11F.122; RT, 99]

Trilogies. I notice that in science fiction there's a frequently repeated form of a trilogy (usually) in which a new world is created: Frank Herbert's Dune books, Asimov's Foundation, Ursula LeGuin's Earthsea or something, Zelazny's Amber books, and a set by Philip Jose Farmer called *Riverrun,* hardly up to the others. These trilogies owe a great deal to the prestige of Tolkien, and are rather routinely and drearily compared to Tolkien in the blurbs. But the Eddison Memison books were in the field earlier, and Morris, though he wrote no trilogy as such, certainly wrote a lot of damn long books about some world at the end of ours. [NOTES 54-13.2]

Trinity. Power, wisdom and love are three persons in one substance. [NOTES 53.34; LN, 2:619]

True Gods. The real "gods" are not forces within nature, but forces within the human transformation of nature. That is, the true gods are the gods of words, numbers, tones and colors that produce the arts. [NOTES 54-1.20; LN, 2:668]

The true gods are the Muses, except that there are six of them: literature, painting, sculpture, architecture, mathematics and music. There is a seventh God who combines all these and creates us, rather than being the means of our own creation. It is this God who deserves a day of a week set aside for him, who is entitled to first-fruits and to the study of his myths and rituals that recreate us as we recreate the world through our arts. That's what Blake meant by saying you're not a Christian if you're not an artist, though I certainly wish he'd said it in a more cautious way. The six gods are both servants and masters, as every practitioner of them knows. They are servants of humanity, but masters of their priests: *ego dominus tuus,* as the god of poetry said to Dante. (He was the god of love too, of course: they're all forms of Eros, the reverse of the Agape that belongs to the seventh. [NOTES 54-1.30; LN, 2:670]

Truth. One should think of truth, not only statically as the correct formulation of propositions, but dynamically, as the normal current of the energy

293

of the soul. These correspond to the allegorical & moral levels in Dante. A lie is to the intellect what a neurosis is to the emotions, a blocking point which dams up the current; a stone around which it forms whirlpools. Hence imaginative people who keep spinning spider-webs in their minds make the best liars, as they make the best use of neuroses. For vigorous extroverted people "living a lie" is an intolerable burden, & confession for them has the quality of a physical compulsion. A great deal is said about the psychological rightness of Catholic auricular confession: as usual, the priest absorbs both the indwelling Christ & the social community. The point about "know thyself" is to pervert self-deception, so that the lies one is obliged to tell in the interests of the *persona* won't stay in the mind— thus Johnson's "clear your mind of cant." Probably one has to lie to men— certainly to women—but not to know that one is lying is to lie to God. Honesty with oneself carries off social lies in a private excretion. Honesty with others follows: you can't interpret James's "confess your sins to one another" as the Oxford Group does, because shitting in a group is a perversion, or rather a fixation of childish curiosity. One has always to remember the dynamic nature of truth, and hence of reasoning. "My father has money; I shall have it when he dies; I need money now; he must die now." Depending on the extent of one's capacity for parricide, that sequence may be anything from irrefutably logical to unthinkable. [NB 3.161; RT, 64]

The ideologue identifies truth with whatever promotes his cause: the trouble with that is the mortality of causes. Truth, like the classic in literature, is whatever won't go away, and keeps returning to confront us. I don't know what "the truth" is in most matters, only that it's likely to be connected with whatever returns until we deal with it. (Logical positivism went under because it was the exact opposite of "the truth": only statements that make no sense at first have any continuing validity.) [NOTES 53.213; LN, 2:653]

Trying God's Patience. Jan. 1, 1980. I continue to try the patience of God, yet I still hope for some improvement. [NB 11B.77; RT, 359]

Two Worlds. Man lives in two real worlds, one spiritual, the other natural, physical, or psychic. In the spiritual world God exists in us and we in him: a paradox that only metaphorical language can begin to express. In this world nature exists in us and we in it, but here the centralizing principle, or ego, is constantly trying to isolate itself. The spirit interpenetrates with its world but never violates: our interpenetration makes war, as Heraclitus said, the center of all activity, because it's always withdrawing to objectify. [NB 50.810; LN, 1:415-16]

U

Ultimate Concern. Is ultimate concern a primary concern? I think not. No one can live a day without being concerned with food: anybody can live all his life without being concerned about God. In my table of metaphors, animal & vegetable are food, mineral shelter (for living & dead) & direction, the human itself sexual. The superhuman categories have to do with leisure, concern for survival (of death), intelligence (a need according to me), and vision. [NB 27.428; LN, 1:78]

Unconscious Symbolism. The corporal punishment of the child in the Victorian home or school is a kind of black mass, & corresponds point for point to a church service: the preparation or approach, defining the approacher as a sinner, then the proclaiming of the Word in a legal-punishment instead of a gospel-forgiveness sense, proving guilt from the record historically, & from general principles morally, then the announcement of the intention to punish as a *nunc dimittis:* then the period of bodily contact with the law: the command to approach & kneel, the disrobing corresponding to the opening of the mouth; the elevation of the buttocks, the descent of the holy rod, the transubstantiation into real blood, the burst of tears & the benediction ("let this be a lesson to you")—every detail has its analogies. [NB 34.68]

Underground Religion. The poetic imagination is earth-centered: I'm getting a little close to my feeling about Christianity being really an underground religion. That is, it's really the death on cross-harrowing of hell-resurrection pattern, and the nativity-ministry-ascension ghost of it is the romantic idealism of an ascendant social class. [NB 11F.104; RT, 94]

Unforgivable Sin. Nietzsche says that it's hard to get rid of God when we still believe in grammar. I'd say, as all "good" words are part of the Word, we can't get rid of God except by misusing or perverting language. The latter is the unforgivable sin against, not the Word, but the Spirit responding to it: unforgivable because it cuts off the possibility of its own forgiveness. [NB 50.635; LN, 1:385]

Ungodly Question. The question "Is there a God?" can only be answered "No," because any question beginning with "is there" is an ungodly question. [NB 11B.67; RT, 358]

Union Jack. Whenever I look at a Union Jack, a superb piece of abstract design in which centuries of history are expressed with the greatest possible pungency & wit, a pure cabalistic sign in the sense I'm beginning to attach to that word, I realize, not only the expressive power of the sign as a piece of cabalism—dying fighting for the flag is the commonest form of cabalism in society—but also the fact that there is such a science as heraldry, & that it's an essential aspect of iconography. Its association with a fighting aristocracy rings true, too: the purest cabalism today is the solder's uniform, where it's possible to read off his whole military history. [NB 34.36]

Uniqueness. Uniqueness is not in itself worth studying, the world's worst poem being as unique as the best; second, uniqueness is unknowable. We cannot know the literary work except in terms of what is typical. [NB 11F.246; RT, 129]

United Church of Canada. I wonder why the information that so-&-so has turned Roman Catholic depresses me so. I think it's not so much that Church, though, as a liberal Protestant democrat, I hate & fear this total-itarian, sleepless, relentless, anti-liberal, anti-Protestant, anti-democratic machine. It isn't the fact that Catholic converts have to assent that they believe absurd doctrines that bothers me. It's really, at bottom, resentment against Protestantism, especially this fatuous United Church, for being so miserably lacking in intellectual integrity. Protestantism is done for here, unless it listens to a few prophets. I don't want a Church of any kind, but if, say, a student of mine were quavering over conversion to Catholicism, I'd like to be able to point to something better than a committee of temperance cranks, which is about all the United Church is now. [D 49.27; DNF, 59-60]

Unity. Man is sectarian. That's why he's instinctively a polytheist. As I say, concern must have an enemy. God is, among other things, unity: monotheism is a lot more than just economy of hypothesis. So when man is confronted by God with a demand for unity which is wholly other than man's nature, man's rationalizations for avoiding it are interminable. His notion of charity is to say: God wants us to unite, so you can bloody well unite with me on my terms. When that doesn't work, he relapses into "tolerance," & says, I'll let you live in your way as long as you let me live in mine. [NB 21.433; RT, 219-20]

University. The university impinges on the adolescent at the climax of his adolescence, just when he is beginning to get the idea that all knowledge proceeds from the knower, & provides him with the community of learning which paradoxically completes & organizes his sense of individual freedom. The university, like the Protestant Church & the democratic state, does not define itself dialectically. It forms the keystone of life, between a childhood where the subjective has reality & an adult life in which the objective dialectically determined social unit has reality. It concerns itself, not with the dialectic choice which properly follows it, Plato's state & Newman's Church, but with the disinterested community of vision, which includes the dialectic, Plato's symposium & Newman's liberal conversation. To the Protestant it's *that* that embodies Christian liberty, the pure act of listening to the Word which enfranchises both Church & State & breaks down all the dialectic barriers. [D 49.351; DNF, 197]

University as Community. The whole fallacy about university life is that it isn't regarded as a community of learners, but as a dichotomy of scholar-

teachers & students, & the false analogies from democracy that build up student government separate them & drive the teachers into the graduate school, where they feel they can find their community.
[D 49.171; DNF, 119]

Utopia. The Utopia is a vision of the rational form of society, & it is best seen, not as an end, but as an informing principle. It's the objective aspect of what in subjective terms is ideal education. The Utopia & the educational treatise are closely linked in the 16th century: in Rabelais, Castiglione, Spenser, where we have idealized courts and universities. Besides, education is the only way to develop the ritual habits needed, so Utopianism & the theory of education are inseparable, hence they must both be in my book. Educational theory hooks itself on somehow to the conception of the order of words. [NB 19.88; TBN, 20]

$\mathcal{V}$

Value-Judgments. Value-judgements are worn as blinkers by conventional critics to prevent themselves from seeing the real facts of literature. Karl Shapiro in Indiana spoke of Jung's references to Rider Haggard as showing what crude & undeveloped taste in literature Jung had. Maybe Jung's taste is crude, but Shapiro's real feeling was that once we start making serious allusions to "inferior" writers, the whole system of valuation which makes Shapiro an interesting & distinctive person will be overthrown. Closely connected with this is the bad analogy between reading and eating, which a lot of people have without knowing it. In eating a large amount of the involuntary & automatic goes on: a baby's pablum builds up the baby's nervous & muscular energy without consciousness being involved. Taking the analogy seriously gives us the theory of educational magic: the notion that one cannot help improving one's mind by being exposed to Shakespeare or Dante. The negative side of this is the impulse behind censorship: the analogy of poison, the notion that certain arrangements of words will, like a mushroom full of prussic acid, automatically & involuntarily do harm. There is an educational rhythm to be followed, analogous to not giving beef-steak to babies; but knowledge, being conscious, is based on character, & has no automatism. To the true critic there is nothing poisonous, because poison, unlike food, works automatically in the mechanical, not the organic, sense. I haven't got all this clear yet. [NB 18.33-4]

Venus and Mars. I have occasionally played around with the idea that all determinisms are elements in a manifold criticism. Thus every literary work would have its sexual, "Freudian," erotic, or fetishistic aspect; also a cultural or class "Marxist" aspect; also a historical "Spengler" aspect, and perhaps a primitive or Frazerian aspect. The first two, the green & the red, the conjunction of Venus & Mars, seem to me particularly obvious. They're both evolutionary; the other two are regressive. [NB 19.45; TBN, 12-13]

Verbal Formulations. My whole life is words: nothing is of value in life except finding verbal formulations that make sense. Yet the great secret in reserve is something you can't reach unless you shut up. That's what Zen has to communicate. And how does it communicate? By flooding the world with books about silence. Words are to us what water is to a fish: dwelling-house of being, says Heidegger. [NB 50.52; LN, 1:267]

Verbal Formulas. All religions are, Blake says, different forms of the Poetic Genius, so that there's objective religion as well as objective art. My job in this world appears to be that of a mantra-gleaner, a picker up (inventor) of possibly useful verbal formulas. One set has to do with the role of art as a potential liberator of whatever gets liberated. Again, I suspect (and I hope, rather than at present believe) that Christianity has at least as much to be said for it as any other religion, & I'd like to keep this comparative aspect of my Bible book open. If I could suggest this I'd be very grateful. [NB 24.198; TBN, 323]

I sometimes think I am looking for the truth in the sense of tremendous insights or intuitions that will illuminate the meaning of life—and of death. But of course I'm not: all I'm looking for is verbal formulations, to fit somewhere in some damn paper. Truisms are never true: the verbal expression of truth has to be sharply pointed to skewer an experience in the reader; but of course it doesn't directly communicate experience. Nor does it necessarily represent anything more than a potential one. [NB 19.290; TBN, 66]

With the Fall man lost good & got the knowledge of good & evil, a cyclical & interpenetrating knowledge of good & evil, a cyclical & interpenetrating knowledge in which evil is primary & good a secondary derivation from it. So much I've always got clear. Man also lost life, life which is the *opposite* of death, life where death is an alien & non-existent possibility like unicorns, and got the interpenetrating cycle of life & death, where death is not only natural & inevitable, but implied in the very conception of life itself. I'm intellectually a prisoner of my own profession: for me, to know anything is to find a verbal formula for it. Hence the above represents something I've always known but never really knew. I suppose the good-evil & life-death cycles are only aspects of a total pattern of double-gyre or antithesis which can "exist" only in that form, as *The Critical Path* says. Youth & age, male & female, master & slave, & so on. So the cycle is the demonic analogy of interpenetration. [NB 24.184-5; TBN, 319]

It isn't much to do for the Liberation, but there's always the hope that my industrious search for koans & verbal formulas may be useful. In some contexts they could outlast the thoughts of Chairman Mao. Anyway, that's the sort of thing I should keep in front of me. [NB 24.207; TBN, 325]

Verbal Outline. The aphorism is a verbal *perception:* that is, it's a verbal analogy of a *Gestalt* perception. We often speak of it as a perception. And the quality I so admire in Burton and struggle for myself is *verbal* outline, a verbal analogy of powerful sketching that contains a great mass of facts. [NB 19.110; TBN, 25]

Vices. One of the most important of literary virtues consists in the art of concealing an author's personal vices. For the revelation of vice is direct address, & so boring. I don't mind the erotic fantasies in William Morris' romances, but the masochistic fantasies of Swinburne bore me & bother me, in that order, because Swinburne is just jerking off. However, lechery is, next to gluttony, the easiest vice to conceal. The hardest one, I think, is envy. Wyndham Lewis bores me because his motive for writing is envious. Perhaps it isn't concealment but sublimation that's the essential. Pope doesn't conceal spite, for instance. [NB 18.137]

Victoria College. My restlessness is due to a loss of faith in Victoria's future, but I sure as hell don't want to leave Canada or stop being a Canadian, yet technically I've reached the end of the line in Canada for my kind of job. Theoretically, there ought to be many advantages in being in the University of Toronto and not under its jurisdiction. But Victoria's position in federation is indefensible now [1950], and can't be rectified without financial loss which we can't very well stand. [D 50.386; DNF, 366]

Virgin Birth. The most primitive societies think of their significant acts as repetitions of myth: repetition in the present is what ritual is all about: the "truth" of the Virgin Birth is not whether the accounts in Matthew & Luke are historical facts, however factual, but in, say, Meister Eckhart's sermon telling us that every Christian has an obligation to become a virgin and bring the Word to birth in his own soul. [NB 50.364; LN, 1:328]

I don't "believe in" the Virgin Birth as a historical fact, but I "believe in" it as a poetic myth. That could mean (though it doesn't) that I don't take historical facts seriously. It certainly does mean that I take myth (and literature) very seriously indeed. That doesn't mean (once again) that I take seriously what they *say*: what I take seriously is the structure of what they present. [NB 50.495; LN, 1:357]

Virgin Mother. Is the reader, when he becomes the hero and narrative principle of the Bible, to be then identified with the virgin mother, the highest of creatures about to liberate the unborn God? Is that why so many Old Testament types, like the burning bush in Chaucer, get attached to her rather than Jesus? Gideon's fleece too. Has our attention been distracted towards "God" as the entity we should claim for ourselves rather than the Mary who is an immaculate conception in the genuine sense? Is she the lost phallus Lacan talks about? Is she the incarnate Pneuma, as Jesus is the incarnate God? The Mary who kept all these sayings in her heart may be the reader who is possessor & narrative principle of the Gospels, at least, & their archetypal author. [NB 11A.7; RT, 342]

Virginity. Artemis was the goddess who mostly presided over women in labour, yet she was a virgin. Maternity is of course a specifically female function: the virginity symbolizes the fact that she wasn't assisting pregnant women in a context of male supremacy. That's more or less what the virginity of Mary symbolizes too: not conformity with male-oriented standards of "purity," but asserting that maternity is self-imposed and not male-imposed. [NOTES 52.980; LN, 2:607]

Virtue. There has to be, I think, a more or less conscious renunciation of all virtue that lies outside the immediate love of vision & opportunity: the superego is always plunging at the horizon of virtue & getting into trouble. It's a Boy Scout who, seeing bedtime approaching with his good turn undone, leaps into the street & drags an old woman across the road who wanted to stay where she was. [NB 3.41; RT, 20]

Virtuous Heathen. The most subversive question that can be asked of any myth of concern is: what about the success or prosperity or virtue or wisdom of those who reject it or have never heard of it? Medieval Christendom simply turned off its hearing-aid when it thought of the virtuous heathen: Pope Gregory could get Trajan out of hell because he was impressed by his merits & an emperor was conspicuous enough for a Pope to have heard of him. Legend, but it represents a real truth. As soon as one concedes that some people can live just as well outside the myth, the whole *missionary* aspect of it is considerably weakened. And of course a missionary enterprise can hardly restrict itself, say, to pure religion: the whole social & political setup of the myth it's attached to, or at least its whole cultural set up, is inseparable from it. [NB 11F.192; RT, 118]

Visible and Invisible Worlds. Travelling on a train in Canada one looks out the window at a passing landscape. As it gets darker, more & more of the window reflects the inside of the carriage. Eventually there's nothing but reflection: one could assume that there was no world out there at all. A few lights appear that are difficult to reconcile with this thesis, but they

could be ignored or explained away, like…flying saucers. But when the train stops, & you have to get out at a station, it's probably a help to believe it's there. That's a parable of the dilemma of trying to keep the subject-object split between a visible & an invisible world.
[NB 19.145; TBN, 33]

Vision. So many of my students want to believe that the visionary writers of the Bible "just saw" what they said they saw. That's *our* conditioning, the acceptance of a separation of subject & object. There would have been a large subjective element in their vision. That, again, isn't something they made up themselves: that's the same conditioning. The supreme fiction, the illusion that is reality, that's the vision of existential metaphor.
[NB 27.415; LN, 1:75-6]

One of the things relevant to the intensifying of consciousness, the growth from seeing into vision, is beauty, the sense of the purposelessness in Kant's *Critique of Judgment*. Whenever we insist on purpose we stick ourselves with another god. [NOTES 52.645; LN, 2:549]

The main personal problem for me in writing this book [on romance] is to progress from learning about what vision is about to learning about vision. [NB 31.31]

Visions of Creation. The transcendence of resurrection has its counterparts in the speech of God in Job, the Buddhist tankas and mandalas of the wheel of life, the Kabbalistic tree with its demonic reflection. These are all visions of creation, presented in the present, stretching from the sons of God to leviathan, from the ascension of Christ to the leviathan of hell he left behind. [NOTES 53.227; LN, 2:655]

Vogue. Re the Cambridge Classicists—Frazer, Cornford, Murray, Harrison—critics are lazy, and can't hold things in their minds that aren't in vogue. It's an easy step from "I forget the stuff" to "that stuff's out of date." It's a still shorter step from there to "well, it must have been discredited by somebody." [NB 44.345; LN, 1:177]

Vulgar Marxism. In the present situation Marxist countries demand the subordination of the arts and literature to their political concerns; this subordination is sometimes part of what Marxist intellectuals living in non-Marxist countries call "vulgar Marxism," but is commonly the announced policy of Marxism whenever it comes to power. In the U.S. there were also frenzies like the Comstock and McCarthy movements, which fell into the regular pattern of regarding serious culture as their enemy rather than as the spokesmen of genuine concern.
[NOTES 52.201; LN, 2:465]

Vulgate. I've been wondering if I could find any evidence for tendencies in the "vulgate" to build up inflectional endings out of the present mass of slurred particles. The reason it interests me is that at the other end of speech poets are trying to cut out the mass of analytic prepositions & stuff in order to put their images (nouns & verbs) more directly together— hence so much obscurity. For one thing, the vulgate tendency to break down sentences with subordinate clauses into a series of coordinate ones gives conjunctions a quite new syntactic ambiguity. I think of the man in the hospital who said to me "I'm the guy that the tractor fell on his foot." To translate that into conventional grammar we'd need two sentences, one personal ("I'm the guy on whose foot the tractor fell") and one impersonal ("I'm the guy of whom it is said: 'the tractor fell on his foot'"). Or I think of the "no trunks only" sign I saw at a swimming pool—the concentration of that is like many grammatical devices in modern poetry.
[D 52.49; DNF, 482]

W

Walking. I finally got a headache from too much sedentary idling, and went out for a walk. It was a desperately dull and gloomy day, and the streets were largely deserted. I show little enterprise in my walks: I've always preferred obvious paths. I want to think when I walk, and I can't both think and wonder where the hell I'm going next. [D 50.3; DNF, 215]

War and Peace. So much talk about pacifism is too vaguely moral. Peace is an economic system functioning. War is an economic system breaking down. States are healthy in war and degenerate in peace because of original sin and because anarchy is the best form of government. [NB 4.89]

War of the Sexes. In literature I find the war of the sexes a most unheroic theme. I'm enough of a disciple of Blake to believe that the domination of the female will is evil, and therefore I just don't find the wife-beats-husband theme funny. James Thurber does, or pretends to; Bernard Shaw does, & pretends not to, the comic strips do & the movies do. I'm sorry, but I don't. I don't find Mrs. Pinchwife's final line funny; I don't find the Venus of *The Merchant's Tale* funny; I just don't find any irresistible female funny. And it's not funny now because it's not the inverse of a convention. True, women's labor is exploited more than that of men, & the various prostitute rackets that are allowed to run, notably the alimony, the "breach of promise" and the "rape" rackets, are superficial compared to that fact. But there is no real subjection of women today of the kind that makes *Bringing up Father* a criticism of life. I don't want male authority reestablished: I just want the whole silly business of inferior sexes and self-conscious "equality" of sexes dropped & forgotten about. It's no longer amusing, if it ever was. [D 42.78; DNF, 32]

Watching. We must not *do* things, but let them happen. This is the Chinese *wu wei*, Keats' negative capability, which imitates Milton's God in withdrawing from the causation sequence and simply watching with prescience. In Frye's thought this faithful watching is the literal apprehension of art, the willing suspension of disbelief which is the prelude to all understanding (at least all *detached* understanding). [NB 3.151; RT, 61]

Weight and Drive. I want two things from this book [*The Great Code*]: epigrammatic weight and cumulative drive. [NB 11E.40; RT, 326]

What Poets Say.
They say that everything is everywhere at once.
They say that all nature is alive.
They say that creation is dialectic, separating heaven & hell.
They say that the material world neither is nor isn't, but disappears.
They say that the created world neither is nor isn't, but appears.
They say that the containing form of real experience is myth.
They say that time & space are disappearing categories.
They say that men are Man, as gods are God.
[NB 18.121]

The White Goddess. I suppose there's no male equivalent symbol of the irreversibility of time corresponding to woman's loss of virginity. The White Goddess has the power to renew hers because goddesses are above time. The motive for rape may sometimes be the urge to pull the woman down into the stream of time. [NB 27.411; LN, 1:75]

Whitehead. Whitehead's *Science and the Modern World* is a book that's influenced me so profoundly I often reproduce its conceptions when I think I'm thinking. [NOTES 53.12; LN, 2:615]

The Whole Show. The spiritual community or church moves toward the City of God, the panoramic apocalypse, which is the second coming or full epiphany of the Word, and provokes the response of the participating apocalypse, which starts just after the Bible ends and winds up the whole show. [NOTES 52.551; LN, 2:534]

Wigless Reader. The merging of reader and icon leads to interpenetration, but at that stage the reader is no longer an individual but one with the universal reader. The poet doesn't purify his authority until he's got rid of his ego, and the critic is not a real reader until he's taken his wig off & stopped trying to be a judge. [NB 44.415; LN, 1:193]

Will. The difference between a mechanism and an organism is not one of intellectual capacity or even consciousness. I have no difficulty whatever with machines thinking or being intelligent: they clearly can calculate a lot faster than brains can now: they've only started on their development, and eventually, I suppose, we'll have machines that stand in the same relation to the ordinary human brain of today that the jet plane of today does to ordinary human feet. But unless computers are equipped with DNA molecules and genetic codes impelling them to fight every instant of their lives for survival, competition and reproduction of their own species, I don't see how they can escape from the category of machines, who can do anything we like but have no will to do it left to themselves. A car can run faster than we can, but left unused in a garage it will rust away to nothing without the slightest sign of impatience. The difference between a mechanism and an organism is in will, not in capacity. [NOTES 52.189; LN, 2:461]

Will of God. I'm very suspicious of interpreting submission to the will of God as acceptance of anything that comes along. That substitutes the idolatry of "Providence" for God, & assumes that He wills the course of temporal events, for which I see no evidence. All he wills is liberation, & one may have to accept responsibilities so that one's life looks from the outside like an ambitious climb for power & a constant calculation of the main chance. It all depends—that's a mystical enough phrase, by the way. I know that a lot of my cheerful resignation is just laziness, just as a lot of my friendliness is just cuddling. [NB 3.56; RT, 25]

Will to Power. The only thing that gives Nietzsche away—and I haven't got the clue to that yet—is the unvarying contempt of women in his writing. Blake is disturbing enough on this, but at least his poetry is concerned with nameless shadowy females that are not women. The spirit *and the bride* say come, and Nietzsche's self-transcending man is a male. Sublimating love through violence (will to *power*) won't work. [NB 50.652; LN, 1:389]

Will-Religion and Enlightenment-Religion. Christianity says you got born but you don't die; Buddhism says you die but you never got born. One is a will-religion thrown forward to the future, Kierkegaard's "repetition," the other, which is closer to Plato, is an enlightenment-religion thrown back to a "recollection" of reality before the fall. [NB 6.28; TBN, 111]

Will-Worship. The theory of democracy about the will of the people being the source of government is, in that form, just will-worship like Calvin's. [D 42.127; DNF, 46]

Winding Up. I am 75 years old, and my wife is dead. There are a lot of what look like winding-up symbols—the Italian conference, the Governor General's medal, the Oxford degree, the San Francisco meeting—but I know they're not connected to other symbols or processes. I have what seems like one more major book in me, which I might conceivably finish before too long—perhaps by the time I reach the age at which Helen died. I don't feel suicidal: I just have no more resistance to death, though of course I still have the normal anxieties about it. [NB 44.433; LN, 1:197]

Windows. There are two kinds of people who realize that the Church should be the window & not the mirror of the Word, & who regard the autonomy of the Church, which produces the interior reflective monologue, as the silver on the back which makes it opaque. One kind is the Protestant who wants a church service focussed on the sermon or recreating the Word. The other is the dramatic or epic poet…who turns the Church into a window by recreating the Word out of the Church & so dissolving the silver & destroying the anonymity. [NB 7.9]

The Winter's Tale. *The Winter's Tale* has got to be the profoundest stage play ever written. Man faces his emanation, which he now knows he loves now that he's in his right mind again; she's a statue to be brought to life but also one to be separated from all projections of mother, wife, girl friend, and fantasy figures. The Great Work is not, as I used to think, the begetting of a child on her, but the recognition that the child already exists: Our Perdita is found. So Perdita isn't the dying and reviving female; she's the child who refuses to die, and she isn't born, she's found. … Four fathers are associated with her, three kings and a shepherd, and she's the end of the magic journey. All the magi begot Jesus, and yet none of them did. [NOTES 54-5.62; RT, 284]

Wisdom. The Promised Land appears in the distance from the ex-hodos [out+way], but wisdom reaches the kindergarten. [NOTES 52.461; LN, 2:515]

Witch-Finders. Reading Margaret Murray's book on witchcraft, one can't believe any part of her argument that assumes an actual religious organization, but that some subconscious demonic parody of Christianity was extended from all those poor creatures under torture is quite obvious, and its consistency doesn't surprise me: it's the same kind of thing primitive tribes produce, often by self-administered torture. The witch-finder himself was a psychopath, or soon became one by sticking pins all over naked women, and so they were linked in a communal dream. [NB 18.108]

Woe. The idealism of youth is inseparable from its egotism, & moral denunciations of hypocrisy are proclamations of self-righteousness, superego squallings of the "O daddy, why did you do it all so wrong?" type. The evils of society are the same kind of bitchup the human situation has always been in. The young will have the responsible jobs twenty years on; they'll make the same balls of it that everyone else in human history has made, & by that time their children will be whining at them. [NB 11F.77; RT, 87]

A century ago, the sense of continuity was reinforced by teleological art, virtues like thrift & independence, the authority of seniority, & so on. Craftsmanship was a continuity element also. Now we have an anti-teleological art, the assertiveness of youth, inflation (which is the transvaluation of the one real value, stable money), and technological obsolescence, even planned obsolescence, & an economy of waste—a kind of revived potlatch mentality. One hopes that it will be James' moral equivalent of war, with its phony sacrificial symbolism. Meanwhile, the compulsory continuity of the social order keeps going, with all these forces discouraging it. [NB 11F.78; RT, 87]

Womb of the Tomb. The fact that Jesus took on flesh in the Virgin's womb has certainly been dinned into Christian ears often enough; but the fact that he took on flesh in the womb of the tomb at the Resurrection, and that there's a female principle incorporated in the spiritual body, seems to have got strangled. The real tomb of Christ was the male-guarded church. [NB 50.358; LN, 1:327]

Women's Books. I think I start with those two wonderful books of Gertrude Levy's: she's really one of the wise women. (And why so many women? Maud Bodkin, Jessie Weston, Gertrude Levy, Helen Flanders Dunbar, Madame Blavatsky, Frances Yates, Enid Welsford, Jane Harrison, Bertha Phillpotts, Ruth Benedict: whatever the level of scholarship, a woman's book seems to meet me wherever I turn.) [NB 19.316; TBN, 71]

Word and Spirit. We think of words as human inventions, and of spirit as dissolved in nature outside us. In the New Testament the Word comes from and goes back to a world of mysterious remoteness, while the spirit works from within man, taking over first the "humanistic" world of language. [NB 44.294; LN, 1:166]

Words. Is there a point where we really get past words? The Buddhists & others keep yapping about this: words certainly seem to have an incarnational context for me. Also the sense of community seems involved. [NB 11E.13; RT, 321]

Words of Power. Wonder if the reason why gods are so anxious to punish boasts is that the boast could be or might become a word or power, and so genuinely threaten their supremacy? The implication would be that the Word is a power supreme over all divine wills in polytheism, the real form of the oath of power (swearing by the Styx). Warriors boast before battles, perhaps to strengthen themselves by what might be words of power. [NOTES 54-5.14; RT, 273]

Work and Play. The interpenetration of work and play is also the interpenetration of necessity and freedom. If we define genuine work as creative act (vs. drudgery or exploited & alienated work), what we have to do and what we want to do are the same thing. [NB 44.147; LN, 1:132]

I'm beginning to think, perhaps too much, about the word "mimesis." In Kant's *Critique of Judgment* the relation between purpose and purposiveness without purpose is the difference between work and play. Biology excludes or brackets teleology because the work of God is a notion that undercuts their work. The beauty that might be seen as the play (=wisdom) of God is a stimulus to human recreation, which is a mimesis of the divine creation (if the latter phrase really describes anything). Time is the endless Sabbath when God rests and we work. [NB 44.411; LN, 1:192]

World as Anything. The goal of Eastern training appears to be a world in which the imaginative, the imagined, the imaged & the imaginary are all the same, a world which is not nothingness because nothing is a dogmatic antithesis to something. It would be better described as anything, a world of total potentiality. Now according to the East, the difference between the imaginative & the imaged, the conscious & unconscious perception, is accounted for by a *habitus* built up over a series of previous existences, which is all right with me if we give the previous "habit" (life) a Samuel Butler interpretation. But in the East's revolutionary conception of break with habit there is, having entered the world of anything, no reason for doing one thing rather than another. [NB 34.47]

World's Profoundest Poem. I am about to write the world's profoundest poem, with apologies to William James, the only one who has touched my level of genius:

> *Hogamus, higamus,*
> *God is polygynous.*
> *Higamus, hogamus,*
> *Christ was androgynous.*

[NB 50.88; LN, 1:274]

Writing. Intelligent and sensitive people who have been through, say, a war seldom talk about it much. If you've shared the experience you don't need to be told about it, and if you haven't telling of it somehow subtly makes the experience untrue. This, apparently, is because the basis of conversation is casual & associative. Writing about it brings in a mythical shaping form that makes it true. Yet this truth often goes with a departure from fact. In writing you'd say "June 18 dawned foggy and cold" and still feel you were about to tell the truth, whereas you'd hesitate to say that in conversation, because it was neither foggy nor cold on June 18 and you weren't up until long past sunrise. [NB 18.143]

Why do I want to write books? Not to make money, obviously: to acquire fame & a better job? These things are as easily got as money by quicker means. To increase my self-respect with the sense of a job well done? I could do without that. To make me happier? That's closer, for happiness is a by-product, but not a goal, much less a final cause. Because there's a deeper compulsion in me that says I must? Bullshit. I don't want to write books at all: I just intend to write them, & doing so is a completely unmotivated act. [NB 3.37; RT, 18]

The main difficulty in my writing, as I've often said, is in translating discontinuous aphorisms into continuous argument. Continuity, in writing as in physics, is probabilistic, and every sequence is a choice among possibilities. Inevitable sequence is illusory, & especially so in logic, where, just as q is always followed by u, so "rigor" is always followed by "mortis."
[NB 27.112; LN, 1:21]

I've never started a book, even an essay, knowing exactly where it was going & how it would end. [NB 11F.252; RT, 130]

I want to have a book to write that (without being a diary) will be more fun to write than any book will be to read. [NB 11F.260; RT, 132]

I'm not waiting for more or new information: I'm waiting to see what shape the information I actually have actually has. [NB 11F.272; RT, 135]

I've taken to starting everything I write with a personal reminiscence, because I want to involve myself, as the reader I know best, with what I'm reading. I also want to distinguish the subjective possession of an object from a model in the mind around which the lifestyle is shaped. It's linked to Kierkegaard's either-or dilemma, but the context is very different.
[NB 44.392; LN, 1:187]

The form in which an idea is expressed is part of its truth. If I set down ideas without punch or wit or vivid imagery or a vitally logical connection, & then revise the passage so that it becomes more readable, with more punch & wit & so on, *it thereby becomes more true*. A work on the inner

315

mysteries of profound intellectual disciplines which is dull & hard to read is simply not a true picture of those disciplines. Now I know there are all sorts of difficulties & dangers & necessary qualifications to be made to this, but the central intuition is true. That's why a discipline founded on oral teaching can get only so far—though it may get farther in other respects, derived from the teacher's knowledge of the character of his pupil.

[NB 30N.20]

X

X. Because a lot of things seem to be converging on Yeats' double gyre or hourglass figure, of which the X is one form: a conscious world where the mind is at the center or top; a lower world where the mind is looking into itself below. "Poetic Cosmology": it sounds like Vico. [NB 12.243; TBN, 190-1]

X, Malcolm. I must read Malcolm X to see why the hell a black revolutionary would turn to the religion of the Arab slave-traders. I suppose it's a vulgarization of the black-Hebrew anti-Egyptian Queen of Sheba let-my-people-go alliance. Because the Queen-Bride is certainly black (reversed into white), whatever suit I'm expounding. [NB 21.283; RT, 193]

Xenophon and Plato. What are the highest genres in prose? The most usual answer given was that it was the vision of a model society. There were two forms of this, the description of an ideal state and the account of the ideal education of the prince, the classical examples of which were, respectively, the *Republic* of Plato and the *Cyropaedia* of Xenophon. English literature made one very great contribution (though it was written in Latin) to the former in More's *Utopia*. [LS, 68]

ϒ

Yeats. Got Yeats' *Vision* out of the library. Now Yeats is neither fool nor liar, & if I have received any help from spirits myself in the course of writing on Blake I am very grateful for it. But I'm sure he's all wrong. Submission to automatic writing is relaxation or passivity of the mind. If it's imaginative, it creates the spirits itself—Yeats himself has difficulty in not believing this. His spirits seem to be a rather dim-witted bunch of boobs and if he'd told them to go to hell, where they perhaps belonged, & worked his system out himself, it would have been clearer, surely. [D 42.15; DNF, 9]

Yoga. If I may now make an attempt to codify a program of spiritual life for myself according to the eight stages of Yoga: I do not at the moment see clearly beyond the first three, & only the outline of the fourth.
[NB 3.78; RT, 32]

The "yoga" intuition is founded on the notion of transforming the body, & I don't know if there's any Christian alternative answer to it. Our present body is almost wholly unknown to the consciousness which inhabits it. Yoga creates an imaginative body in its place, & goes to work on that. Christian imagery concentrates on the social body, the city & garden which are also the body of the one man who achieved resurrection. The next step connects with the contrast between the crumbling monument & immortal because dying & rebirthing papyrus, & somewhere in here is the mystery of why the Bible tells a story. [NB 24.233; TBN, 330-1]

Yoga is the voluntary suppression of the involuntary actions of the mind.

We're all born with a natural yoga: we're freed by objective energy and our consciousness freezes it into matter. Matter is *mater,* the mother. Materialism, dogmatism, the authority of elders and impotent kings, all assist the freezing process. A higher discipline that would freeze the mind could liberate the spirit. [NB 11H.24; LN, 2:716]

Z

Zero. The fascination the Lankavatara has for me has something to do with my feeling that art is the zero of knowledge, the no-fact that turns out to be the essential fact, the unnumbered Fool of the greater trumps, my eighth book & Blake's eighth eye. There seem to be two antithetical forces here: there is the Hegelian dialectic of A and not-A, which leads to revolutionary dialectic action by turning ideas into half-ideas, truths into half-truths, in order to sharpen their cutting edge; and there is the cultural dialectic of spiritual authority, the dialectic of A and non-A, of "this is" and "let this be," the ultimate in conservation & the ultimate in liberality. [NB 3.168; RT, 66-7]

Glossary

Adam Kadmon. In the Kabbala, the universal man whose limbs contain all heaven and earth.

Akasa. Pali for "the all pervasive," a term that Frye adapted from Madame Helena Petrovna Blavatsky. In the *Upanishads* it means "ether" or "space."

Albion. Blake's name for humanity or the universal human being.

Alchimie du verbe. "Alchemy of the word," the title of Rimbaud's second delirium (the story of one of his journeys into madness) in *A Season in Hell.*

Anabasis of Kore. Literally, "the ascension of Kore" (Persephone), a reference to the restoration from Tartarus of Persephone: Zeus had commanded that Hades return Persephone to Demeter for a portion of every year.

Anima Mundi. The soul of the world, a pure ethereal spirit, pro-claimed by some ancient philosophers to be diffused throughout all nature.

Anima naturaliter Christiana. "The soul in its nature is Christian," a phrase from Tertullian that Frye attributes to Augustine.

Avatamsaka sutra. A massive, dense, extravagant, and repetitive Mahayana text that forms the basis of the Chinese Hua-yen school of Buddhism; it stresses the interpene-tration of all elements in the world.

Bardo. In *The Tibetan Book of the Dead,* the "in-between" state that connects the death of individuals with the rebirth that follows.

Begriff. Concept or notion, in Hegel's *Logic* and elsewhere.

Belacqua fantasy. In Canto 4 of Dante's *Purgatorio,* Belacqua remains outside the gates of Purgatory with the Indolent, excusing his failure to begin the climb by claiming that he will not be allowed beyond the gates until he has spent as much time in the Antepurgatory as he spent delaying his repentance during his lifetime (ll. 127-32). The title character in Samuel Beckett's *Murphy* feels an affinity with Belacqua.

Beulah. One of Blake's four states of being. Eden is the apocalyptic heaven or unfallen world, the world of creator and creature; Beulah is the state of innocence, the world of lover and beloved and the potentially creative world of dreams and childhood; Generation is the subject-object world of experience; and Ulro is Blake's hell or the fallen world of ego and Satan.

Bodhisattva. In Sanskrit, "enlightenment being"—a being who seeks buddhahood through the systematic practice of perfect virtues but who renounces entry into nirvana until all beings are saved.

Brynhild. A character in the *Volsungasaga* who promises to marry whoever will ride through her flaming fire and slay her enemies.

Casa Loma. An eccentric stone mansion, built by Sir Henry Mill Pellatt, which became a Toronto landmark.

Chik-hai bardo. The first period of the after-death state of bardo (*see above*), followed by the subsequent states, Chönyid and Sidpa.

Claritas, integritas, consonantia. Terms from an aphorism by St. Thomas Aquinas about the three things required for beauty. In Joyce's *A Portrait of the Artist as a Young Man* Stephen Dedalus translates the passage as "Three things are needed for beauty, wholeness, harmony and radiance."

Covering Cherub. Blake's term (from Ezekiel 28:16) for the angel with the flaming sword who keeps humanity out of Eden; thus, the fiery serpent or Satan in his dragon or leviathan form. The Covering Cherub is one form of what Blake called the Selfhood, the anti-creative death-principle that keeps humanity blocked from paradise.

Da capo **aria.** A three-part aria, in ABA form.

Deteriora sequor. From Ovid, *Metamorphoses,* Bk. 7, ll. 20-1: "Video meliora, proboque; / deteriora sequor" (I see the better and approve it; I follow the worse).

DeWitt, Norman Wentworth (1876-1958). Canadian linguist and historian who advanced the thesis that world history was the evolution of the unintended and that government was the administration of the unforeseen.

Diogenes Teufelsdröckh. "Devil's Dung," the imaginary professor whose speculations are the basis of Thomas Carlyle's *Sartor Resartus* (1833-34).

Do ut des. I give that you may give; the principle of reciprocity.

Écriture. Jacques Derrida's notion, argued in *Of Grammatology* and elsewhere, that writing is prior to speech.

Ego dominus tuus. "I am your Lord," the words of a mighty figure in Dante's dream in the *Vita Nuova*. W.B. Yeats uses the words as a poem title.

Erdgeist. The Spirit of Nature that Faust conjures up in Goethe's play.

Esse est percipi. "To be is to be perceived," which, according to Bishop Berkeley, is the most basic feature of all sensible objects.

Faute de mieux. "For want of a more satisfactory alternative."

Fisher, Peter. One of Frye's students in the late 1940s and early 1950s; he wrote a thesis on Blake, introduced Frye to certain Mahayana Buddhist texts, and was, by Frye's account, the most brilliant student he ever taught.

Ganz anders. A phrase used by Karl Barth to describe a God who is "completely different" or "wholly other."

Gauleiter. Leader of a district under Nazi control.

Generation. *See* "Beulah," *above.*

Glasnost. Literally, "openness." The policy, promoted by Mikhail Gorbachev in the USSR in the late 1980s, of openness in public discussions about current and historical problems.

Guna. In Vedantic philosophy, one of the three qualities of nature, which are activity (Rajas-guna), inertia (Tamas-guna), and harmonious balance (Sattva-guna).

"Hid divinity" tradition. The tradition beginning with the anonymous fourteenth-century contemplative text *The Cloud of Unknowing,* which advances the idea that God may know us but whatever apprehension we have of God is finally beyond language.

Homo ludens. Human beings at play.

Homunculus. A little man living in the flask in Goethe's *Faust*. He lies outside of the domain of nature, a soul and spirit without a proper material body.

Hortus conclusus. "Garden enclosed" (Song of Songs 4:12).

Hypnerotomachia. The earliest of the Renaissance emblem books or collections of symbolic pictures, printed by Aldus in 1499.

Ishvara. In Sanskrit, "the lord of the universe"—the concept of a personal God as the creator of the world.

Jnana. In Sanskrit, "to know"; in Mahayana Buddhism, *jnana,* the tenth stage in the development of the bodhisattva, refers to mastering the rational teachings in the Hinayana scriptures.

Kaivalya. In Sanskrit, literally, "uniqueness, complete release"; in Hinduism, the state of the soul that realizes it is perfect and its consciousness is pure.

Lankavatara sutra. A major text of Mahayana Buddhism, stressing an inner enlightenment that erases all dualities.

Lisible. A "readerly" text, as opposed to a *scriptible* or "writerly" text; a distinction made by Roland Barthes, Jacques Derrida, and others.

Los. In Blake's mythology, the creative imagination in the fallen world; the archetype of the poet-prophet.

Martha-world. In the story of Jesus' visit to Mary and Martha in Luke 10:38-42, Martha is said to be "cumbered about" and "distracted with much serving," and Mary is said to have chosen the good part of the one thing that is needful. This one thing is the word of Jesus, for she sits at his feet and listens to his teachings, while Martha busies herself with practical matters. Martha represents the anxious, frantic search for novelties or skills or even luxuries that don't really matter because they detract from the one thing she really needs and wants. On another level, Martha has come to represent the way of salvation through action, Mary through contemplation.

Maya. Literally, in Sanskrit, "deception, appearance"—in Hinduism, the universal principle of Vedanta; the basis of mind and matter, which veils our vision so that we see only diversity; *maya,* however, is inseparably united with *brahman,* the principle of absolute unity.

Metis. A Titaness, the daughter of Oceanus and Tethys and the mother of Athena by Zeus.

Nel mezzo del cammino. "In the middle of life's journey," from the opening line of Dante's *Commedia.*

Nunc dimittis. From "*Nunc dimittis*

servum tuum, Domine" (Vulgate) ("Lord, now lettest thou thy servant"), the first words of the canticle that Simeon uttered when Jesus was presented at the temple in Luke 2:29.

Orc. The spirit of revolution in Blake's prophetic poems.

Paravritti. Sanskrit for "the highest wave of thought," meaning, in Frye's use of the term, the complete conversion of the mind. See entry for "Paravritti," p. 210.

Poète maudit. "Accursed poet," a phrase first applied by Paul Verlaine to the poet as an outcast of modern society, whose rulers fear the poet's penetrating insights into their spiritual emptiness.

Psychikos. Greek adjective used to describe the soul-body (*soma psychikos*) as opposed to the spiritual body (*soma pneumatikos*), as in 1 Corinthians 2:14; the noun forms (*soma psychikon* and *soma pneumatikon*) are translated as "natural body" and "spiritual body" in the AV (1 Corinthians 15:44).

Rajas. *See* "Guna," *above.*

Robins, John (1884-1952). Frye's undergraduate teacher and later his colleague at Victoria College.

Rochdale. A student residence that provided undergraduates in the late 1960s with an alternative to the University of Toronto system of instruction. It became a center of counter-culture activities and was eventually closed—in May 1975—for mortgage arrears.

Sacrificium intellectus. "Sacrifice of the intellect"—a phase used by Jung and others to describe those who elevate faith above religious experience.

Spectre of Urthona. In Blake's mythology, the Spectre of Urthona is, as Frye says in *Fearful Symmetry,* "the isolated subjective aspect of existence in this world, the energy with which a man or any other living thing copes with nature."

Tabula rasa. Blank tablet. The Latin phrase originated with the scholastics, but the idea of the mind as a *tabula rasa* is most often associated with John Locke's contention that there are no innate ideas.

Tamas. *See* "Guna," *above.*

Temenos. Sacred space.

Tertium quid. Something intermediate between two things or related to two things though distinct from them.

Toute pensée émet un coup de dés. "All thought emits a throw of the dice," the final line of Mallarmé's *Un Coup de Dés.*

Trahison des clercs. A phrase from Julien Benda's book of that title (1927). He described the attitude of some intellectuals between the world wars as a *trahison,* meaning that they had betrayed the causes of justice and truth because it would have been inconvenient to defend them.

Ubi sunt. A verse form in which the poem or its stanzas begin with the Latin words *ubi sunt* ("where are") or their equivalent in another language and which has as a principal theme the transitory nature of all things.

Ulro. See "Beulah," above.

Urizen. One of the four Zoas who make up the four-fold individual in Blake's mythology. Generally, Urizen represents reason.

Ut pictura poesis. "As is painting so is poetry": the phrase originates with Horace (*Ars Poetica,* l. 361), though the analogy was an ancient one.

Wiseman, Adele (1928-92). Canadian writer; the author of *Memoirs of a Book Molesting Childhood and Other Essays* (1987), the book to which Frye refers.

Wu wei. In Taoism and Zen Buddhism, unmotivated action; in Chinese, literally, "nondoing."

Yama. The first of the eight stages of Raja-Yoga, consisting of five ethical practices.

Young Woodbury. J.C. (Jack) Woodbury, one of Frye's students; he attended the University of Toronto from 1951 to 1954.

Za-zen. Zen meditative practice of free-thought not directed toward an object; it is taught as the most direct route to enlightenment.